EMERGING TRENDS IN WEB COMPUTING

EMERGING TRENDS IN WEB COMPUTING

Vijay Kumar Gupta

MD PUBLICATIONS PVT LTD
NEW DELHI
www.mdppl.com

Published by :

MD Publications Pvt Ltd
"MD House", 11, Darya Ganj,
New Delhi - 110 002
Phone : +91-11-45355555
E-mail : contact@mdppl.com
Website: www.mdppl.com

ISBN : 978-81-7533-333-8

Published and Printed by Mr. Pranav Gupta on behalf of **MD Publications Pvt Ltd** at Times Press, Delhi.

PREFACE

The World Wide Web is becoming accessible to the common man day by day. Moreover, the world we live in has become flooded with computer technologies. It has become the utmost need to ponder numerous upcoming technologies. Hyperbole aside, cloud computing, real-time content, and advancements in browser speed and capabilities made the Web more compelling than ever before. This book has four main themes, covering different aspects of Web Technology, Web Applications, Multimedia and Computing Technologies. Robust infrastructure can now be leased with just a few clicks of the mouse. Instant information, characterized by tweets and Flickr updates sent from anywhere at any time.

Fortunately, the Web doesn't stand still and a great deal of research and development continues to go into evolving the mechanics of today's online social universe. There are presently many new efforts under way to refine and improve the world of social media, some of which we'll explore here and many which are just beginning.

Sincere thanks to all the resource persons who spared their time from busy schedules for submitting papers for this book. Hoping that this book on emerging web technologies would enhance the knowledge quotient of the readers.

I am very grateful to Mr. Pranav Gupta, Director of

MD Publications Pvt. Ltd., New Delhi, for his kind cooperation and support for this book.

Vijay Kumar Gupta

CONTENTS

1

Unique ID Project 'Aadhaar'

Issues, Challenges and Solutions

Sukhvinder Singh Deora, Dr. (Mrs) Pushpa R. Suri***

Abstract – *Introduction of a Unique Identification (UID) for citizens of India is a step towards highly controlled database of all citizens in line with Social Security Number (SSN) in America. The number will be a 12 digit number with which we can fetch information related to the person, his bank accounts and other government identities. Utilization of UID can be used to trace almost each and every activity of the person while his stay in the country. We have critically analyzed the UID Project so as to address the issues, challenges and possible solutions to those.*

I. INTRODUCTION

The world's first ID project where biometric data is used to provide unique identification numbers for India's billion-

*Associate Professor, Deptt. of Computer Sc. & Applications, NC Institute of Computer Sc., Israna

**Associate Professor,Deptt. of Computer Sc. & Applications, Kurukshetra University, Kurukshetra

plus citizens rolled out today with Prime Minister Manmohan Singh and UPA chief Sonia Gandhi handing over the first set of 12-digit numbers to 10 tribals.[1]

With the start of handing over of the UID cards to some tribal citizens near Mumbai, India's most tech savvy initiative called 'Aadhaar'(base) has taken a "historic step" to provide identity to each and every citizen for the use in various Government activities. This card will provide almost all information related to the person involved and will contain information using which the person can be verified with best of the available biometric parameters.

The UID project would be completed in 5 years and would cost a sum of Rs 3127 crores to the Government. UID Authority of India (UIDAI) has been formed which is headed by Nandan Nilekani, eX-corporate of Infosys Technologies will take care of the project. The UID card is actually a smart card containing details about Name, Unique ID Number, FatherID, MotherID, DOB, marriages, BankAccountData, RationCardData apart from this the Left hand thumb print scan and Iris scan etc. According to Nilekani, it would be voluntary for the citizen to possess the UID Card, but situations like banks not opening the bank account, schools not offering admissions, non-transference of land in revenue papers etc will force the persons to go for it well in time.

II. PROJECT 'AADHAAR' AND THE UID

Project 'Aadhaar' will provide UIDs that will become "a single source of identity verification". It will provide a one-time verification system to which all other records of the government will be linked. The major objective of Project 'Aadhaar' is to divide wealth equitably. The Government is aiming at providing various kinds of helps through public schemes like Sarva Shiksha Abhiyaan, National Rural Employment Guarantee Scheme (NREGS), Bharat Nirmaan etc. It will be then the only single identity, using which; one can learn anything about an Indian citizen. Under this scheme people will be provided UID, a plastic card with memory in form of a smart card. This card will have limited data and service related data would be incorporated in other cards like the National Rural Employment Generation Scheme (NREGS), Voter card, Ration card or Driving License.

III. OBJECTIVES OF ISSUING UIDs

The initial objective Unique Identification Authority of India is to assign a unique identification number to each resident in the country and to eliminate the need for multiple identification mechanisms. This unique number will be the basis for a positive and accurate identification of citizens on which e-Governance platforms and services can be built around it.[2] However, with the passage of time, the possession of UID at the time of opening bank accounts, seeking admissions, reservation, governmental benefit schemes, proving identity etc may be made mandatory. Since the card contains information regarding parents, address, personal information, bank accounts, passport, license information in related databases, it will prove out to be beginning a transparent e-Governed society. E-Governence has the potential to tackle with corruption in various domains. In fact, various government departments can be linked with each other to build a strong database containing latest accurate information about persons living in India. In this way, government can control law and order, security, public distribution systems, NREGS like government services in the country. Also the holders of the UID cards will enable them to take all such services and many more with ease.

IV. SIMILAR PROJECTS

The Unique Identification Number is a part of series of measures carried out in other Countries such as US, Malaysia, and Thailand, to name a few.[3] These projects have also faced opposition from the general public on the basis of right to privacy, which prevents governmental interference in intimate personal relationships or activities, freedoms of individual to make fundamental choices involving himself, his family and his relationship with others from public scrutiny. UIDs may also allow the government to routinely mine the primary and secondary databases — from drivers' licenses to bank statements to telephone records — to compile trends or behavioral studies, buying patterns etc related to the person.

V. ISSUES AND CHALLENGES

The Government of India (GOI) has initiated the process at some tribal village near Mumbai, but we feel there are still some issues and challenges before it to resolve and implement the project successfully.

(1) With the population of the country more than 110 crores, it will take many years to issue the UIDs to all the citizens of the country. This means we have to deploy many organizations who can make and distribute the UID cards in parallel.

(2) The UID cards use biometrics other than the regular data, so will require comparatively larger memory in the smart cards and related databases.

(3) As the UID uses fingerprint recognition technique, the issue related to fade fingerprints and changing of the fingerprints in highly cold and high temperature situations will fail the recognitions.

(4) The biometric of Iris detection is also used other than fingerprints so as to use multiple biometrics for verifications of persons. But the liveliness of the iris has not taken into account. This may result to an attack based on artificially constructed iris structure.

(5) If this UID has to be issued to each and every Indian then the children with age more than 5 years must also be included in the list. The fingerprints of the child can change a bit with the passage of time. This means, we have to update our UID records at least after every 10 years so as to incorporate the latest

changes in their biometric properties. This is definitely one biggest challenge and will increase the cost factor for continuously providing the services.

(6) The collaborated information in the government databases will contain details at much smaller granularity; the protection of this private information will be another challenge before the government.

(7) Like the cloning of the mobile sim-cards, debit and credit cards, the cloning of UIDs may pose a big security threat for the country.

(8) In India, where private information can be had with less than 1$ per person, as reported by some Australian reporters way back in 2006 from BPO company, what will be the security of information stored about each person in the UID databases? Companies may learn our consumption patterns, bank transaction trends, using our information to influence us from time to time.

(9) The usage of UID in other than the claimed areas, i.e. government schemes for up-gradation of the society and the backward, will lead to a digital surveillance of the society. For instance, transaction data gleaned from credit card usage could be matched with tax records. Payment of sales taxes when you buy some product or VAT on the raw material when bought by the industrialist will require just a few tracks.

(10) The data should be stored in the dabases that are available over the Internet so that it can be accessed at any instance of time. Appropriate number of servers have to be maintained for this.

VI. POSSIBLE SOLUTIONS

We provide some solutions to the problems, issues and challenges mentioned in the previous section of the article, which when carried out may reduce the vulnerabilities in the system.

(1) The GOI should distribute the work of making and distribution of the UIDs at the State level so that the work can be carried out in parallel.

(2) The databases which are used to store primary and secondary information of the UIDs should be distributed databases with replicas for uninterrupted access to the information.

(3) Multiple finger impressions at different temperature and pressure have to be stored to increase the availability of data.

(4) Live Iris detection should be used instead.

(5) Challenge of updating the information periodically needs some commitment from the government. As one can learn that the electoral cards, which just contain a photo other than the text data, are not even updated for years for many persons due to cost factor.

(6) Data Protection Law needs to be enforced with greater determination and that too on all private & public sector organizations dealing with this project. There should be some organization which will take the responsibility for data protection and will be held liable for any breach of Privacy and data theft.

(7) Digital personation should be strictly dealt with.

(8) Data Protection Law of the Information Technology Act should be abided at all stages of information collection, storage, usage and manipulation. We may use encrypted databases rather than simple databases. Data stored in such databases will require special software to understand in the form of information. However, that may turn out to be an overhead in the process also.

(9) Use of UIDs to look over the activities is intrusion to ones' personal life, but we feel that it is most important to smash down corruption and detect theft of taxes at various levels.

(10) Distributed database servers must be maintained for uninterrupted supply of information at all times.

REFERENCES

[1] Press Trust of India, Tembhli (Maharashtra) September 29, 2010, 16:01 IST

[2] Krishna Chilukuri, "UIAI and India's First Steps Towards e-Governance", at http://online.wsj.com/article/SB125474159669964289.html

[3] C.R. Sridhar, "Unique Identification Number: The Politics of Privacy and Information" at http://desicritics.org/2010/05/02/054859.php, May C2, 2010

[4] Tapash Gan Choudhury, "Legal & Commercial Dictionary", sixth ed., 2006, Eastern Law House.

❑❑❑

2

Agile Methodologies in Web Engineering

*Mandeep Kaur Chawla**

Abstract – *Agile software development approaches have gained widespread interest in last some years. It is a family of methodologies that has been developed to tackle the problems associated with classic heavy-weight software engineering processes. One of the biggest advantage is that work can begin ahead of all the requirements are recognized. Features on the priority list are implemented first and fully working deployable versions are released. System is evolved through various iterations as the client gets clear picture of what is required from end-product. In this paper, first a core idea of agile development and various methods has been described. How this field relates to web engineering has been explained thereafter. Finally, a conceptual framework for agile-based development process is depicted.*

*Department of Computer Sci. & Applications, MCMDAV College for Women, Chandigarh.

I. INTRODUCTION

In the last three decades, several distinct software engineering approaches have been introduced, of which only a handful have made their mark practically and rest remained topics of theoretical interest or are used in conjunction with other more effective techniques. With fast growing business world, Internet industry and emerging technologies, expectation of rapid accomplishment of end product with ever-changing requirements is inevitable. The issue of delivering earlier, better, cost-effective and maintainable solutions has generated a lot of interest and anxiety among software community.

Traditional approaches of software development such as waterfall model, spiral model, iterative and incremental models have been much discussed, followed and popularized till date. Some reaped the fruits and some paid the price depending upon their expectations, time and money involved.

The conventional waterfall model assumes that the requirements of a software can be fully conceived and accumulated at the onset of the project and does not allow to loop back or revisit the specifications and design ideas in view of changes in the environment or client needs. Though other ad-hoc and iterative models allow the uncertainty and modifications to set in, but does not guarantee efficient, consistent and maintainable code in the light of somewhat unorganized amendments. In the recent past, the adoption of agile methodologies by experienced practitioners has had a massive impact on the complex development processes. Agile software development represents a major departure from traditional, plan-based approaches to software engineering [1].

The literary meaning of Agile denotes "nimbleness, quick in motion, promptness for action, readiness to perform" - software engineers are in constant search of devising techniques that enable them to have quick and clean software development processes. In the real world, there would be hardly any system which is so simple that it can be fully visualized and its layout can be designed in complete detail in advance. The inherent ambiguous and complex nature of them encourages us to undertake adaptive techniques so as to deal with uncertainty and a good count of unforeseeable variables.

II. AGILE METHODS: WELCOMING CHANGES

Because the foundations of software development are inherently unstable and unreliable, organizations developing software must realize variables exist that are largely outside of management control [2]. Broadly, there are four control variables that demands balancing – Requirement specifications, Money, Time and Quality. When one factor modifies, others are prone to change. Therefore software development can be described as a non-linear process which cannot be predicted in advance. People need to see and feel something before they really know what they want. The "I'll Know it When I See It" (IKIWISI) law says that software development customers can better describe what they really want after seeing and trying working, functional software[2].

Agile values a high visibility and customer involvement. The frequent demonstration and release of software common in Agile approaches gives customers a chance to "try software" periodically and provide feedback. Agile helps companies produce the "right product". An iterative approach allows customers to delay decisions as well. Decisions can be delayed to some future iteration when better information or technology is available to optimize the choice [2]. Project is seen as a series of relatively small tasks conceived and executed as the situation demands in an adaptive manner.

In a system following Agile methods, at the end of an iteration doesn't stand a prototype, but a fully functional, fully tested, potentially deployable system, containing the highest priority features on the requirement list. Agile methods are considered light-weight because emphasis is on delivering working product and reacts promptly to changes.

III. AGILE METHODOLOGIES

Some of the leading Agile Development methodologies are:

1. **Extreme Programming (XP)**: Encompasses a set of rules and practices that occurs within four framework activities – Planning, design, coding and testing. With close interaction with the customer, set of stories are created to describe required features and functionality for software to be built. Then they work together to decide how to group stories into the next release. Some of the main characteristics of XP are short iterations with small releases and rapid feedback, close customer participation, constant communication and coordination, continuous refactoring, continuous integration and testing, collective code ownership, and pair programming [3].

2. **Scrum**: Project is divided into small units named sprint, lasting 2-4 weeks generally. Deliverable, which is visible and usable increment, is decided for each sprint. It is a team-based approach for controlling the chaos of conflicting interests and needs [4].

3. **Feature Driven Development (FDD)**: FDD emphases quality aspects throughout the process and includes frequent and tangible deliveries, along with accurate monitoring of the progress of the project. It consists of five sequential processes and provides the methods, techniques and guidelines needed by project stakeholders to deliver the system [5]. These processes are - Develop Overall Model, Build Features List, Plan by feature, Design by feature, Build by feature.

4. **Adaptive Software Development (ASD)**: Adaptive Software development works on the principle of continuous adaptation. The three major phases are – speculation, collaboration and learning. The method encourages incremental and iterative development, with constant prototyping [3].

In addition to above Agile Modeling, Crystal methodologies, Dynamic Systems Development Methods

(DSDM), Lean software development are also well known techniques.

IV. CHARACTERISTICS

Various characteristics can be summarized as under-

1. Time slots are measured in weeks rather than months and work is performed in highly structured teams and in collaboration with clients.
2. It does not insist on big, up-front design.
3. Most Agile philosophies involve "test-first" methods.
4. Refactoring is an integral part of the software development cycle: developers alternate between adding new tests and functionality and refactoring the code to improve its internal consistency and clarity.
5. It follows the principle of shallow structure to effectively achieve its objectives.
6. Planning is kept to minimum to accommodate various unforeseen requirement changes.
7. Active customer involvement is encouraged.
8. Agile development focuses on talent and skills of individuals, molding the process to specific people and teams.

V. WEB ENGINEERING – AGILE WAY

In most cases, development of Web-based systems has been ad hoc, lacking systematic approach, and quality control and assurance procedures. Hence, there is now legitimate and growing concern about the manner in which Web-based systems are developed and their quality and integrity [6]. Web Engineering is the application of systematic, disciplined and quantifiable approaches to development, operation, and maintenance of Web-based applications. It is both a pro-active approach and a growing collection of theoretical and empirical research in Web application development [7]. Generally one can observe that, the large projects of earlier times are being replaced by highly interactive, small web developments. These small projects are being done using different technology as well. These trends are motivated by the move to quicker-paced developments [8]. Expectation of shorter development life cycles fades away the need of developing software from scratch which used to follow rigid development stages. Instead, components are combined following an agile process and a – hopefully – useable design is being created "on the job" by means of refactoring [9].

The importance of understanding End-User usage has never been so critical to the success of a class of software applications as it is with Web engineering projects. Consider the number of different ways information in a Web application can be displayed to End-Users, and the ease with which End-Users can find and change to alternative Web-based solutions should they lack satisfaction with their current usage experience [10]. Besides, there is no denying that the developers and the establishment involved in the engineering of a certain the web-based application are the prime factors in the failure or success of the final solution. Hence agile methods' focus on welcoming change and people, tightly-knit small development teams with quick results and feedback makes it strong contender for web engineering.

VI. FRAMEWORK OF AGILE BASED DEVELOPMENT

The complexity of Web based applications has grown significantly - from information dissemination (consisting of simple text and images to image maps, forms, CGI, applets, scripts and style -sheets) to online transactions, enterprise-wide planning and scheduling systems, Web-based collaborative work environments, etc [6]. To achieve sound system solutions and to give away with potential web crisis, there is earnest need for steady development approaches, assessment and quality control, overall project management; notwithstanding little turn-around time. In Figure 1, we can identify all the key phases which need to be followed essentially in web environments.

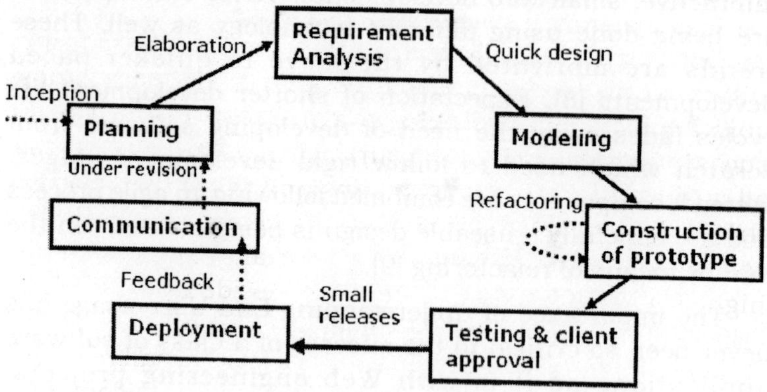

Fig. 1. Conceptual framework for Agile-based development process.

Being an iterative and incremental process, this counts for—

(a) Early and incessant delivery of working software

(b) The ability to accommodate design modifications even late

(c) Periodical quality reviews

At the end of each iteration development team is supposed to evaluate and ponder the development process through feedback channels to make it sustainable.

VII. SUCCESS FACTORS

The parameters that affect the success of projects advocating agile methodologies can be derived as follows-

(i) Adequate client participation

(ii) Short decision timeframes

(iii) Project planning and control

(iv) Degree of uncertainty in project environments

(v) Proficiency in technical domain

(vi) Team composition and distribution

(vii) Communication and Negotiation

VIII. CHALLENGES

Everyone involved in contributing to the deliverables on a Web application, whether it be graphics, business objectives or database designs are responsible for the success of their Web-based endeavors. It is essential that all involved realize the importance of their contribution and that of the other members of the team. This requires collaboration, compromise, education, understanding and high degree of professionalism. Should these developer criteria be seriously lacking amongst those responsible for the development of Web-based systems then one must question the effectiveness of the agile approach [10]. In view of this, below mentioned are the additional challenges that one is expected to cope with—

(a) Persuading customers to invest valuable time during development process and keeping them all-time motivated;

(b) Management should be less bureaucratic and allow teams to take decisions to empower them;

(c) Besides being highly skilled, team should have a great infrastructural support;

(d) Numerous iterative cycles must not discourage maintenance of documentation;

(e) Quality is non-negotiable.

Nevertheless, the power lies in the fact that at the inception of a project, we are not obligated to capture all the requirements beforehand. Customers find it difficult to mention specifications completely without seeing it working and practically trying hands on it. Having said that, it is suggested that practitioners cautiously study unique characteristics of their anticipated software and other prerequisites before adopting a suitable engineering approach.

REFERENCES

[1] Tore Dybå, Torgeir Dingsøyr: Empirical studies of agile software development: A systematic review, Information & Software Technology, 2008.

[2] Victor Szalvay: An Introduction to Agile Software Development. Danube Technologies, Inc., 2004.

[3] Abrahamsson, P., Warsta, J., Siponen, M. T., and Ronkainen, J. New Directions on Agile Methods: A Comparative Analysis. In Proceedings of the 25th IEEE International Conference on Software Engineering (ICSE), Portland, Oregon, May 03 - 10, 2003.

[4] P. Meso and R. Jain, "Agile Software Development: Adaptive Systems Principles and Best Practices," Information Systems Management, vol. 23, no. 3, 2006, pp. 19–30.

[5] P. Abrahamsson, O. Salo, J. Ronkainen, J. Warsta, Agile software development methods: review and analysis, VTT Technical report, 2002.

[6] S. Murugesan, Y. Deshpande, S. Hansen, and A. Ginige. Web engineering: A new discipline for development of web-based systems. Lecture Notes in Computer Sci, Springer Berlin/ Heidelberg, 2016, 2001.

[7] Deshpande, Y., Murugesan, S., Ginige, A., Hansen, S., Schwabe, D., Gaedke, M., and White, B. "Web Engineering," Journal of Web Engineering (1:1) 2002, pp 3-17.

[8] D.C. Reifer, Estimating Web Development Costs: There Are Differences, CrossTalk – The Journal of Defense Software Engineering, pp. 13-17, June 2002.

[9] K. Schwaber, M. Beedle, Agile Software Development with Scrum, Prentice Hall, 2002.

[10] McDonald A., Welland R.: Agile Web Engineering (AWE) Process, Department of Computing Science Technical Report TR-2001-98, University of Glasgow, Scotland, (2 December 2001)

3

Analysis of Emerging Trends in Information Technology

Cloud Computing

*Rupinder Kaur**

Abstract – *The service provider industry especially the information technology is changing the way services were provided in the past. This shift has already been started with the evolution of cloud computing. All industry types from small to large enterprises are challenged to contain and even reduce the technology cost while at the same time responding to the expectations of the "New Millennial Generation". In this paper we will analyze the cloud computing from various aspects – what all type of services it provides, how it helps the organizations, security concerns and its impact on information technology.*

Keywords – *Cloud computing, segments of cloud computing, software development trend.*

*Department of Computer Science; Punjabi University, Patiala, India.
e-mail: rupadeo@gmail.com

1. INTRODUCTION

"Cloud computing" has dramatically changed how business applications are built and run. At its core, cloud computing eliminates the costs and complexity of evaluating, buying, configuring, and managing all the hardware and software needed for enterprise applications. Instead, these applications are delivered as a service over the Internet.

Cloud Computing is all about using Information Technology as a service over the network. Everyone has an opinion on what is cloud computing. It can be the ability to rent a server and run an application on the most powerful systems available anywhere. It can be the ability to rent a virtual server, load software on it, turn it on and off at will, or clone it ten times to meet a sudden workload demand. It can be storing and securing large amounts of data that is accessible only by authorized applications and users [1]. Cloud computing can be the ability to use applications on the Internet that store and protect data while providing a service — anything including business application hosting, email, sales force automation. It can be, using a storage cloud to hold application, business, and personal data. In general, cloud computing customers do not own the physical infrastructure, instead avoiding capital expenditure by renting usage from a third-party provider. They consume resources as a service and pay only for resources that they use [2].

In Section 2, we discuss more about cloud computing and how this is useful for end user. Then we will discuss in detail various segments of cloud computing, there benefits and companies offering these services in Section 3. Next, we analyze the security concerns of cloud computing model and discuss the specific security issues customers should raise with vendors before selecting a cloud vendor. Finally, we conclude and discuss future trend in Section 5.

2. CLOUD COMPUTING

It is a technology that uses the internet and central remote servers to maintain data and applications. Cloud computing allows consumers and businesses to use applications without installation and access their personal files on any computer with internet access. This technology allows for much more efficient computing by centralizing storage, memory, processing and bandwidth. Cloud promises real cost savings and agility to customers [3]. Through cloud computing, a company can rapidly deploy applications where the underlying technology components can expand with the technology advancements and business life cycle. Traditionally, once an application was deployed it was bound to a particular infrastructure, until the infrastructure was upgraded. The result was low efficiency, utilization, and flexibility. Cloud enablers, such as virtualization and grid computing, allow applications to be dynamically deployed onto the most suitable infrastructure at run time. This dynamic aspect of cloud computing allows applications to scale and grow without needing traditional 'fork-lift' upgrades.

A simple example of cloud computing is Yahoo email or Gmail etc. You don't need software or a server to use them. All a consumer would need is just an internet connection and you can start sending emails. The server and email management software is all in the cloud (internet) and is totally managed by the cloud service provider Yahoo, Google etc. The consumer gets to use the software alone and enjoy the benefits. All the users or consumers need is to get the benefits of using the software or hardware of the computer like sending emails etc., Consumer need not to buy software /hardware [4],[5]. In figure 1, we presented the conceptual diagram of cloud computing, where various computers are connected to the cloud, using the services provided by cloud vendors.

3. SEGMENTS OF CLOUD COMPUTING

Cloud computing is broken down into three segments: "applications," "platforms," and "infrastructure." Each segment serves a different purpose and offers different products for businesses and individuals around the world.

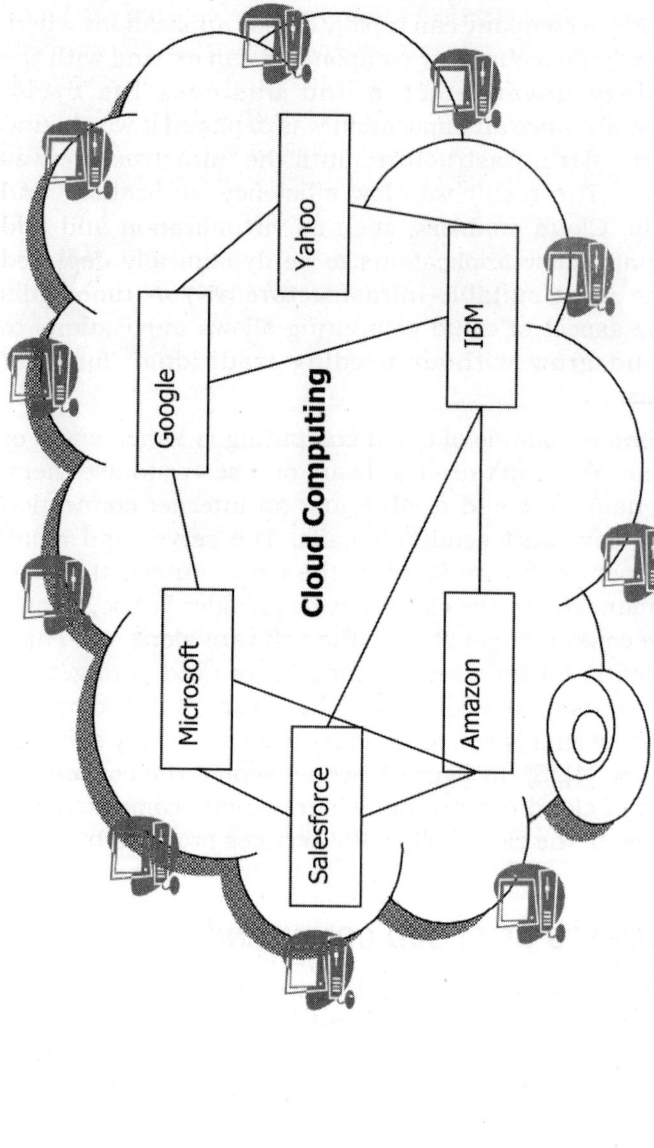

Fig. 1. Cloud Computing example

3.1 Applications

Cloud Computing application services or "Software as a Service (SaaS)" delivers software as a service over the Internet, eliminating the need to install and run the application on the customer's own computers and simplifying maintenance and support. In the past, the end-user would generally purchase a license from the software provider and then install and run the software directly from on-premise servers [6]. Using a cloud application service however, the end-user pays the software provider a subscription fee for the service. The software is hosted directly from the software providers' servers and is accessed by the end user over the internet [7].

The companies which are already providing cloud computing application services:

- Salesforce.com
- Google
- PayPal
- Banking Payment Gateways
- Net Suite
- Telco

3.1.1 Benefits

- Save money by not having to purchase servers or other software to support use.
- Focus Budgets on competitive advantage rather than infrastructure.
- Monthly obligation rather than up front capital cost.
- Reduced need to predict scale of demand and infrastructure investment up front as available capacity matches demand [8].
- Multi-Tenant efficiency.
- Flexibility and scalability.

3.2 Platforms

Cloud platform solutions are development platforms for which the development tool itself is hosted in the cloud and accessed through a browser. With "Platform as a Service (PaaS)", developers can build web applications without installing any tools on their computer and then deploy those applications without any specialized systems administration skills [9]. The platform segment of cloud computing refers to the products that are used to deploy applications. It facilitates deployment of applications without the cost and complexity of buying and managing the underlying hardware and software layers [10].

Examples of PaaS solutions today include:

- AppEngine from Google: based on Python and Django
- Force.com from SalesForce: based on the SalesForce SaaS infrastructure and Apex language
- Bungee Connect: visual development studio based on Java
- LongJump: based on Java/Eclipse
- WaveMaker: visual development studio based on Java and hosted on Amazon EC2

3.2.1 Benefits

The benefits of cloud platform service lie in greatly increasing the number of people who can develop, maintain and deploy web applications. In short, it offers to democratize development of web applications. Today, building web applications requires expert developer with three, highly specialized skill sets:

- Back end server development
- Front end client development
- Web site administration.

Platform service offers the potential for general developers to build web applications without needing specialized expertise. This allows an entire generation of general developers to start building web applications without the huge learning curve.

3.3 Infrastructure

Cloud infrastructure services or "Infrastructure as a Service (IaaS)" delivers computer infrastructure, typically a platform environment as a service. Infrastructure vendors provide the physical storage space and processing capabilities that allow for the all the services described above. Rather than purchasing servers, software, data center space or network equipment, clients instead buy those resources as a fully outsourced service. The service is typically billed on a utility computing basis and amount of resources consumed (and therefore the cost) will typically reflect the level of activity [11], [12].

Below are companies that provide infrastructure services:

- Google (GOOG) - Managed hosting, development environment
- International Business Machines (IBM) - Managed hosting
- SAVVIS (SVVS) - Managed hosting
- Terremark Worldwide (TMRK) - Managed hosting
- Amazon.com (AMZN) - Cloud storage
- Rackspace Hosting (RAX) - Managed hosting & cloud computing

3.3.1 Benefits

- Infrastructure as a service results in IT services that easily conform to the changing requirements of a business. Because the infrastructure does not reside on the premises, obsolete equipment, upgrades, and retrofits no longer play a role in the company's decision to adopt new technology: the IaaS provider takes care of that seamlessly, allowing the business to focus on its mission.
- Cost effectiveness augments the convenience of IaaS. Because the IaaS provider has massive platforms segmented for each customer, the economies of scale are enormous, providing significant cost savings through efficiency. The need for every company to maintain its own infrastructure is eliminated through IaaS.
- The power of IaaS brings the resources needed to service government and enterprise contracts to

businesses of every size. IaaS improves reliability because service providers have specialized workers that ensure nearly constant uptime and state-of-the-art security measures.

4. SECURITY CONCERNS

The number of companies using cloud computing continues to increase because it saves money and effort and, furthermore, provides for high flexibility, because the activity of the leased service can be adjusted according to the customers' needs. In the last few years, cloud computing has grown from being a business concept to one of the fastest growing segments of the IT industry. Now, companies are increasingly realizing that simply by tapping into the cloud they can gain fast access to best-of-breed business applications or drastically boost their infrastructure resources, all at negligible cost [13].

But as more and more information on individuals and companies is placed in the cloud, concerns are beginning to grow about just how safe an environment it is. What happens in the case of a service failure? Who guarantees that the company secrets are secure on the external servers? Which security risks evolve when a cloud service subcontractor access the cloud systems? Are the data destroyed after deletion? These and similar questions should be resolved before a company decides if and what cloud service to use. The strategy of outsourcing into the cloud on the one hand allows the companies to concentrate on their core competencies and to develop new business opportunities [14]. But on the other hand the dependency on external IT systems is increasing, and a failure of these systems due to technical failures, malware or hacker attacks may not only cripple communication but can disrupt even whole business or production processes.

Companies should review a cloud provider's security function individually and decide also on an individual basis, whether the supplied security mechanisms are sufficient for the specific requirement of the company [15]. Here are few of the specific security issues customers should raise with vendors before selecting a cloud vendor.

- **Privacy** – The confidential company data processed outside the enterprise brings with it an inherent level of risk, because outsourced services bypass the "physical, logical and personnel controls" IT shops exert over in-house programs. The organizations should ask the vendor to provide all the information related to data security – how and who manage your data.
- **Compliance** – Customers are ultimately responsible for the security and integrity of their own data, even when it is held by a service provider. Traditional service providers are subjected to external audits and security certifications.
- **Legal** – When you use the cloud, you probably won't know exactly where your data is hosted. In fact, you might not even know what country it will be stored in. Ask providers if they will commit to storing and processing data in specific jurisdictions, and whether they will make a contractual commitment to obey local privacy requirements on behalf of their customers.
- **Data Recovery** – Even if you don't know where your data is, a cloud provider should tell you what will happen to your data and services in case of a disaster. Any offering that does not replicate the data and application infrastructure across multiple sites is vulnerable to a total failure. Ask your provider if it has "the ability to do a complete restoration, and how long it will take.
- **Sustainability & Availability** – There are also concerns about a cloud provider shutting down for financial or legal reasons, which has happened in a number of cases.

5. CONCLUSION

Cloud computing helps the companies to meet the expectations of new age customers at lowest possible cost available across globe, without worrying about latest in-house technical expertise and infrastructure. Business and industry have long recognized the value and efficiencies of cloud computing. The number of companies moving towards cloud computing is increasing and this trend will continue in future. John Hagel and John Seely Brown, in an article titled "Your Next IT Strategy" (Harvard Business Review, October 2001), write that "Companies will in the future buy their information technologies as services provided over the Internet rather than owning their own hardware and software."

REFERENCES

[1] Gruman, Galen (2008-04-07). "What cloud computing really means". InfoWorld. http://www.infoworld.com/d/cloud-computing/what-cloud-computing-really-means-031. Retrieved 2009-06-02.

[2] "The Rise of Cloud Computing." Michael Otey. April 2010". windowsITpro.com. 2010-04-26. http://www.windowsitpro.com/article/cloud-computing2/The-Rise-of-Cloud Computing/2.aspx. Retrieved 2010-08-22.

[3] Wikinvest "Cloud Computing and Business Adoption of cloud computing" Dave Cleveland,Andrew Lewis

[4] "The Internet Cloud". Thestandard.com. http://www.thestandard.com/article/0,1902,5466,00.html. Retrieved 2010-08-22.

[5] "Cloud Computing Savings – Real or Imaginary?". Appirio.com. 2009-04-16. http://www.appirio.com/blog/2009/04/cloud-computing-savings-real-or.php. Retrieved 2010 08-22.

[6] Software as a Service: Strategic Backgrounder, Software & Information Industry Association, http://www.siia.net/estore/pubs/SSB-01.pdf, retrieved May 2010

[7] "SaaS 2.0: Saugatuck Study Shows Rapid SaaS Evolution to Business Platforms". April 2006. Archived from the original on October 29, 2006.

[8] Why You Need A SaaS Strategy. Michael Biddick. Jan. 16, 2010. Retrieved 2010-03-10.

[9] Comparing Amazon's and Google's Platform-as-a-Service (PaaS) Offerings | Enterprise Web 2.0 | ZDNet.com

[10] Cloud application delivery platform for dynamic Case Management Solutions, Eccentex

[11] "IEEE Technical Committee on Services Computing". Tab.computer.org. http://tab.computer.org/tcsc. Retrieved 2010-08-22.

[12] "IEEE International Conference on Cloud Computing (CLOUD)". Thecloudcomputing.org. http://www.thecloudcomputing.org. Retrieved 2010-08-22.

[13] Study on the Security of Cloud Computing, 26-Feb-2010, Fraunhofer-Gesellschaft

[14] Gartner,Cloud Computing Security Risks, Networkworld , April 2010

[15] "Security of virtualization, cloud computing divides IT and security pros". Networkworld.com. 2010-02-22. http://www.networkworld.com/news/2010/022210 virtualization-cloud-security-debate.html. Retrieved 2010-08-22

4

Analysis of Major Cyber Threats in Wireless Networking

Vikram Mangla, Dr. S. N. Panda***

Abstract – *Wireless Networking is another way to connect to the network without wires. Wireless networks are experiencing unprecedented growth in the recent years. Wireless computing promises greater user convenience and ease of usability. The wide proliferation of laptops, PDAs, and mobile phones means that there are an increasing number of devices on the move and hence there is a greater need to support such devices. In wireless domain, there is more need of safety of corporate resources and maintaining the functionality needed. Many security protocols have been defined, but still much work is to be done. In this paper, we explore different kind of major cyber threats occur in Wireless networking and the threat analysis.*

*Asstt. Professor, Chitkara Institute of Engg. & Technology, Punjab. Email id: mangla.vikram@gmail.com

**Professor, Regional Institute of Management & Technology, Mandi Gobindgarh, Punjab. Email id: panda.india@gmail.com

Keywords – *Wireless networking, Wireless threats, Active and Passive Eavesdropping, Man-in-middle attacks, Unauthorised access, Cyber Security, Threat analysis, WEP, Cryptography.*

1. INTRODUCTION

Wireless Local Area networks are increasing in popularity day by day. WLANs are not limited by network jacks nor are they limited by geography. The initial advent of wireless infrastructures and associated technologies were originally overlooked by most within the technological community. This was mostly due to the infantile nature of the technology, as well as its failure to address absolute critical issues such as security. With the rapid adoption of wireless networks by the IT departments of the organisations everywhere, the security has now become the major concern which involves an entirely new dimension of vulnerability to malicious hackers and casual intruders. As an extension to existing wired infrastructure, Wi-Fi helps companies achieve better customer responsiveness and improvements in the bottom line. The downside is that making corporate data accessible through Wi-Fi networks means intruders and other unwanted visitors can easily access such networks if proper precautions and tools aren't used to protect them. In this paper different kind of major cyber threats, which occur in Wireless networking, are studied in detail and the analysis of each threat in the organisation are studied.

2. THREATS IN WIRELESS NETWORKING

There are many threats in wireless networking which can be classified as insider and outsider attacks. The outsider has access to the wireless network and the software and hardware that can be purchased or otherwise obtained publicly. The insider is a valid user of wireless network whose goal is to obtain the access to information which he would not otherwise be entitled. The insider has valid software, hardware and certificates for both the wired network and WLANs. There can be data attacks in wireless networking also which affects the data of the user. The different types of threats are:

- Passive Eavesdropping
- Active Eavesdropping
- Man-in-the-middle attacks
- Unauthorised access
- Session high jacking
- Replay attack

Out of the above, first two threats violate the confidentiality or privacy of the session, whereas the third one violate the confidentiality and integrity and the last three threats violate the integrity of the network traffic. The details of first three attacks are explained as under:

A. Passive Eavesdropping – In this attack the attacker passively monitors the wireless session (Figure 1) and the payload. If the payload is encrypted, this includes breaking the encryption to read the plaintext. The only precondition is that the attacker has access to the transmission.

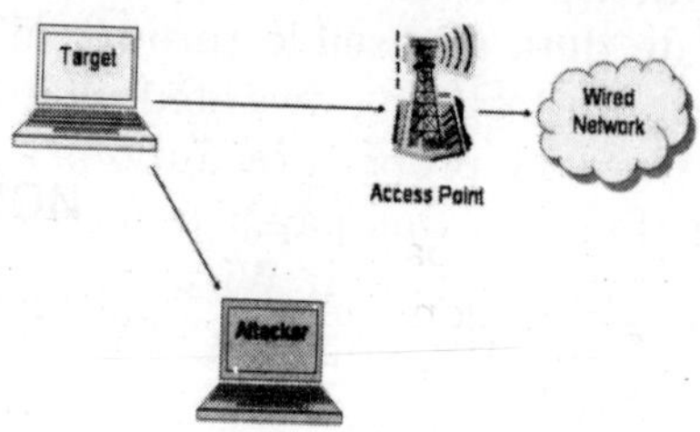

Fig. 1. Passive Eavesdropping

Passive eavesdropping in wireless communications may cause significant risk to an organization. This attack cannot easily be stopped by using the physical security measures. Because of the extended range of 802.11 broadcasts, enemies can potentially detect transmission from a parking place or the nearby roads. The 802.11 signals can travel outside the building or there can be an "insider" through which this attack can happen. An adversary or enemy may be able to listen in and obtain sensitive information including proprietary information, network IDs and passwords, and configuration data. This kind of attack, performed through the use of a wireless network analyzer tool or *sniffer*, is particularly easy for two reasons: 1) frequently confidentiality features of WLAN technology are not even enabled, and 2) because of the numerous vulnerabilities in the 802.11 technology security, determined adversaries can compromise the system. The impact of this kind of attack is that not only the privacy of the data is lost, but also the information gleaned is an important precondition for other, and that is more damaging attacks. In a wireless environment it is usually impossible to detect this attack, as it does not produce any new traffic in the network. For example Bluetooth has been vulnerable to passive eavesdropping attacks, since secrecy has been based on weak symmetric cryptographic algorithm and typically short PINs.

B. Active Eavesdropping – The active eavesdropping technique involves the attacker injecting data into the communication to help decipher the payload. An example of active eavesdropping with partially known plaintext is IP spoofing. In order for the hacker to perform IP spoofing on the packets being sent between the wireless device and the wireless router the hacker needs to know the IP address of the destination of the packet. The hacker also needs to have another machine connected to the Internet in order for this type of attack to work, they also have to know the IP address of their other machine. When a hacker intercepts the packet, they determine the bit difference between the original IP address, and the new IP address, which will be the IP address of his other machine. Using this knowledge, the hacker replaces the destination IP address with the IP address of their other machine. When the modified packet is sent to the wireless router, it decrypts it and sends it to the hackers other machine, completely getting rid of the WEP encryption. The advantage of this method is the user sending the original packet has no idea that this is happening because their original packet is still being sent to the original destination IP address. This is possible because WEP uses a cyclic redundancy check (CRC) to verify the integrity of the data in the packet, where an attacker can modify the messages and the change cannot be detected. Another active eavesdropping method requires the hacker to know the contents of the original packet. This attack is performed by having the hacker with an offsite computer send a packet to a computer within the wireless network. This packet could be anything from an email message, to a chat conversation. When the hacker monitors the packet in the wireless network it is in its encrypted form, so now, the hacker knows the original packet, the encrypted packet, and the Initialization Vector used to encrypt the packet.

C. Man-in-the-middle Attacks – A Man in the Middle attack, often abbreviated as MITM, is accomplished by inserting a third party into a two party communication and hiding that fact from the original two participants. The man in the middle then gets access to the data and can secretly alter it for his own purposes. The man-in-the-middle attacks violate the integrity of the session. Man-in-the-middle was developed to be used on switched LANs, where it could only affect hosts on a particular network segment, but it can easily work on wireless systems just the same. This is a real-time attack, means it occurs during a target machine's session. The data may be read or the session is modified as it occurs. The attacker will know the contents of the message prior to the intended recipient receiving it, or change the message en route. In wireless networking, the MITM scheme is implemented in a number of ways. One is to operate a rogue access point resembling a legitimate wireless hotspot. Often the real access point is jammed or blocked while the rogue, with the same SSID, is in the clear with a strong signal. Another method is to break a client's connection and lure the client's hardware into reconnecting to the middleman. In this case the middleman has faked the access point MAC address.

Since 802.11 authentications is not mutual between the access point and the client, and the default encryption (WEP) is easy to crack, the man-in-the-middle attacks are somewhat trivial on 802.11 networks. These attacks are not limited only to wireless networks; there have been the cases of proxy servers faking security for SSL/HTTPS communications. Banking, secure mails, or other sensitive connections have been compromised in the man-in-the-middle attacks. ARP attacks are particularly dangerous subsets of MITM attacks because these attacks can be directed against targets on the wired component of the network, not just wireless clients. The attacker has to access the network to make this attack happen. The attacker sends the forged ARP reply message that changes the mapping of the IP address to the given MAC address. The attacker acts as the man-in-the-middle between any two hosts in the broadcasts domain. These attacks are more dangerous than the other attacks. They affect the integrity of data more.

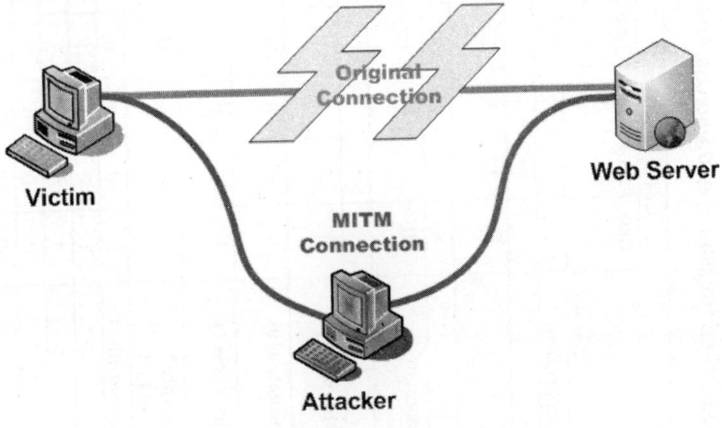

Fig. 2. Man-in-the-middle attacks

3. ANALYSIS OF CYBER THREATS

Each threat discussed above have its own effects. While analysing each threats many things are considered such as their effect on the organisation, each layer in the network and data on which they effects. Even a single security hole in an otherwise bullet-proof application can potentially wreak embarrassing and costly chaos in the hands of the wrong person. To create a completely secure application, every

Table 1: Cyber Crimes/Cases Registered and Persons Arrested under IT Act during 2003-2006

S. No.	Crime Heads	Cases Registered				% Variation in 2006 over 2005	Person arrested				% Variation in 2006 over 2005
		2003	2004	2005	2006		2003	2004	2005	2006	
1	Tampering computer source department	8	2	2	10	0	6	0	10	8	-20.0
2	Hacking computer systems										
	a. Loss/Damage to computer resource/utility	13	14	33	25	-24.0	11	31	27	34	25.9
	b. Hacking	8	12	41	34	-17.1	7	1	14	29	107.1
3	Obscene publication/transmission in electronic form	20	34	88	69	-21.6	17	21	125	81	-35.2
4	Failure										
	a. Of compliance/orders of certifying authority	0	0	1	0	-100.0	0	0	0	0	–
	b. To assist to decoy or the information in interception by Govt. Agency	6	0	0	0	–	12	0	0	0	–
5	Unauthorized access/attempt to access of protected computer system	1	0	0	0	–	0	0	0	0	–
6	Obtaining license or digital signature by misrepresentation/suppression of fact	0	0	0	0	–	0	0	0	0	–
7	Publishing false digital signature certificates	0	0	0	0	–	0	0	0	0	–
8	Fraud digital/signature	1	0	1	1	0	2	0	3	0	-100
9	Breach of confidential/Privacy	3	6	3	3	0	0	7	13	2	-84.6
10	Other	0	0	0	0	–	0	0	0	0	–
11	Total	60	68	179	142	-20.7	55	60	192	154	-19.8

member of every object in the application must be carefully analyzed to determine every conceivable way each member could be invoked. Doing a thorough job of this requires analysis of other many application details such as the data, user roles, technology choices, use cases, and external dependencies. This analysis should be done in the design phase for optimal efficiency, because security threats found and dealt with in the design phase are far easier and cheaper to fix. Additionally, all these details must be thoroughly reviewed every time any design detail changes. For all but the simplest of applications, manually mapping out the seemingly infinite combinations of all the above details for every member in an application is a foreboding task indeed. That's why this time consuming, error prone, and potentially budget busting task is rarely done properly in the real world.

3.1 Meaning of Threat Analysis

In network systems, two important steps in developing architecture and designing the protocol are to define the problem and to lists the characteristics of acceptable solution. Once the problem is defined, a list of characteristics for an acceptable solution, often called *requirements*, serves to limit the solution space in order to direct design energy toward the most promising architectural solution. The equivalent activity for security – identifying the threats and figuring how attacks can be mounted – is called a *threat analysis*. In most cases the threat analysis starts from an existing architecture, design or system design. Ideally the threat analysis should start with the existing system and security. A threat analysis is conducted by finding opportunities for disruption or compromise of communication. Architectural solutions are not always the best way to handle a threat. For example, in the case of an 802.11 microwave oven attack, the defence is to find the microwave oven and close the door. The alternative solution of locking up all the microwave ovens in the building and requiring some kind of credentials check to use them is unrealistic and not really commensurate with the threat. If the threat is not architectural in nature, then architectural solutions are obviously not the right way to address it. After threats have been identified, the next step is to generate some realistic assumptions about the nature of the attacker. If the assumptions are too strict, the security solution may be over engineered for the actual threat. A standard assumption about the attacker when conducting a threat analysis is that the attacker is able to see all traffic between legitimate parties to the protocol. While this assumption may not be true for most wired networks, it is almost always true for wireless networks. A threat analysis cannot assume that known users will never be a threat. An important consideration when performing a threat analysis is to clearly identify the value of the threatened activity or the severity of the disruption. If the value of the activity is low or the severity of the disruption is slight, measures to counteract the threat should be similarly lightweight. The process of doing threat analysis is unfortunately is very heuristic and not very quantitative.

3.2 Security Services

Following are the security services required to mitigate the above threats.

1. Identity management in the form of authentication and authorization addresses threats involving unauthorized entities. Identity verification of the terminal by the network mitigates the threat of unauthorized network access service or access to a service level above the authorized level. Identity verification of the network by the terminal mitigates the threat of a rogue access point or base station attempting to steal the terminal's traffic.
2. Key management establishes keys for cryptographic algorithms used in further security services. The initial authentication and authorization process includes key management to ensure that the keys are tied to a verified terminal or network identity.
3. Data origin authentication using the keys established during authentication and authorization mitigates the threat of session stealing, both on the current access point and during handover.

4. Confidentiality protection using the keys established during authentication and authorization mitigates the threat of eavesdropping.

3.3 Counter Measures

To diminish the risks which are involved in these attacks, architecture should have the following four components:

a. Mutual Authentication
b. Block cipher encryption of the payload.
c. Strong cryptographic protection.
d. Firewall

These components should be present between the wireless and the wired components of the system. The absence of any of these components leave the network unsecured and any unwanted outsider can enter into the network and can disturb the integrity of the system. These components, properly implemented and configured, will result in a wireless network component that offers little to no additional threat to the network as a whole. Neglecting any one of these components exposes the network to a significant increase in risk.

4. CONCLUSION

As the use of wireless networks are increasing day by day, so as the threats. More and more wireless devices are coming to the market by the different vendors. The user is using the devices without taking much care of the security of the devices and their use. Interfering with the wireless network is very easy to do and difficult to stop. The current trends of increasing threats shows the need for increased cooperation among the security companies, governments, academics and other organisations and individuals to reduce these threats. The stress will be on organisations, institutions, and other knowledgeable groups to come together for the benefit of the effected regions and try to minimize the effect of the attacks. Internet threat activity is truly global and malicious activity allowed to flourish in one area could quickly spread worldwide. With the increasing adaptability of malicious code developers and their ability to avoid detection, different organisations are working in this context. The large increase in the number of new malicious code threats, coupled with the use of the Web as a distribution mechanism, also demonstrates the growing need for more responsive and cooperative security measures. While antivirus signature scanning, heuristic detection, and intrusion prevention continue to be vital for the security of organizations as well as end users, newer technologies, such as reputation-based security, will become increasingly important.

REFERENCES

1. *Rony Hasinur Rehman, Nusrat Nowsheen, Mahbubul Azam Khan, Asif Hossian Khan* - Wireless Lan Security : An Indepth Study of the threats and vulnerabilities.
2. *Antonietta Stango, Neeli R. Prasad* - A Threat analysis methodology for Security Evaluation and Enhancement planning.
3. *SANS Institute InfoSec Reading Room* – SSL Man-in-the-Middle Attacks.
4. *Karan Singh and Rama Shankar Yadav* - Overview of Secure Network System.
5. *John Peter Jesan, Nova Southeastern University* – Major threats to Information Security.
6. *Robert Boncella* – Wireless Threats and Attacks.
7. Wireless Lan Security Research Paper – Sara Nasre
8. Barken, Lee. How Secure Is Your Wireless Network? Saddle River, NJ: Prentice Hall PTR, 2004
9. Dan Schade. Wireless Attacks and Defense.
10. Arbaugh, William. "Wireless Security is Different." Computer. Volume 36, Issue 8, Aug. 2003: 99–101.
11. Donald Welch. Wireless Security Threat Taxonomy. Proceedings of the 2003 IEEE Workshop on Information Assurance.
12. Internet Security Systems, Wireless LAN Security: 802.11b and Corporate Networks. ISS Technical White Paper. Webpage online available at http://documents.iss.net/whitepapers/wireless_LAN_security.pdf
13. Chickinsky, Alan, Wireless LAN Security Threats. Document IEEE 802.11-01/258

14. Arbaugh, William, Narendar Shankar and Y.C. Justin Wan, Your 802.11 Wireless Network has No Clothes. Department of Computer Science University of Maryland. Web page online available at http://www.cs.umd.edu/~waa/wireless.pdf.
15. Carey, Allan, Wireless Security Vulnerabilities continue to Surface: Cigital Identifies the Latest. White Paper by Cigital, Inc. http://www.cigital.com. October 2001.
16. Andrei A. Mikhailovsky, Konstantin V. Gavrilenko, Andrew Vladimirov. Wireless Hacking: Breaking through.
17. Wired and Wireless Security Best Practices. Trapeze Networks.
18. Information Warfare – How to survive Cyber Attacks. Ebook by Michael Erbschloe, Osborne/McGraw-Hill.
19. Maximum Wireless Security – Cyrus Peikari, Seth Fogie , Sams Publishing.
20. Wireless Security Handbook – Aaron E.Earle, Aurebach Publications.
21. "Protecting Data from Cyber Theft – A virulent disease", *Vikram Mangla, Dr. S. N. Panda*, JETWI, Vol 2 No 2.

❑❑❑

5

Cloud Computing Architecture

An Overview

Dr. Soni Ritu, ^Anil Saini, Ashwani Goel ***

Abstract – *Resource sharing is one the key aspects being looked in to in the field of computer networking application with its optimum utilization. In the time when cost cutting is one of the major focus areas along with the quality by the companies, cloud computing has the solution for them. To make the best use of cloud computing we need to understand the architectural aspect along with the security as there are more than one entity using the same resource simultaneously or at different times. Cloud computing has its applications in almost all possible fields due to its positive results in terms of cost cutting, efficiency, reliability, scalability. This paper discusses the various architectural models of different companies. It also gives a*

*Associate Prof & Head, DCSA, G.N.G, Yamunanagar, e-mail: ritusoniynr@yahoo.com

**Lecturer & ^Head, Lecturer DCSA, GIMT, Kanipla, e-mail: anilsaini1042@gmail.com, ashwani30goel@gmail.com

comparative insight view of different companies with respect to various cloud computing parameters.

I. INTRODUCTION

Cloud[1] computing is relatively new way of utilizing the shared resources and can be considered as an alternative to the private server based applications. Cloud computing considers a large number of servers along with other resources and allows users to utilize them, as and when required by them on there demand, as a chargeable service. The end users need not to worry about the physical location of the resources and these services can be used around the globe.Cloud computing application development depended largely on its architect because the infrastructure used in cloud computing is demand oriented and releases as soon as the purpose is solved. With the greater advantages and utilization of cloud computing, we must not forget that the data/information is open to public domain and thus can be accessible to all. Thus security in terms of data & infrastructure is the major concern in cloud computing. As shown in fig. 1, number of applications like ERP , BI , CRM

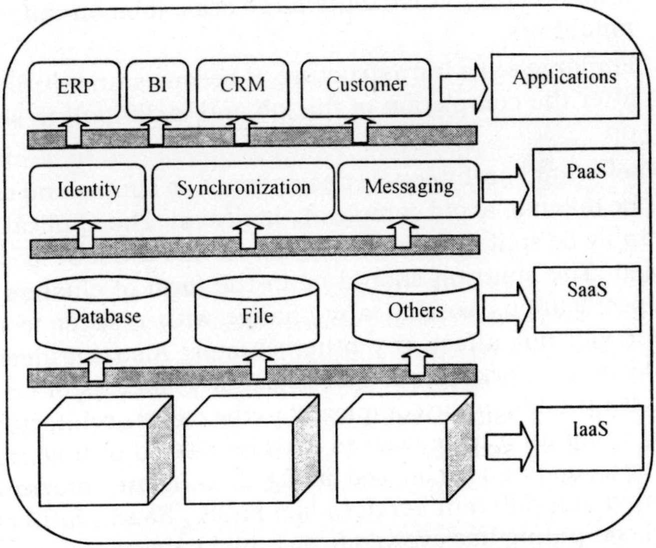

Fig. 1. Examples of Cloud Architecture

etc can be developed with cloud architecture. Conversion of word files to PDF, OCR to editable text, changing the size /resolution of images, websites are few applications that make use of cloud architecture.

II. ARCHITECTURAL CONSIDERATION

Architecture, be of any field, evolves over time. With the introduction of Personnel computers, the demand of network and infrastructure grew at a great pace leading to separation of the application tier and server tier. With the advancement in technology and passage of time services became more and more distribute, Cloud computing has become the distributed virtualized solution. There[2] are a number of reasons for effective architecture of cloud applications and networks as compared to traditional networks. Few of them are:

1. An application might require large number of machines which is very difficult to manage.
2. It is difficult to manage machines on time.
3. It is difficult to distribute large scale jobs on different machines.
4. For large scale infrastructure, it becomes underutilized after the completion of the job and is difficult to scale up.

The[1] cloud architecture design must be simple and care must be taken to avoid complexity in design. The application preferably be split into different systems and must be loosely coupled .The splitting should be in the form of clusters as per specifications so that any change with respect to the cluster will not affect any other cluster. Also the design should be network based. The scalability factors of cloud computing adds to the complexity to the cloud architecture. Cloud computing have evolved with he passed of time from different states as discussed in fig 2. Difrrent companies are providing different services like PaSS , SaaS , IaSS etc. Cloud computing has evolved from initial networking i.e grid computing through utility computing to its current stage. As shown in fig. 2 Grid computing solved large problem with parallel computing. Utility computing offered the resources as a metered service. SaaS was introduced as a network based subscription to the application.

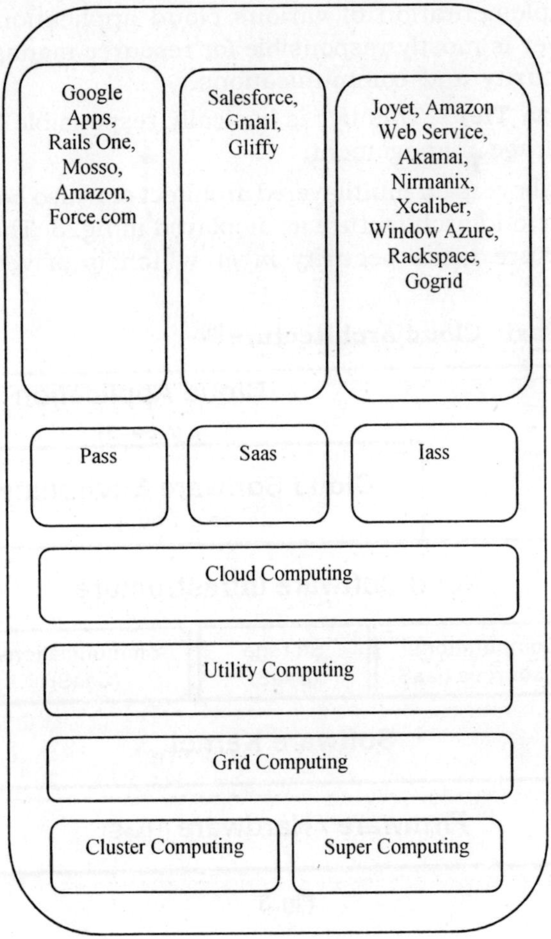

Fig. 2

There are various architectural models that can be implemented for designing a cloud. For instance we can have multi-tier architecture

- **Presentation Tier** – This tier usually provides the user interface for any application. This interface can be

with respect to software environment or software infrastructure.

- **Logic Tier** – This tier provides back end logic implementation of various cloud applications. This layer is mostly responsible for resource management, security and communications.
- **Data Tier** – This tier is basically responsible for data storage management.

The above said multilayered architect can also be related to basic cloud architecture as displayed in fig. 3. This basic architecture lacks security layer which is of very high concern.

A. Basic Cloud Architecture [6]

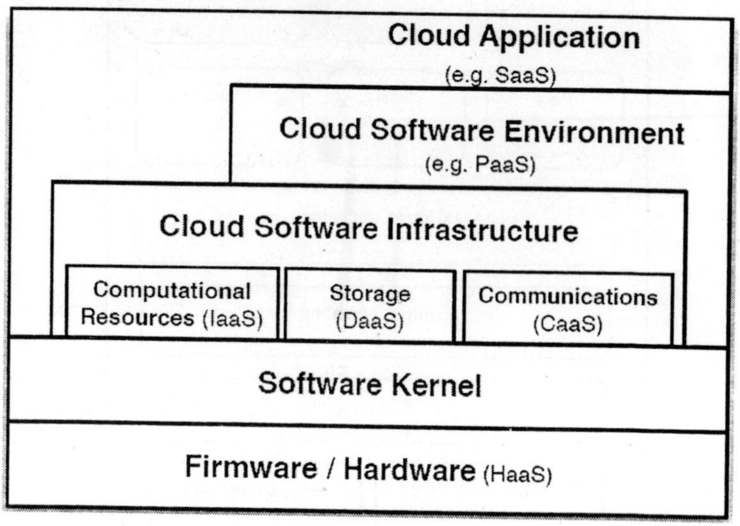

Fig. 3

With this basic cloud architect, various companies have developed there own architecture to provide cloud services in the market. We will be discussing the architect of CISCO, AT&T and Oracle here.

B. CISCO Cloud Architecture [7]

The Architecture of CISCO Cloud is represented in fig. 4. The hosting of services in the cloud for the users is done by the network/storage/compute blocks. The Architecture of CISCO Cloud is represented in fig. 4. The hosting of services in the cloud for the users is done by the network/storage/compute blocks. The security is taken care by security layer and the resource mapping/service details are stored in orchestration layer. As compared to basic cloud architecture the SaaS layer is taken care by cloud service consumer, PaaS by Service delivery and management, Iaas /DaaS/Caas by Network/Storage/Compute.

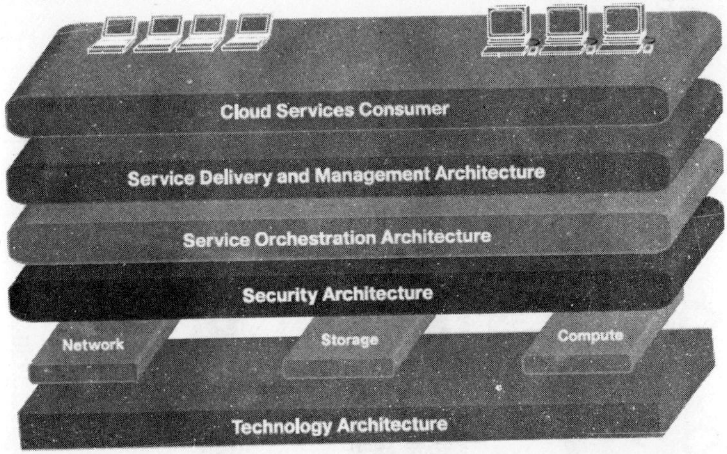

Fig. 4

In addition to architecture with respect to hardware, service providers also implement service based architecture. Fig. 5 and fig. 6 displays the architecture of AT&T and IBM[8] respectively.

C. AT&T Cloud Architecture

As shown in fig 5, the user accesses the cloud service after passing through the security checks at the initial stage. This architecture helps in accelerating the communication process. The user enjoys the services through virtual environment where PaaS, IaaS and DaaS are part of it.

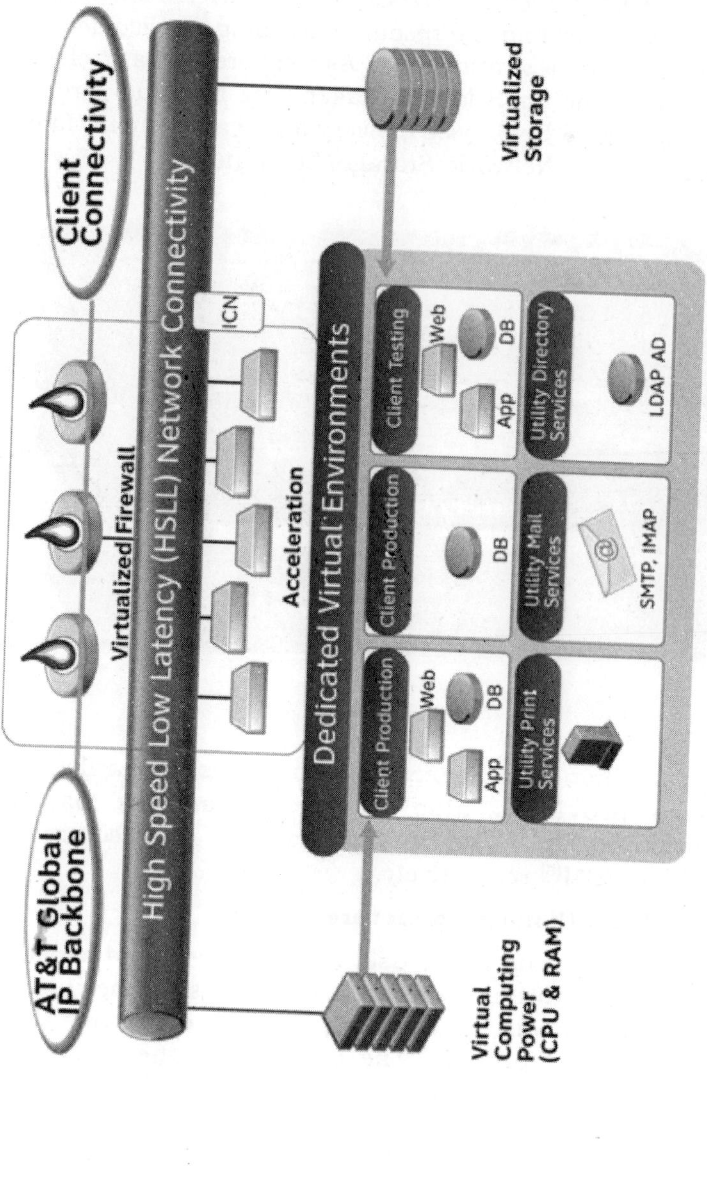
AT&T Global IP Backbone
Client Connectivity
High Speed Low Latency (HSLL) Network Connectivity
Virtualized Firewall
ICN
Acceleration
Dedicated Virtual Environments
Client Production
App
Web
DB
Client Production
DB
Client Testing
App
Web
DB
Utility Print Services
Utility Mail Services
SMTP, IMAP
Utility Directory Services
LDAP AD
Virtual Computing Power (CPU & RAM)
Virtualized Storage

Fig. 5

D. IBM Cloud Architecture

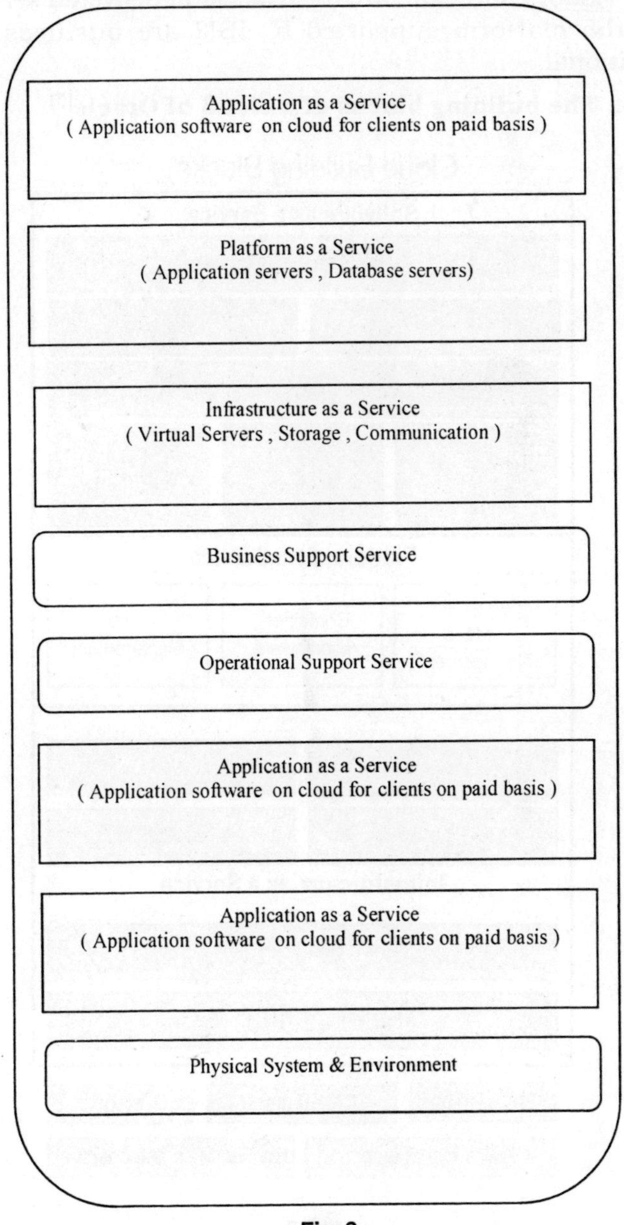

Fig. 6

` IBM cloud architecture is self explanatory as shown in fig. 6. AaaS, PaaS, IaaS are the IBM cloud delivered services and the platform supported by IBM are business and operational.

E. The building blocks of a cloud of Oracle[5]

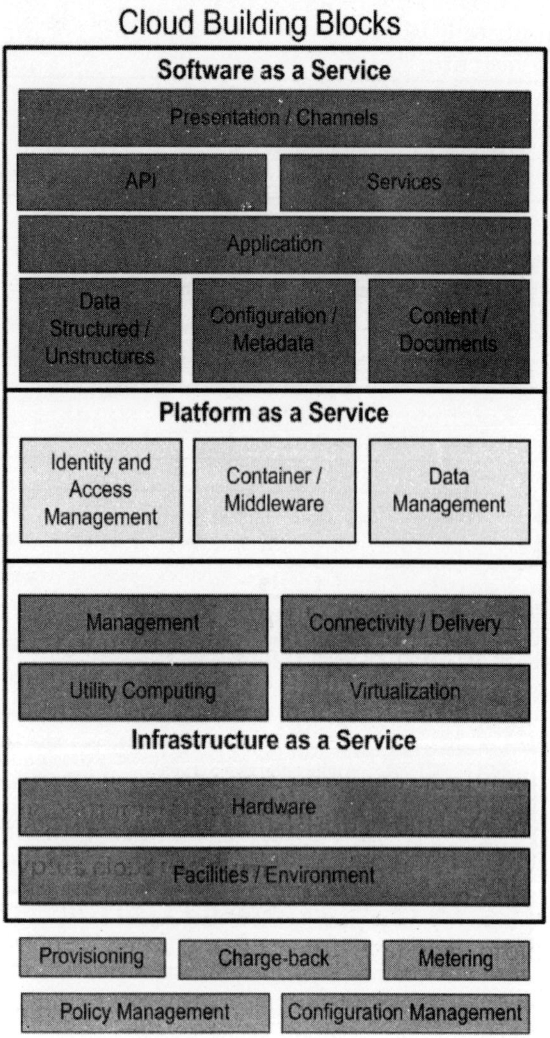

Fig. 7

As shown in fig. 7 , Oracle provide services in the form of software, platform and infrastructure. The software service includes the user interface and applications. The platform service consists of data management and security. Hardware management is the part of infrastructure management. The policies, configuration in addition to the charges applicable to the user and charge-back are also dealt with extreme care.

3. CLOUD COMPUTING PARAMETERS

While designing any architect the following parameters are to be considered.

- **Services Used** – Various cloud services like SaaS, PaaS, IaaS etc that are provided to the customers.
- **Platform Supported** – The operating systems that would support the applications of the cloud service provider.
- **Integrated DB supported** – Various external database that a cloud service provider would support for backup.
- **SLA availability** – The service level agreement that would indicate the uptime for network and /or Service
- **Cloud services and tools** – Various tools supported / provided by the cloud service provider to its users
- **Maximum limits** – The amount of memory space that would be available to the user for the data storage.
- **Support Pricing, Policy** – The policies and pricing for the support to any of the users for the services enjoyed by them.
- **Support response Time** – Response time from the cloud service provider to the user .
- **Service credit for an outage** – The rebate to be given to the customers in case the uptime as per SLA is not met.
- **Data backup** – It is about the responsibility of backing up the user data, whether at user level or at service provider's level.

- **Data security –** Security being the most critical aspect of cloud computing , here the security aspect is taken care of.
- **Virtualization –** Decoupling and separation of the business service from the infrastructure needed to run it.

There are a number of cloud service providers in the market. Amazon, Google, Force.com, Go Grid, Windows Azure, IBM , Oracle, AT&T are to name a few. Services, platform, Database used, SLA, cloud tools, price, backup, security are certain parameters based on which the service providers can be compared. A brief comparison with respect to mentioned parameters is mentioned in the Annexure-I[9]

As observed from Annexure-I, Amazon, Google and Force.com provide Platform services whereas Windows, Rackspace and Go Grid provide Infrastructure service. It is also observed that Google has free user support but doest not commit the user for the support response time and with no service credit. Some service providers take the responsibility take ensure proper backup of data whereas others have passed on the responsibility to the user.

4. CONCLUSION

In the era when nothing can be thought of without computers and internet, we need such services that will suffice our needs with minimum cost and maximum output and reliability, cloud computing is the solution. With proper architecture and security measures, cloud computing has taken networking and internet to new heights and has made there right utilization. Keeping in mind the basic architecture of cloud, companies implement there own architecture depending on there service priorities and there perspective about the cloud. While analyzing the various architectures, both at service level and hardware level, a lot work can be done in almost all the areas of services, be it at software level, platform level or infrastructural level .

REFERENCES

1. Application Architecture for Cloud Computing (www.rpath.com)
2. Varis Jinesh, Cloud Architectures, Technology Evangelist, Amazon Web Services
3. An Oracle White Paper in Enterprise Architecture, August 2009
4. Expert Reference Series of White Paper (www.globalknowlege.com)
5. Mather Tim, Kumarswamy Subra, Latif Shahed, Cloud Security and Privacy
6. Lamia Youseff University of California, Santa Barbara Maria Butrico, Dilma Da Silva IBM T.J. Watson Research Center Yorktown, New York, Toward a Unified Ontology of Cloud Computing
7. Cisco Cloud Computing -Data Center Strategy, Architecture ,and Solutions Point of View White Paper for U.S. Public Sector
8. IBM Point of View: Security and Cloud Computing Cloud computing White paper November 2009
9. Cloud Computing Services – A comparison

Annexure - 1

	Amazon	**Google**	**Window Azure**	**Force.com**	**Rackspace**	**Go Grid**
Services Used	PaaS, IaaS	PaaS	IaaS	PaaS	IaaS	IaaS
Platform supported	**Operating systems** • IBM DB2 • Red Hat Enterprise Linux • Windows Server 2003/2008 • Open Solaris • Microsoft SQL Server & many more	**Runtime** • Java Runtime Environment • Python Runtime Environment	**Operating systems** • Windows 7 • Windows Server 2008 • Windows Vista	**Software** • Unlimited real-time database customizations • Programmable user interface • Programmable cloud logic	**Operating systems** • Linux • Mac OS X • Windows	**Operating systems** • Windows server 2008 • Windows server 2003 • Redhat Linux 5.1
Integrated DB supported	MySql	GAE doesn't support external databases; it provides a data store of its own.	Sql azure	Not applicable	MySQL, Microsoft SQL Oracle	MSSQL 2008 Workgroup, Microsoft SQL Server 2005, Microsoft SQL Server 2005 Workgroup Edition
SLA availability	Amazon S3 - available with a Monthly Uptime Percentage of at	100% Uptime	99.9% Uptime	99.9 + % Uptime	100% Network Uptime	100% Uptime

	Amazon	Google	Window Azure	Force.com	Rackspace	Go Grid
	least 99.9% during any monthly billing cycle & Amazon EC2 - available with an Annual Uptime Percentage of at least 99.95% during the Service Year					
Cloud services and tools	Amazon CloudWatch API Tools Auto Scaling API Tools Elastic Load Balancing API Tools AWS Toolkit for Eclipse AWS Management Console Amazon EC2 API Tools Amazon EC2 AMI Tools	Google Secure Data Connector Private gadgets Google Visualization API Google Apps APIs Google web toolkit IDE support	Windows Azure Platform Training Kit Windows Azure Software Development Kit Microsoft Visual Studio 2008 Service Pack 1	Apex Language Code Editor Enhanced Metadata Support Upgrade Wizard	Beanstalk – Hassle-free Subversion Hosting Attachment fu in Ruby Cloudvox Nautilus Cloud Files Plugin by Chmouel Boudjnah Paperclip-Cloudfiles Olark Live Website Chat	Go Grid's Cloud control Command Line Tool Cloud Wizard's Open Source Cross Cloud Scripting Language Mitch Denny's Windows Power Shell Snap-in

	Amazon	Google	Window Azure	Force.com	Rackspace	Go Grid
Maximum limits	Amazon S3 - Store object up to 5 GB Amazon EC2 Volume sizes ranging from 1GB to 1TB	Automatic scaling is built in with App Engine No matter how many users you have or how much data your application stores, App Engine can scale to meet your needs	Azure has a 64MB limit on individual blobs and also allows you to split a blob into blocks of 4MB each	In the unlimited edition, Number of sites - 252,000 Database objects Total storage 120MB/user API calls/day - 5,000/user, 5 million total Page views/month - 1,000,000 Sites bandwidth/day - 40GB	Infinite scalability	Horizontal server scaling Vertical server scaling Server parking This is ideal for users that don't want to pay for an entire month of service for a server used only a few days per month
Support pricing policy	Premium, Silver and Gold support available	Free Support is available	Developer support is charged on a per incident basis.	Basic and Premier Support with Administration.	24x7x365 Live Support	FREE 24/7 Phone and Premium Support
Support response Time	Urgent - 1 hour High - 4 business hours Normal - 1 business day Low - 2 business days	Not available	Not available	Basic Support - 2 business days Premier Support - 2 hours Premier Support with Administration - 2 hours	24 x 7 x 365 online live chat and toll free phone	EMERGENCY Cases - 30 minutes All other Cases - 120 minutes
Service credit for an outage	Amazon S3 Equal to or greater than	Not available	Microsoft will provide a 10 percent credit if	Not available	Not available	A "10,000% Service Credit" is a credit

	Amazon	Google	Window Azure	Force.com	Rackspace	Go Grid
	99% but less than 99.9% - 10% less than 99% - 25% Amazon EC2 (If the Annual Uptime Percentage for a customer drops below 99.95% for the Service Year, that customer is eligible to receive a Service Credit equal to 10% of their bill)		compute connectivity falls below 99.95 percent uptime; a 10 percent credit if role-instance uptime or storage falls below 99.9 percent uptime. If it falls below 99 percent availability across anything, 25 percent credit will be provided			equivalent to one hundred (100) times Customer's fees for the impacted Service feature for the duration of the Failure
Data backup	Amazon RDS automatically patches the database software and backs up the database Amazon AWS	The user is solely responsible for securing and backing up the Application and any Content. Google has no responsibility or	The user is solely responsible for securing and backing up the data.	All networking components, SSL accelerators, load balancers, Web servers, and application servers are configured in a redundant	Although the Rackspace Cloud service may be used as a backup service, you agree that you will maintain	Whether or not Customer's Signup calls on Go Grid to maintain back-ups, Customer will have to keep a back-up

	Amazon	Google	Window Azure	Force.com	Rackspace	Go Grid
	may delete, without liability of any kind, any of the Amazon SQS Content	liability for the deletion or failure to store any content and other communications maintained or transmitted through use of the Service.		configuration. All customer data is stored on a primary database server that is clustered with a backup database server for redundancy	at least one additional current copy of your programs and data stored on the Rackspace Cloud system somewhere other than on the Rackspace Cloud system.	copy of all data hosted by Go Grid.
Data security	Amazon Elastic Compute Cloud (EC2) provides Host Operating System, Guest operating system and a complete firewall solution.	App Engine runs Java applications using the Java 6 virtual machine (JVM). The JVM runs in a secured "sandbox" environment to isolate your application for service and security.	• Filtering Routers Firewalls • Cryptographic Protection of Messages • Software Security Patch Management • Centralized monitoring, correlation, and analysis systems	User authentication features such as SAML through to IP range restrictions on logons, session security and auditing. Security Addresses all layers Physical Security Logical Network Security Host	Enterprise firewalls, email accounts include antivirus and spam protection. SSL capabilities available as an add on service	Provided via Serve Path's secure infrastructure and telecom facility

	Amazon	Google	Window Azure	Force.com	Rackspace	Go Grid
			• Network Segmentation Service Administration Access Physical Security	Security Transmission Level Security Database Security		
Virtualization platform	EC2 uses modified Xen virtualization	Not available	Modified Hyper-V hypervisor	Not available	Xen virtualization	Xen virtualization

❑❑❑

6

Security Concerns in Cloud Computing

A Review

*Dr. Ritu Soni, **Ashwani Kumar, Anil Saini*

Abstract – *This paper will discuss some security concerns of cloud computing. Cloud Computing provides several services in the market, such as Infrastructure as a Service (IaaS), Platform as a Service (PaaS) and Software as a Service (SaaS). There are many service providers in the cloud computing who manages all services. Users can consume their services at a rate that is set by the providers. There are significant security concerns that need to be discussed when data is exchanging between the clouds.*

1. INTRODUCTION

In the last few years, cloud computing has grown from being a promising business concept to one of the fastest

*G.N.G College, Yamunanagar, e-mail: ritusoniynr@yahoo.com, **Kanipla, *GIMT,* Kurukshetra, e-mail: ashwani30goel@gmail.com, anilsaini1042@gmail.com

growing segments of the IT industry. [1] Power grids, traffic control, healthcare, water supplies, food and energy, along with most of the world's financial transactions, now depend on information technology. An emerging IT delivery model-cloud computing - can significantly reduce IT costs & complexities while improving workload optimization and service delivery. Cloud computing is massively scalable, provides a superior user experience, and is characterized by new, internet-driven economics. Cloud computing is a class of the next generation highly scalable distributed computing platform in which computing resources are offered 'as a service'. Cloud based services include software-as-a-service (SaaS) and platform as a service (PaaS). Amazon's Elastic Compute Cloud (EC2) [2] and IBM's Blue Cloud [3] are example of cloud computing services [4]. These clouds have different architecture based on the services they provide. The data is stored on to centralized location called data centers having a large size of data storage. The data as well as processing is somewhere on servers. So, the clients have to trust the provider on the availability as well as data security[5][6].

One of the major issues slowing cloud computing growth is security. Despite the proliferation of security management tools, along with numerous reliability assurances from cloud providers, complications with data privacy and data protection continue to plague the market. This primer on cloud computing security contains all our recent cloud security news stories, tips and interviews. Thus to take full advantage of the power of cloud computing, end user need comprehensive security solution to attain assurance of the cloud's treatment of security issues[4]. In the end, one prevalent question remains: Will things get better or worse for security in the cloud?[7].

2. BACKGROUND WORK

The concept of cloud computing has been evolving for more than 40 years. In the 1960s, J.C.R. Licklider [8] introduced the term "intergalactic computer network" at the

Advanced Research Projects Agency. This concept served to introduce the concept that the world came to know as the Internet.

Since the sixties, cloud computing has developed along a number of lines, with Web 2.0 being the most recent evolution. However, since the internet only started to offer significant bandwidth in the nineties, cloud computing for the masses has been something of a late developer.

One of the first milestones for cloud computing was the arrival of Salesforce.com [10] in 1999, which pioneered the concept of delivering enterprise applications via a simple website. The services firm paved the way for both specialist and mainstream software firms to deliver applications over the internet.

The next development was Amazon Web Services in 2002 [10], which provided a suite of cloud-based services including storage, computation and even human intelligence through the Amazon Mechanical Turk.

Then in 2006, Amazon launched its Elastic Compute cloud (EC2) [10] as a commercial web service that allows small companies and individuals to rent computers on which to run their own computer applications.

Another big milestone came in 2009, as Web 2.0 [11] hit its stride, and Google and others started to offer browser-based enterprise applications, though services such as Google Apps.

"*The most important contribution to cloud computing has been the emergence of "killer apps" from leading technology giants such as Microsoft and Google. When these companies deliver services in a way that is reliable and easy to consume, the knock-on effect to the industry as a whole is a wider general acceptance of online services,*" said Dan Germain [12], chief technology officer at IT service provider Cobweb Solutions.

Other key factors that have enabled cloud computing to evolve include the maturing of virtualization technology, the development of universal high-speed bandwidth, and universal software interoperability standards, said UK cloud computing pioneer Jamie Turner. Turner added, "As cloud computing extends its reach beyond a handful of early-adopter Google Docs users, we can only begin to imagine its scope and reach. Pretty much anything can be delivered from the cloud."

From a technical perspective, cloud computing includes service oriented architecture (SOA) and virtual applications of both hardware and software. Within this environment, it provides a scalable service delivery platform. Cloud computing share its resources among a cloud of service consumers, partners, and vendors. By sharing resources at various levels, this platform offers various services such as an Infrastructure cloud, a software cloud, an application cloud and a business cloud [9].

3. CLOUD PROVIDERS

There are so many Cloud Service Providers which provide their services according to cloud models. Some of them are based on Iaas, PaaS and others are on SaaS. Prominent Cloud Computing Service providers are:

Table 1: Prominent Cloud Providers

Cloud Provider	Cloud Type
Microsoft	SaaS
Zenith InfoTech	IaaS
TCS	IaaS & SaaS
Cynapse India	IaaS & SaaS
Wipro	SaaS
Netmagic Solutions	IaaS
Reliance Data Centre	IaaS, PaaS & SaaS
Infosys	SaaS
Salesforce.com	SaaS
Amazon AWS	PaaS & IaaS
Google App. Engine	PaaS
Go Grid	IaaS
Rackspace	IaaS
Force.com	Paas

4. SECURITY CONCERNS

Cloud computing brings benefits across three categories: economic, architectural, and strategic. First, it helps reduce IT costs. Second, it improves the experience of end-users. Third, it helps companies focus on their core competencies. While cost and ease are two great benefits of cloud computing, there are major security concerns which are to be discussed when data is moving from one cloud to another cloud. To address these concerns, the cloud provider must develop sufficient controls to provide the same or greater level of security. There are some security concerns to review in cloud computing.

1. Data Storage: Within the Cloud Computing, different countries have different requirements and controls placed on access. Because data resides in different physical locations, the cloud provider should agree in writing to provide the level of security required for customers.

2. Controlled User Access: Access control is a key concern, because insider attacks are a huge risk. A potential hacker is someone who has been entrusted with approved access to the cloud. Anyone considering using the cloud needs to look at who is managing their data and what types of controls are applied to these individuals.

3. Genuine Cloud: Cloud providers must be genuine and authorized by proper security agencies. You must ensure that your cloud provider is able to meet these requirements and is willing to undergo certification, accreditation, and review.

4. Audit Rights: The cloud service providers should agree in writing to the terms of audit.

5. Trained Employers: Employees of the cloud service providers should be well trained because people will always be the weakest link in security. How the cloud providers trained their employees is also an important item to review.

6. Data Location: When we use the cloud, we exactly don't know where the data is stored. The cloud service provider must ensure the data security. They should ensure that proper encryption technique is used in the access of data[13].

7. Security Service Levels: The SLA serves as a contracted level of guaranteed service between the cloud provider and the customer that specifies what level of services will be provided.

8. Providers Reliability: How long has the cloud provider been in business and what is their track record. If they go out of business, what happens to your data? Will your data be returned, and if so, in what format? The failed company left behind unhappy users and focused concerns on the reliability of cloud computing.

9. Recovery & Backup: While you may not know the physical location of your services, it is physically located somewhere. All physical locations face threats such as fire, storms, natural disasters, and loss of power. In case of any of these events, how will the cloud provider respond, and what guarantee of continued services are they promising?

10. Security Breach: Now a Days one of the most popular concept is social networking sites, most of the people are using these sites regularly and they uploading their personal details, pictures & videos. However, this leads to the problem that, if such a set of facts can be used to establish your own identity, then it is equally possible for an attacker to steal your identity if this set of facts is acquired. Identity theft is a huge concern for those who spend a great deal of their time online. [14]

11. As an online service provider: We will also tackle the cloud as a service provider. This covers Software as a Service (SaaS), web-hosting services, and so on. A SaaS application traditionally has the following characteristics [16]:

- Network-based
- Centralized access (by the end-user) and management (by the vendor)
- (Usually) one-to-many model

Currently popular SaaS systems are SAP Business by Design, Microsoft Dynamics and Google Apps. Gartner estimates that by 2012, 80 per cent of Fortune 1000 companies will be using SaaS [17].

5. CLOUD COMPUTING SECURITY ATTACKS

In the following, we present a selection of security issues & attacks related to Cloud Computing. Each issue is explained briefly and accompanied with a short discussion. Some of the potential attack vectors criminals may attempt include:

1. Denial of Service (DoS) attacks: In a denial-of-service (DoS) attack, an attacker attempts to prevent legitimate users from accessing information or services. By targeting your computer and its network connection, or the computers and network of the sites you are trying to use, an attacker may be able to prevent you from accessing email, websites, online accounts (banking, etc.), or other services that rely on the affected computer. [18]

2. XML Signature: A well known type of attack on protocols using XML Signature for authentication or integrity protection is XML Signature element wrapping [19] (denoted as wrapping attack). [20]

3. Browser security: In a Cloud, computation is done on remote servers. The client PC is used for I/O only, and for authentication and authorization of commands to the Cloud. It thus does not make sense to develop (platform dependent) client software, but to use a universal, platform independent tool for I/O: a standard Web browser. [20]

4. Side Channel attacks: Side Channel attacks are based on "Side Channel Information". Side Channel Information is information that can be retrieved from the encryption device that is neither the plaintext to be encrypted nor the cipher text resulting from the encryption process. [18]. So an attacker could attempt to compromise the cloud by placing a malicious virtual machine in close proximity to a target cloud server and then launching a side channel attack.

5. *Authentication attacks:* Authentication is a weak point in hosted and virtual services and is frequently targeted. There are many different ways to authenticate users; for example, based on what a person knows, has, or is. The mechanisms used to secure the authentication process and the methods used are a frequent target of attackers.

6. *Man-in-the-middle cryptographic attacks:* This attack is carried out when an attacker places himself between two users. Anytime attackers can place themselves in the communication's path, there is the possibility that they can intercept and modify communications. [21]

7. *Transaction security:* The old saying that 'money is the root of all evil'. The fact that online transactions use a central system means that if a cyber criminal manages to get control of the transaction servers, everyone is affected regardless of how cautious or security-aware they are. For example, database breaches such as those that affected debit card processor Heartland were reportedly due to malware that infiltrated the company's systems [22].

According to the indictment of suspect Albert Gonzalez, SQL injection was the primary attack vector, and in some cases custom-made malware was installed in certain systems, which allowed the suspects to evade anti-virus programs, scan for data, and delete log files [23]. Spoofing and phishing are two social engineering techniques that have emerged solely from the development of the cloud. [14].

6. CONCLUSION

In Cloud computing all the data is stored on the centralized server so the Cloud providers must ensure the proper security mechanism or procedure for the safety of data. Client should review a cloud provider's security function individually and decide also on an individual basis, whether the supplied security mechanisms are sufficient for the specific requirement of the company. Lot of work already been done to minimize the attacks.

REFERENCES

[1] "Top Five Security Concerns", http://www.puterweekly.com/Articles/2010/01/12/235782/Top-five-cloud-computing-security-issues.htm

[2] Amazon Elastic Compute Cloud[URL],http://aws.amazon.com/ec2, access on Oct. 2009.

[3] IBM Blue Cloud project [URL]. http://www.03.ibm.com/press/us/en/pressrelease/22613.wss, access on Oct. 2009

[4] "A Layered Security Approach for Cloud Computing Infrastructure", July 19, 2010 from IEEE Xplore

[5] "Cloud Security Issues" July 2009 IEEE Xplore

[6] "IBM Smart Business" http://www-07ibm.com/in/ibm/cloud/?ca=googleaw&gclid=CIe838v97KMCFQdB6wodbkhM2

[7] http://searchcloudcomputing.techtarget.com/generic/0,295582,sid201_gci1372033,00.html

[8] http://www.computerweekly.com/Articles/2009/08/03/236832/Distributed-systems-grid-and-cloud-ssential-Guide.htm

[9] http://thecloudcomputing.org/2009/2

[10] wwww.computerweekly.com/.../A-history-of- cloud computing.htm

[11] www.computerweekly.com/.../2009/.../A-history-of-cloud-computing.htm

[12] http://www.itbstorage.com/pr/35012

[13] "Data Security in the World of Cloud Computing", July 19, 2010 from IEEE Xplore

[14] "The Cloud or The Mist?" Virus Bulletin Conference September 2009

[15] Software & Information Industry Association. Software as a Service: Strategic Backgrounder. February 2001. http://www.siia.net/estore/ssb-01.pdf.

[16] Taudt, E. Konary, A. 2005 Software as a Service Taxonomy and Research Guide. IDC Research Report. June 2005.

[17] Miller, C. Cloud security: Is it raining in the cloud? SC Magazine. March 2009. http://www.scmagazineus.com/CloudsecurityIsitraininginthecloud/article/128 308.

[18] "National Cyber Alert System", http://www.us-cert.gov/cas/tips/ST04-15.html

[19] M. McIntosh and P. Austel, "XML signature element wrapping attacks and countermeasures", in SWS '05: Proceedings of the 2005 workshop on secure Web Services. ACM Press 2005, pp. 20-27

[20] "On technical Security Issues in Cloud Computing", July 19, 2009 from IEEE Xplore.

[21] "10 Security Concerns of Cloud Computing",http://www.globalknowledge.ae/knowledge%20centre/white%20papers/virtualisation%20white%20papers/10%20security%20concerns%20for%20cloud.aspx

[22] Krebs, B. Payment Processor Breach May Be

[23] Largest Ever. Security Fix/Washington Post.

January 2009. http://voices.washingtonpost. com/securityfix/2009/01/payment_processor_breach_may_b.html.\http://securosis.com/blog/heartland-hackers-caughtanswers-and-questions/.

7

Component Based Software Development

A Technology Overview

**Dr. Rachna Soni, **Shivani Soni*

Abstract – *Software systems are becoming increasingly complex and providing more functionality. To be able to produce such systems cost-effectively, suppliers often use component-based technologies instead of developing all the parts of the system from scratch. The motivation behind the use of components was initially to reduce the cost of development, but it later became more important to reduce the time to market, to meet rapidly emerging consumer demands Component-based software development is a new trend in software development. The main idea is to reuse already completed components instead of developing everything from the very beginning each time. Use of*

*Associate Professor & HOD, Dept of Computer Sc & Appl, DAV College for girls, Yamuna Nagar. **Shri Atmanand Jain Institute of Management & Technology, Ambala City

component-based development brings many advantages: faster development, lower costs of the development, better usability, etc. To be able to successfully develop component-based products, the organizations must introduce new development methods. In this paper, we survey current component-based software technologies, describe their advantages and disadvantages, and discuss the features they inherit and comparisons of various technologies are also discussed.

1. INTRODUCTION

Modern software systems become more and more large-scale, complex and uneasily controlled, resulting in high development cost, low productivity, unmanageable software quality and high risk to move to new technology [1]. Consequently, there is a growing demand of searching for a new, efficient, and cost-effective software development paradigm. One of the most promising solutions today is the component-based software development approach. This approach is based on the idea that software systems can be developed by selecting appropriate off-the-shelf components and then assembling them with well-defined software architecture [2]. This new software development approach is very different from the traditional approach in which software systems can only implemented from scratch. These commercial off-the shelf COTS) components can be developed by different developers using different languages and different platforms. This can be shown in Fig. 1, where COTS components can be checked out from a component repository, and assembled into a target software system.

Component-based software development (CBSD) can significantly reduce development cost and time-to-market, and improve maintainability, reliability and overall quality of software systems [3] [5]. This approach has raised a tremendous amount of interests both in the research community and in the software industry. The life cycle and software engineering model of CBSD is much different from that of the traditional ones. This is what the component-Based Software Engineering (CBSE) is for used. Software component technologies are an emerging technology, which is far from being matured. Here is no existing standards or guidelines in this new era, and we do not even have a unified definition of the any item "component". In general, however, a component as three main features: 1) a component is an independent and replaceable part of a system that fulfills a clear unction; 2) a component works in the context of a well-defined architecture; and 3) a component communicates with other components by its interfaces [5].

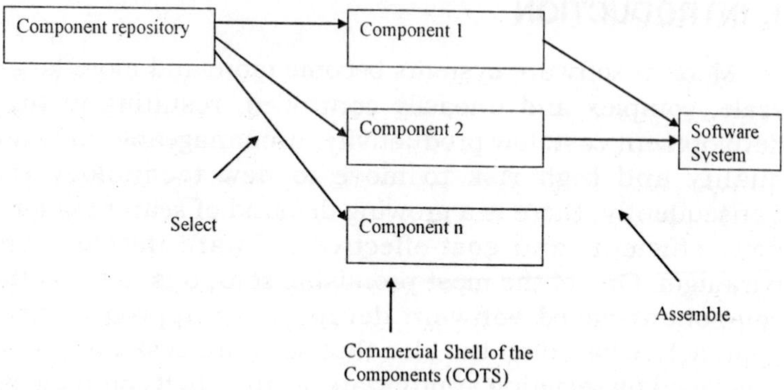

Fig. 1. Component based Software Development

Looking into Oxford Advanced Learners Dictionary, we can find:

A component is any part of which something is made.

"Software components are binary units of independent production, acquisition, and deployment that interact to form a functioning system" [6]

2. COMPONENT MODELS

The component models define the standards forms and standard interfaces between the components. They make it possible to components to being deployed and to communicate. The communication can be established between components on the same node (computer) or between different nodes. Component models are the most important step to lift the component software off the ground. If components are developed independent of each other then it is highly unlikely that components developed under such conditions are able to cooperate usefully. The primary goal of component technology, independent deployment and assembly of components is not achieved.

A component model supports components by forcing them to conform to certain standards and allows instances of these components to cooperate with other components in this model.

Among the component infrastructure technologies that have been developed, three have become somewhat standardized: OMG's (Object Management Group) CORBA, Microsoft's Component Object Model (COM) and Distributed COM (DCOM), and Sun's JavaBeans and Enterprise JavaBeans.

3. COMMON OBJECT REQUEST BROKER ARCHITECTURE (CORBA)

The Common Object Request Broker Architecture (CORBA) is a standard that has been developed by the Object Management Group (OMG) in the beginning of the nineties. The OMG provides industry guidelines and object management specifications to supply a common framework for integrating application development. Primary requirements for these specifications are reusability, portability and interoperability of object based software components in a distributed environment.

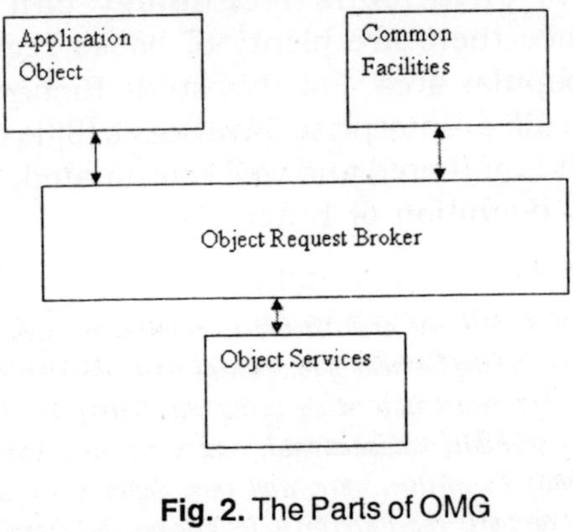

Fig. 2. The Parts of OMG

CORBA is part of the Object Management Architecture (OMA which covers object services, common facilities and definitions of terms.

The most important part of a CORBA system is the Object Request Broker (ORB) [7]. The ORB is the middleware that establishes the client-server relationships between components.

Object services are for instance naming, persistency, events, transactions and relationships. These can be used when implementing applications. Common facilities provide general-purpose services like information, task and system management. All services and facilities are specified in IDL. An object request broker (ORB) provides the basic mechanism for transparently making requests and receiving responses from objects located locally or remotely. Requests can be made through the ORB without regard to the service location or implementation. Objects publish their interfaces using the Interface Definition Language (IDL) as defined in the CORBA specification.

Objects are stored in an interface repository where they can be found and activated on demand from the clients. The stubs and proxies are generated from the IDL specification that each object provides for its interfaces.

4. ENTERPRISE JAVA BEANS (EJB)

Enterprise JavaBeans technology can be easily discovered since there are plenty of books regarding this favorite and popular area. For this study Richard Monson-Haefel's book called Enterprise JavaBeans [8] is chosen and all information is gathered and well coordinated. Firstly Sun Microsystems' definition of Enterprise

JavaBeans is:

The Enterprise JavaBeans architecture is component architecture for the development and deployment of component-based distributed business applications. Applications written using the Enterprise JavaBeans architecture is scalable, transactional, and multi-user secure. These applications may be written once, and then deployed on any server platform that supports the Enterprise JavaBeans specification.

A Java Bean is a reusable component that support persistency and can inter-operate across all platforms supported by Java. EJB uses Java Beans but it is a lot more than a component model. EJB provides support for transactions and security over a neutral object communication protocol, which gives the user the benefit to implement the application on top of a protocol of choice. EJB is part of the Java 2 Platform Enterprise Edition (J2EE) which includes many other technologies remote method invocation (RMI), naming and directory interface (JNDI), database connectivity (JDBC), Server Pages (JSPs) and Messaging services (JMS).

Fig. 3 shows the architectural style of EJB used in a three-tier application. The clients connect to the server components through either a web server or directly using remote method invocation (RMI). The server components that implement the business logic reside within an EJB container with the support for transactions and security. The data is stored in databases, which are managed with some database management service (DBMS) and is accessed through the data base connectivity component (JDBC). Java server pages (JSP) or servlets are used when the thin web clients access the system through the Internet.

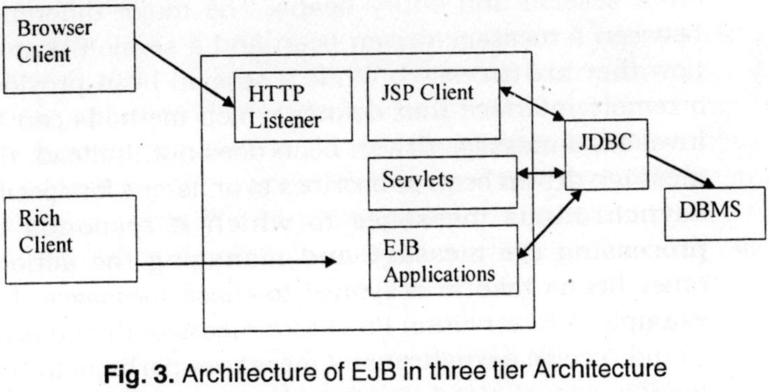

Fig. 3. Architecture of EJB in three tier Architecture

To make a JavaBean an Enterprise bean the JavaBean has to conform to the specification of EJB by implementing and expose a few required methods. These methods allow the EJB container to manage beans in a uniform way for creation, transactions etc. A client to an enterprise bean can virtually be anything, for example a servlet, applet or another enterprise bean. Since enterprise beans may call each other then a complex bean task might be divided into smaller tasks and handled by a hierarchy of beans. This is a powerful way of "divide and conquer".

EJB Component Types

- **Entity beans:** A good rule of thumb is that entity beans model business concepts that can be expressed as nouns. For example, an entity bean might represent a customer, a piece of equipment, an item in inventory, or even a place. In other words, entity beans model real-world objects; these objects are usually persistent records in some kind of database.
- **Session beans:** Session beans are an extension of the client application and are responsible for managing processes or tasks. Session beans tend to manage particular kinds of activities, such as the act of making a reservation. They have a lot to do with the relationships between different enterprise beans.
- **Message-driven beans:** Message-driven beans in EJB 2.0 are responsible for coordinating tasks involving other session and entity beans. The major difference between a message-driven bean and a session bean is how they are accessed. While a session bean provides a remote interface that defines which methods can be invoked, a message-driven bean does not. Instead, the message-driven bean subscribes to or listens for specific asynchronous messages to which it responds by processing the message and managing the actions other beans take in response to those messages. For example, a Reservation Processor message-driven bean would receive asynchronous messages-perhaps from a legacy reservation system-from which it would coordinate the interactions of the Cruise, Cabin, and Customer beans to make a reservation.

A general architecture for component software allows application and systems to be built from different software providers. It is platform dependent, that is, Microsoft platforms Windows and Windows NT. Its language independency is restricted with the number of languages that are supported by Microsoft for example Java is not there.

5. THE COMPONENT OBJECT MODEL

It provides a model for designing components that have multiple interfaces with dynamic binding to other components. COM is an open standard, which has been implemented on many different platforms, but the main platform is of course Microsoft Windows for which it was first developed. Components expose themselves through interfaces and only interfaces. The interfaces are binary which makes it possible to implement the component in a variety of programming languages such as C++, Visual Basic and Java. A COM component can implement and expose multiple interfaces. A client uses COM to locate the server components and then it queries for the wanted interfaces.

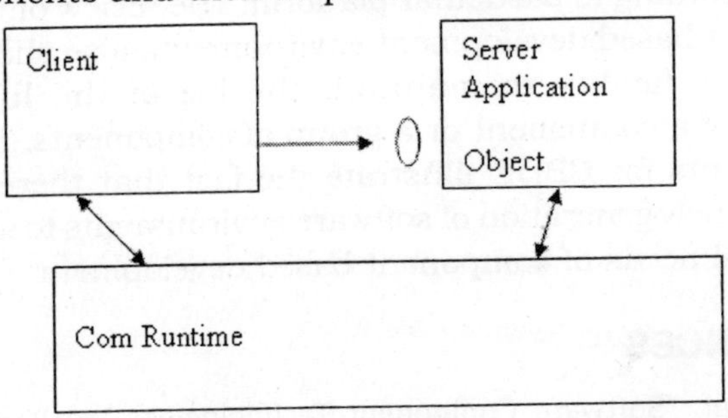

Fig. 4. COM Establish the Connection between Client and Server

DCOM (Distributed COM), as the name suggests, defines the distribution of COMs over a network. COM defines how components and their clients interact. COM set the standards for components to interact on the same machine. However, distributed applications require components on different machines to interact. When client and component reside on different machines, DCOM simply replaces the local interprocess communication with a network protocol. Neither the component nor its client is aware of the network protocols lying between them. DCOM provides location independence, completely hides the location of a component, whether it is in the same process as the client or on a machine halfway around the world. In all cases, the way the client connects to a component and calls DCOM's location independence greatly simplifies the task of distributing application components for optimum overall performance. Suppose, for example, that certain components must be placed on a specific machine or at a specific location. If the application has numerous small components, network loading can be reduced by deploying them on the same LAN (Local Area Network) segment, on the same machine, or in the same process.

6. CONCLUSION

This Paper makes an attempt to present a review of component based software development technologies and their choice according to particular platform. The review of various component based development environments also shows the inadequate facility to maintain the log of the life-time activities of a component or a group of components. Several requirements for CBDE illustrate the fact that there s still need for a new generation of software environments to support the special needs of component based development.

REFERENCES

1. G.Pour, "Software Component Technologies: JavaBeans and ActiveX," Proceedings of Technology of Object-Oriented Languages and systems, 1999, pp. 398 – 398.
2. G. Pour, "Component-Based Software Development Approach: New Opportunities and Challenges," Proceedings Technology of Object-Oriented Languages, 1998. TOOLS 26., pp. 375-383.
3. G. Pour, "Enterprise JavaBeans, JavaBeans & XML Expanding the Possibilities for Web-Based Enterprise Application Development," Proceedings Technology of Object-Oriented Languages and Systems, 1999, TOOLS 31, pp.282-291.
4. G.Pour, M. Griss, J. Favaro, "Making the Transition to Component-Based Enterprise Software Development: Overcoming the Obstacles – Patterns for Success," Proceedings of Technology of Object-Oriented Languages and systems, 1999, pp.419 – 419.

5. A.W.Brown, K.C. Wallnau, "The Current State of CBSE," IEEE Software , Volume: 15 5, Sept.-Oct. 1998, pp. 37 – 46. 26., pp. 375-383.
6. [Heineman 01] G. T. Heineman &W. T. Councill. Component-Based Software Engineering - Putting the Pieces Together. Addison-Wesley, Boston, MA, 2001
7. CAI Xia, LYU Michael R., WONG Kam-Fai, KO Roy, Component-Based Software Engineering: Technologies, Development Frameworks, and Quality Assurance Schemes, http://www.cse.cuhk.edu.hk/~lyu/paper_pdf/apsec.pdf, last access: 01.12.2005
8. MONSON-HAEFEL Richard, Enterprise JavaBeans, O'Reilly, 2001

8

Cloud Computing

An Overview, Issues and Challenges

**Dr. Vivek Mohan Gupta, Dr. B. K. Murthy*

Abstract – *Nowadays Cloud Computing has become a buzz word in the corporate world. It has become a synonymous for infrastructural paradigm shift that is sweeping across the IT industry.*

Cloud Computing minimize large IT infrastructure expenses by moving towards operational expenses for the IT services/ infrastructure required for an Enterprise. This makes it more useful for SMEs and new IT startups where generally in-house IT expertise are not available to take care of implementation and maintenance of IT Infrastructure, and relevant security issues. While there are many advantages towards migrating to Cloud Computing, there are many issues need to be addressed and analysed. The main issues related to the Cloud Computing centers along portability, interoperability, monitoring, data-

*Department of IT, Ministry of Communication and IT, New Delhi, India. e-mail : vm.gupta@nic.in, bkmurty@nic.in

security, jurisdiction, availability and issues relating to migrating legacy systems to the Cloud. There are many big players like Google, IBM, Amazon provide Cloud Computing services. While there are many advantages of Cloud Computing, still there are any myths and challenges in implementation.

This paper presents an overview of the Cloud Computing and describes the three major components, namely; software as a service, platform as a service and infrastructure as a service. It touches upon issues of portability, interoperability, data-security, jurisdiction and issues relating to migrating legacy systems to the Cloud. The paper summarizes some of the potential advantages of Cloud Computing which would be critical companion for this technology in long run.

Keywords – *Cloud Computing, Software as a Service (SaaS), Platform as a Service (PaaS), Infrastructure as a Service (IaaS), Service level Agreement (SLA), Security, ultra-high speed network, low latency network, middleware/APIs, Service Oriented Architecture (SOA), Green Technology, Grid Computing.*

I. INTRODUCTION

Cloud Computing has emerged as the infrastructure paradigm shift from owning an infrastructure to buying the services necessary for the growth of the business. This has opened a new way for the user-group to get IT resources as service and to focus on the main business, without getting too much into building and then maintaining and upgrading the IT resources critical to their business/work. This is more useful for SMEs especially new IT startups, where the companies do not have much in-house IT expertise to take care of implementation, maintenance and security issues related to IT resources.

In Past few decades some important technological improvements has taken place in the IT domain which includes: (i) ever increasing numbers of computing devices got networked, (ii) the computing power of processors per unit cost increasing in almost non linear way, (iii) advancement in network technology with the advent of ultrahigh speed networks, (iv) major advancements in storage technology. In this background the concept of Grid computing evolved to harness the idle cycles of CPU of a large number of computer on a network to work on a very large task. The Computing Grids are a form of distributed computing whereby a "super virtual computer" is composed of many networked loosely coupled computers acting together to perform very large tasks. This technology generally been applied to computationally intensive scientific, mathematical, and academic problems through volunteer computing, and it is also used in commercial enterprises for such diverse applications as drug discovery, economic forecasting, seismic analysis, climate modeling and back office data processing in support for e-commerce and Web services. The Grid has come up as an alternative of supercomputers but at less cost.

The same group of technological improvements has made it possible the concept of Cloud Computing which generally share some characteristics with, but should not be confused with: (i) Autonomic computing, (ii) Client–server model, (iii) distributed application, (iv) Grid computing, (v) Mainframe computer etc.

The basic concept of Cloud Computing is mainly based on consumption and delivery model, which makes Cloud Computing distinct from most of the technologies mentioned above. Like any such model, consumer of Cloud Computing are more interested in consuming the IT services/resources they need rather than creating and owing an IT infrastructure to produce those services for their consumption. The term Cloud is basically an abstraction of underlying infrastructure.

To be more precise technically "cloud computing" refers to the bigger picture basically the broad concept of using the internet to allow people to access technology-enabled services. According to Gartner, those services must be "massively scalable" to qualify as true "cloud computing" [1].

II. COMPONENTS OF CLOUD COMPUTING

Evolution of Cloud Computing over the time can be traced back to the application service providers of 1990's, but in its present form it is a much border concept which may includes at least one out of three main services: (i) Software as a Service (SaaS), (ii) Platform as a Service (PaaS), and (iii) Infrastructure as a Service (IaaS). Though, the concept of Cloud Computing is not limited these three service categories.

The above three main services could be defined as follows:

(i) Software as a service (SaaS) is a business model in which a cloud services company (or private cloud service within the enterprise) provides full applications to customers. Applications are accessed via the Web. SaaS does not require the capital purchase of any software or hardware by the customer [2]. Pricing (or chargeback) is subscription based by user. Some example of application on demand include: Gmail, Google Calendar, document management, Payroll, HR, CRM, IBM Lotus Live.

Some basic characteristic of SaaS include: network based accesses and management to commercially available (or similar) software, application delivery typically one to many, centralized updating, faster new features release, support to prevailing best practices.

(ii) Platform as a service (PaaS) is a business model in which a cloud services company (or private cloud service within the enterprise) provides its customers with a cloud-based infrastructure to develop and configure customer-developed applications using programming languages and tools supported by the services provider [2]. Customers pay (get charged back) only for the resources they use. Some example of it include: AppEngine from Google: based on Python and Django, Force.com from SalesForce: based on the SalesForce SaaS infrastructure and Apex language, Bungee Connect: visual development studio based on Java, LongJump: based on Java/Eclipse, WaveMaker: visual development studio based on Java and hosted on Amazon EC2.

Some basic characteristic of PaaS include:

Multi-tenant development tool: a cloud-based studio must support multiple users, each with multiple active projects; Management and monitoring tools: a cloud based solution must include good management and monitoring tools. The benefits of PaaS lie in greatly increasing the number of people who can develop, maintain and deploy applications. In short, PaaS offers to democratize development of applications.

(iii) Infrastructure as a service (IaaS) is a business model in which a cloud services company (or private cloud service within the enterprise) provides its customers with computing equipment located and accessible in the cloud and is used to support customer operations via the cloud. Infrastructure components may include storage, servers, networking components, and general infrastructure hardware [2]. Customers pay (receives internal charges) only for the IT resources actually used. For example, they may "rent" servers by performance level, network bandwidth, or amount of storage/backup. Some example of it include: IBM Blue house, VMWare, Amazon EC2, Microsoft Azure Platform, Sun Parascale.

Some basic characteristic of IaaS include: virtual instances of Infrastructure like servers, datacenter-resources etc. on demand of customers; the power/capacity of infrastructure on offer can be expanded or decreased as per customer's demand, which in a traditional system may not be always cost effective.

III. CLOUD COMPUTING MYTHS

In general there are some prevailing myths about Cloud Computing some of them are described here:

(i) The Cloud is not Secure: A general perception about security is that it is binary. Security is not something like it exists or it does not exist at all, it is not something binary. In reality it is matter of degree. The key to good security is understanding and managing risks [4]. It's true that an internal network will always be more transparent to the customer than the comparative opacity of a cloud provider. But if one can understand and accurately assess the risks presented by the cloud service, the security it offers might be as good, or even better, than an internal solution. One can make their system more secure in-house, but that assumes they have the budget and the skills available to match those of a cloud provider. The cloud provider has greater incentive in provisioning for and addressing the security issues as it is question of their business.

(ii) **The Cloud is not Reliable:** with the Service Level Agreement (SLA) in place, this concern could be addressed well[4].

(iii) **Sensitive Data not safe in the Cloud:** This concerns mostly well addressed buy the strict rules for handling such sensitive information and data. It more depends on where the Cloud is hosted and the prevailing regulations and compliance mandates applicable on that geography. In other words one can say technologies are available to make sensitive data adequately secure and the Cloud Provider has enough incentive to use enough security elements in their clouds, the only concern cloud be that of appropriate regulatory environment in the geography cloud is hosted in.

(iv) **The Cloud Locks in the Data:** One of the key differences between cloud and on-premise is that the provider looks after the infrastructure. They're maintaining it for you, ensuring that you're always on the latest version and on an up-to-date infrastructure. The best providers let you export your data at any time. This may not be true about some of existing legacy applications.

Often user of such legacy applications find their data is stuck in proprietary formats, and even though they might have control of the hardware, they don't have any way to get control of their data. It's even worse when the system is old and potentially unsupported. Having physical control of your data does not necessarily mean you can do anything useful with it.

IV. CLOUD COMPUTING ARCHITECTURE

The physical architecture and relationship between the components for delivery of Cloud Computing services can be broadly consists of: (i) Cloud Services, (ii) Cloud Platform, (iii) Cloud Storage, (iv) Cloud Infrastructure (Fig. 1). These components communicate with each other over API / common-interface to deliver the desired service to the customer.

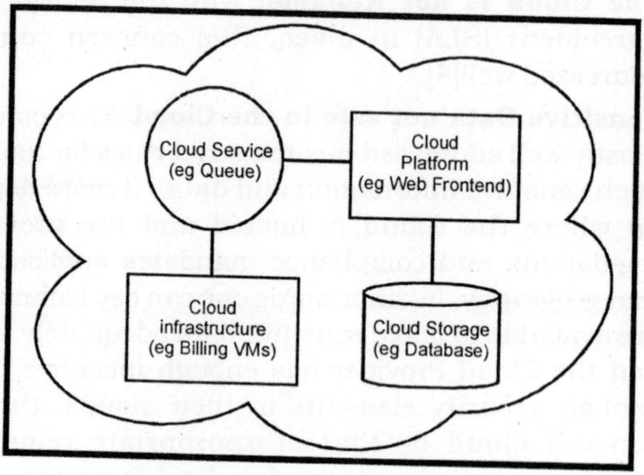

Fig. 1. Cloud Computing Architecture [3]

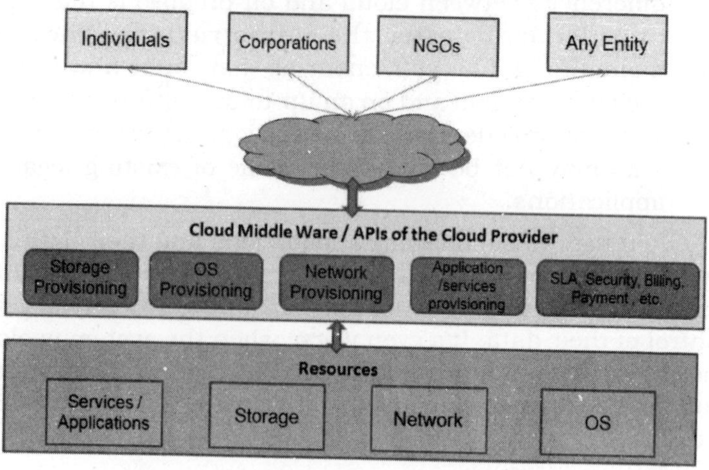

Fig. 2. Cloud Computing Layered Structure

A more elaborated picture of interacting components can be described in terms of Cloud middle-ware/ APIs of the cloud provider, and resources (it can be hardware like: storage, network; or software like OS, Applications). (Fig. 2)

The middle-ware could consist of different interacting components responsible for provisioning of various resources as per the service request from the customer to the cloud. Even implementation of SLA, billing, Security could be a part of this. However different Cloud Computing provider may implement it in different way depending on the requirement.

V. CLOUD COMPUTING ADVANTAGES

Owning an IT Infrastructure could be inefficient and cost ineffective. For example: It has been observed that due to its nature of use the data centers are notoriously underutilized, often idle 85% of the time because of over provisioning, insufficient capacity planning and sizing, improper understanding of scalability requirements, resource constrain to keep it up with latest technology etc.

Because the basic concept of Cloud Computing is mainly based on consumption and delivery model. Once the Cloud Computing come into picture the inefficiency of idle resource, the scaling up requirement, cost of keeping up with the latest technology, remain no longer part of concern of organization consuming IT services but it transfers into the domain of Cloud Provider. It is due to this paradigm shift thought leaders including from Gartner, Forrester, and IDC—agree that Cloud Computing model offers significant advantages for fast-paced startups, SMBs and enterprises alike. It's in a way enhances and expand the scope for penetration of IT usage. Efficient use of resources makes it potential of being a green technology of future.

The main characteristics which makes Cloud Computing advantageous include:

(i) Agility improves with users' ability to rapidly and inexpensively re-provision technological infrastructure resources on demand [3].

(ii) The capital expenditure is converted to operational expenditure. This ostensibly lowers barriers to entry, for one-time or infrequent intensive computing tasks [3].

(iii) Device and location independence enable users to access systems using a web browser regardless of their location [3].

(iv) Reliability is improved if multiple redundant sites are used, which makes well designed cloud computing suitable for business continuity and disaster recovery [3].

(v) Scalability via dynamic ("on-demand") provisioning of resources on a fine-grained, self-service basis near real-time [3].

(vi) Maintenance of cloud computing applications is easier, since they don't have to be installed on each user's computer. They are easier to support and to improve since the changes reach the clients instantly [3].

(vii) Metering : that Cloud Computing resources usage metered per client and application on a daily, weekly, monthly, and yearly basis [3].

(viii) The Cloud Computing concept in a way enhances and expand the scope for penetration of IT usage. Efficient use of resources makes it potential of being a green technology of future.

VI. ISSUES AND CHALLENGES

Although much enthusiasm and excitement exists over the potential benefits of cloud computing, IDC's Cloud Services survey provided the following top 5 IT cloud computing concerns [2]: (i) Security, (ii) Availability, (iii) Performance, (iv) On-demand model costs more, (v) Lack of interoperability standards. To overcome the these concerns would be the biggest challenge for the Cloud Computing

Provider, as this may pose strong reluctance on the part of enterprise IT to aggressively adopt cloud computing in future system deployments.

It is fact that deployment of the Cloud Computing will not change the security requirement of the enterprise in any significant way. But as now a part of solution resides in the cloud it would not be in direct control of the enterprise. The concern would take more complex turn if the user enterprise and the hosting of the Cloud belong to territory of different nation states which may have different cyber laws and compliance mandates. The problem can be sorted out by either evolving security standards for Cloud Computing, which can reduce the conflict and confusion between different compliance mandates across the nations; or by hosting the Cloud in a Territory governed under same kind of cyber laws and compliance mandates as that of the territory the cloud user belongs to.

Another open issue is the lack comprehensive standards for interpretability between the Cloud Providers. This poses a major lock in situation with one Cloud Provider for Enterprise. This would also increase significantly the cost of hopping the Cloud and consequently this diminishes the benefits which were thought to be attached with this new paradigm of Cloud Computing.

Some other Issues and challenges for the Cloud provider include:

(i) Migration from legacy systems to The Cloud: it has been seen that a large portion of time of the Cloud Providers goes into helping their clients to migrate their data from legacy systems to the Cloud.

(ii) Heterogeneous platforms should be able to access the Cloud: the Cloud resources generally accessed through middleware/APIs. These have to be compatible to a host of heterogeneous platforms. The problem of non compatibility can become more complex if the middleware/APIs are not in open source domain, but proprietary in nature. As at present there is no clear compatibility standards are in place, a proprietary middleware/APIs may strengthen the threat for user of the cloud to get lock in with one Cloud Provider. This will deter an enterprise to make their critical business requirements dependent wholly on the Cloud.

VII. CONCLUDING REMARKS

The potential of the Cloud Computing as a Paradigm changer even with the challenges at hand and many open issues would not be diminished. We can broadly point out three major factors acting in support of the Cloud Computing which can be described as follows:

(i) **Low entry threshold for usage:** The reason for this is that the Cloud Computing due to its basis on consumption and delivery model, it provide an opportunity to own a managed IT Infrastructure/Platform/Software in cost effective way, which would act as major enabler for enterprise/business entity (especially SMBs) by effectively reducing the threshold cost of owing and maintaining IT Infrastructure/Platform/Software, nonetheless virtually. The Cloud Computing concept in a way enhances and expand the scope for penetration of IT usage.

(ii) **Pervasive technology:** The Cloud can be accessed from network/web, hence it enhance the reach and availability of a resource which were in a legacy technology bounded to an office premises or geography.

(iii) **Green Technology:** Efficient use of resources makes it potential of being a green technology of future.

REFERENCES

[1] Robert P. Desisto, Daryl C. Plummer, David Mitchell Smith "Tutorial for Understanding the Relationship Between Cloud Computing and SaaS" Gartner Research, 7 April 2008 ID Number: G00156152.

[2] Christian A. Christiansen, Charles J. Kolodgy, Sally Hudson, Gerry Pintal "Identity and access management for approaching clouds"; White paper May 2010, IDC

[3] From Wikipedia, the free encyclopedia

[4] Justin Pirie "Don't Believe the Hype – Understand Cloud Computing Before Jumping In" Cloud Computing Journal 30 September 2010.

□□□

9

Internet Based Cloud Computing
A Review

Vivek Sharma, Gaganpreet Kaur**, Sunil Khullar***

Abstract – *Cloud computing is Internet-based computing, whereby shared resources, software, and information are provided to computers and other devices on demand, like the electricity grid. For enabling the cloud computing we always use Virtualization and it is a core technology for enabling cloud resource sharing. However, most existing Cloud Computing platforms have not formally adopted the service-oriented architecture (SOA) that would make them more flexible, extensible, and reusable. It is a general term for anything that involves delivering hosted services over the Internet. These services are divided into three category Infrastructure-as-a-Service (IaaS), Platform-as-a-Service (PaaS) and Software-as-a-Service (SaaS). Social media channels and many other*

*Mtech Student, BMESC, Muktsar, email: er.viveksharma22@yahoo.com,
**Sr. Lect., RIEIT, Railmajra, email: gagan1492003@yahoo.com,
***Sr. Lect., RIEIT, Railmajra, email: sunilkhullar222@yahoo.co.in

applications use cloud computing as their platform. In this paper the platform of cloud computing, types of cloud computing, characteristics and application, and future of cloud computing etc. are discussed.

1. INTRODUCTION

Cloud computing is a complex infrastructure of software, hardware, processing, and storage that is available as a service. It offers immediate access to large numbers of the world's most sophisticated supercomputers and their corresponding processing power. It interconnected at various locations around the world, proffering speed in the tens of trillions of computations per second. It provides environments to enable resource sharing in terms of scalable infrastructures, middleware and application development platforms, and value-added business applications.

1.1 Features

- Agility improves with users' ability to rapidly and inexpensively re-provision technological infrastructure resources.
- Cost is claimed to be greatly reduced and capital expenditure is converted to expenditure. This ostensibly lowers barriers to entry, as infrastructure is typically provided by a third-party and does not need to be purchased for one-time or infrequent intensive computing tasks.
- Multi-tenancy enables sharing of resources and costs across a large pool of users thus allowing for:
  - Centralization of infrastructure in locations with lower costs (such as real estate, electricity, etc.)
  - Peak-load capacity increases (users need not engineer for highest possible load-levels)
  - Utilization and efficiency improvements for systems that are often only 10–20% utilized.
- Reliability is improved if multiple redundant sites are used, which makes well designed cloud computing suitable for business continuity and disaster recovery.

- Scalability via dynamic provisioning of resources on a fine-grained, self-service basis near real-time, without users having to engineer for peak loads.
- Security could improve due to centralization of data, increased security-focused resources, etc., but concerns can persist about loss of control over certain sensitive data, and the lack of security for stored kernels. Security is often as good as or better than under traditional systems, in part because providers are able to devote resources to solving security issues that many customers cannot afford.

2. CLOUD COMPUTING TYPES

2.1 Public cloud

Public cloud or external cloud describes cloud computing in the traditional mainstream sense, whereby resources are dynamically provisioned on a fine-grained, self-service basis over the Internet, via web applications/web services, from an off-site third-party provider who bills on a fine-grained utility computing basis.

2.2 Community cloud

A community cloud may be established where several organizations have similar requirements and seek to share infrastructure so as to realize some of the benefits of cloud computing. With the costs spread over fewer users than a public cloud this option is more expensive but may offer a higher level of privacy, security and/or policy compliance. Examples of community cloud include Google's "Gov Cloud".

2.3 Hybrid cloud

A hybrid cloud environment consisting of multiple internal and/or external provider "will be typical for most enterprises" By integrating multiple cloud services users may be able to ease the transition to public cloud services while avoiding issues such as PCI compliance.

2.4 Private cloud

Private cloud and internal cloud have been described as neologisms; however the concepts themselves pre-date the term cloud by 40 years. Even within modern utility industries, hybrid models still exist despite the formation of reasonably well functioning markets and the ability to combine multiple providers. These products offer the ability to deliver some benefits of cloud computing whilst mitigating some of the pitfalls. These offerings capitalize on data security, corporate governance, and reliability concerns during this time of transition from a product to a functioning service based industry supported by competitive marketplaces.

3. CATEGORIES OF CLOUD COMPUTING

3.1 Infrastructure-as-a-Service

Infrastructure-as-a-Service like Amazon Web Services provides virtual server instances with unique IP addresses and blocks of storage on demand. Customers use the provider's application program interface to start, stop, and access and configure their virtual servers and storage.

3.2 Platform-as-a-Service

Platform-as-a-service in the cloud is defined as a set of software and product development tools hosted on the provider's infrastructure. Developers create applications on the provider's platform over the Internet. PaaS providers may use APIs, website portals or gateway software installed on the customer's computer.

3.3 Software-as-a-Service

In the software-as-a-service cloud model, the vendor supplies the hardware infrastructure, the software product and interacts with the user through a front-end portal. SaaS is a very broad market. Services can be anything from Web-based email to inventory control and database processing. Because the service provider hosts both the application and the data, the end user is free to use the service from anywhere.

4. SEVERAL CLOUD COMPUTING PLATFORMS

4.1 Abiclod cloud computing platform

Abicloud is a cloud computing platform developed by Abiquo, a company locates in Barcelona Spain that is mainly focused on the development of cloud platform. It can be used to build, integrate and manage public as well as private cloud in the homogeneous environments. Using Abicloud, user can easily and automatically deploy and manage the server, storage system, network, virtual devices and applications and so on. The main difference between Abicloud and other cloud computing platforms is its powerful web-based management function and its core encapsulation manner. Using the Abicloud, user can finish deploying a new service by just dragging a virtual machine with mouse. This is much easier and flexible than other cloud computing platforms that deploy new services through command lines. According to Abicloud, there is no perfect cloud platform. For each user needs his own cloud infrastructures, and every cloud provider has his own management tools, say monitor, billing and so on, so generally it is very hard to deploy a cloud platform according to user's requirement. The best way to meet the requirement of users is to build public or private cloud with homogeneous cloud computing core and extensible infrastructures. Besides, the cloud platform should also have all kinds of interfaces that support the third parties products. With all these characteristics, providers can build the cloud computing platform of their own.

4.2 Eucalyptus cloud platform

Eucalyptus (Elastic Utility Computing Architecture for Linking Your Programs to Useful Systems) project began from California University Santa Barbara, and mainly was used to build open-source private cloud platform. Now it has been run by Eucalyptus System Company. Eucalyptus is an open-source implementation of Amazon EC2 and compatible with business interfaces. It also implements virtualization depending on Linux and Xen as EC2 does. Eucalyptus is an elastic computing structure that can be\used to connect the users' programs to the useful systems, itis an open-source infrastructure using clusters or workstations implementation of elastic, utility, cloud computing and a popular computing standard based on service level protocol that permit users lease network for computing capability. Currently, Eucalyptus is compatible with EC2 from Amazon, and may support more other kinds of clients with minimum modification and extension.

4.3 Nimbus cloud computing platform

Nimbus is an open tool set, and also a cloud computing solution providing IaaS. Put forward based on scientific research in the early stage, Nimbus have supported many nonscientific research domain applications. It permits users lease remote resources and build the required computing environment through the deployment of virtual machines.

4.4 Open nebula cloud computing platform

Open Nebula is one of the key technologies of reservoir plan and the flagship research project in virtualization infrastructure and cloud computing of European Union. Like nimbus, Open Nebula is also an open source cloud service framework. It allows user deploy and manage virtual machines on physical resources and it can set user's data centers or clusters to flexible virtual infrastructure that can automatically adapt to the change of the service load. The main difference of Open Nebula and nimbus is that nimbus implements remote interface based on EC2 or WSRF through which user can process all security related issues, while Open Nebula does not.

5. ADVANTAGES AND DISADVANTAGES

5.1 Streamlining the Data Center

An organization can streamline its data center by taking advantage of cloud technologies, instead of buying and maintaining the hardware and software and hiring the personnel who keep the data center running.

5.2 Scalability on Demand

All organizations have to deal with global changes in their environment. The ability of cloud computing solutions to scale up and down is a major benefit.

Low Startup Costs: For companies that just starting out, organizations in emerging markets, cloud computing greatly reduces startup costs.

Updates: There is nothing more dangerous on the internet than software that cannot be patched or updated. Adaptation to new conditions – Cloud computing is scary for many people, because it puts everything you have in somewhere else.

5.3 Backup Problem

While backup is always good idea, it's not always possible in Cloud Computing or it's not so easy, as with you local system.

Logging: It's obvious to wish to have a way of getting logs back to the company. Because to be sure in authenticity of the logs, this data has to stored on the company's data center. At the same time, transfer log data over the Internet is not great idea.

Required time estimation problem: Time estimation problem one of the biggest shortfalls of the projects is incorrectly allocating time for the project completion. Reason is attributable to new technology, new way of doing things, and more training necessity.

5.4 The Future of the Cloud Computing

The following is a summary of ten cloud computing industry trends:

- Cloud computing is widening, but focus on an open platform mainly.

- Windows Azure is mostly a better platform of Exchange.
- Google would increase the area of investment in the enterprise; more business users will use Google Apps.
- The first batch of SaaS 1.0 companies will face the risk of bankruptcy.
- The number of firms who abandon the use of its own server increased significantly.
- Private cloud computing services have been popular.
- Business Intelligence (BI) will be SaaS's next target.
- SAP or Oracle will enter PaaS (Platform as a Service, PaaS, and Platform as a service) area.
- Enterprise adoption and use of social networks faster.
- Force.com the creation of software products worth at least 1 billion dollar.

6. CONCLUSIONS

Cloud computing is promising for delivering IT services as computing utilities. Clouds are designed to provide services to external users. Acc. To my point of view cloud computing has many applications like in business and in industry by till now it has some limitations like backup and time estimation. After these limitations Google and other companies like Microsoft wants to increase their investment in this project.

REFRENCES

[1] http://cloudcomputing.blogspot.com/Cloud Computing: adoption fears and strategic innocation opportunities".

[2] John Foley "20 Cloud Computing startups you should know." Information Week , September 20, 2008.

[3] Galen Guman," What Cloud Computing Really Means". Infoworld, April 7,2008

[4] J.Nicholas Hoover and Richard Martin,"Demystifying the Cloud", Information Week and Research and Reports,pp 30-37,June 23,2008.

[5] Nicholas Hoover"Outages Force Clouds Computing Users to Rethink Tactics", Information Week,August 16,2008.

[6] Erica Naone,"Computer in the Cloud",MIT Technology Review, September 18,2007.

[7] Jonathan Weber, "Cloud Computing", Times Online,May 5 , 2008.

[8] Brad Stone, "Web Filtering Moves to the Cloud", The New york Times,April 8,2004.

□□□

10

An Optimal Approach for Centralized Routing Using Clustering

*Neha Sharma, Rubal Chaudhry, Sourav Walia**

Abstract – *Routing in a network may involve a complex collection of functions that work more or less independently and yet support each other by exchanging services or information. The complexity arises due to maintaining coordination between all the nodes of the subnet, coping with link and node failures. Complexity of centralized routing control strategies may be reduced by partitioning a network into smaller subnetworks or clusters such that the routing functionality leads to efficient network performance. Hence, each cluster is having one network routing control center. Existing hierarchical and partitional clusters are based upon creating groups consisting of elements that are close to each other w.r.t. the distance or parameters considered in the application. But these algorithms*

*Department of Computers, R.P.Inderaprastha Institute of Technology, Bastara, Karnal, India. e-mail: sharmaneha29@gmail.com, rubal1686@gmail.com

are not adequate and appropriate. For designing and selecting an appropriate routing strategy for a network, a number of factors that influence the behavior of the strategy have to be considered such as traffic patterns, volumes, service requirements, feasibility and optimality of routes with respect to resource utilization etc.

This paper presents an optimal approach for clustering a large network by first choosing appropriate nodes that can act as a NRC's.

Keywords – *Clustering, Clustering types, Network Routing Control Center (NRC), Centralized routing*

1. INTRODUCTION

Cluster is a type of parallel or distributed processing system, which consists of a collection of interconnected stand-alone computers cooperatively working together as a single, integrated computing resource. Clustering is a common technique for statistical data analysis, which is used in many fields; pattern recognition, image analysis, data mining, bioinformatics, machine learning and mechanical process industries. There are several definitions for clustering. We will borrow the one given by Jain and Dubes [1]:

> *"Cluster analysis organizes data by abstracting underlying structure either as a grouping of individuals or as a hierarchy of groups. The representation can then be investigated to see if the data group according to preconceived ideas or to suggest new experiments".*

Clustering[2] is a method in which we make cluster of objects that are somehow similar in characteristics. The criterion for checking the similarity is implementation dependent. In brief, cluster analysis groups data objects into clusters such that objects belonging to the same cluster are similar, while those belonging to different ones are dissimilar. The notions of similarity and dissimilarity will become clear in later section. We can show this with the help of figure1:

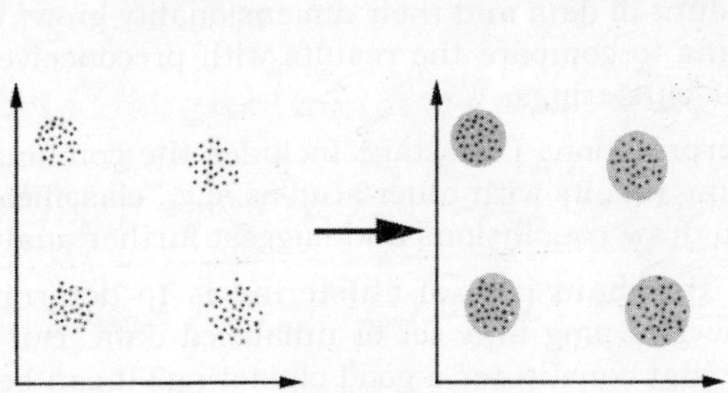

Fig. 1. Different objects in different clusters

The above definition indicates that clustering cannot be a one-step process. In one of the seminal texts on Cluster

Analysis, Jain and Dubes divide the clustering process in the following stages [1]:

Data Collection: Includes the careful extraction of relevant data objects from the underlying data sources. In our context, data objects are distinguished by their individual values for a set of *attributes* (or *measures*).

Initial Screening: Refers to the massaging of data after its extraction from the source, or sources. This stage is closely connected to a process widely used in *DataWarehousing*, called *Data Cleaning* [3].

Representation: Includes the proper preparation of the data in order to become suitable for the clustering algorithm. Here, the similarity measure is chosen, the characteristics and dimensionality of the data is examined.

Clustering Tendency: Checks whether the data in hand has a natural tendency to cluster or not. This stage is often ignored, especially in the presence of large data sets.

Clustering Strategy: Involves the careful choice of clustering algorithm and initial parameters.

Validation: This is one of the last and, in our opinion, most under-studied stages. Validation is often based on manual examination and visual techniques. However, as the amount of data and their dimensionality grow, we have no means to compare the results with preconceived ideas or other clusterings.

Interpretation: This stage includes the combination of clustering results with other studies, e.g., classification, in order to draw conclusions and suggest further analysis.

So, the main goal of clustering is to determine the intrinsic grouping in a set of unlabeled data. But how to decide what constitutes a good clustering? It can be shown that there is no absolute "best" criterion which would be independent of the final aim of the clustering. Consequently, it is the user which must supply this criterion, in such a way that the result of the clustering will suit their needs.

For instance, we could be interested in finding representatives for homogeneous groups (data reduction), in finding "natural clusters" and describe their unknown properties ("natural" data types), in finding useful and suitable groupings ("useful" data classes) or in finding unusual data objects (outlier detection).

2. TYPES OF CLUSTERING

An entire collection of clusters are commonly reffered to as clustering. In this section we distinguish between various types of clustering:

Hierarchical (nested) Vs Partitional (unnested): The most commonly discussed distinction among different types of clustering is whether the set of clusters is nested. or unnested, or in more traditional terminology, hierarchical or partitional.A **partitional clustering** is simply a division of the set of data objects into non-overlapping subsets (clusters) such that each data object is in exactly one subset. Taken individually, each collection of clusters is a partitional clustering. If we permit clusters to have subclusters, then we obtain a hierarchical clustering which is a set of nested clusters that are organized as a tree. Each node (cluster) in the tree (except for the leaf nodes) is the union of its children (subclusters), and the root of the tree is the cluster containing all the objects. Often, but not always, the leaves of the tree are singleton clusters of individual data objects. A hierarchical clustering can be viewed as a sequence of partitional clusterings and a partitional clustering can be obtained by taking any member of that sequence; i.e. by cutting the hierarchical tree at a particular level.

Exclusive Vs Overlapping Vs Fuzzy: Each object when assigned to a single cluster exhibits exclusive clustering. An overlapping or non-exclusive clustering is used to reflect the fact that an object can simultaneously belong to more than one group. For instance, a person at a university can be both an enrolled student and an employee of the university.

In a fuzzy clustering, every object belong to every cluster with a membership weight that is between 0(absolutely doesn't belong) and 1(absolutely belongs).In other words, clusters are treated as fuzzy sets. Fuzzy set is the one in which an object belong to any set with a weight that is between 0 and 1. In fuzzy clustering, we often impose the additional constraint that the sum of the weights for each object must equal 1. This approach is most appropriate for avoiding the arbitrariness of assigning an object to only one cluster when it may be close to several. In practice, a fuzzy or probabilistic clustering is often converted to an exclusive clustering by assigning each object to the cluster in which its membership weight or probability is highest.

Complete Vs Partial: A complete clustering assigns every object to a cluster, whereas a partial clustering does not. The motivation for a partial clustering is that some objects in a data set may not belong to well-defined groups. Many times objects in the data set may represent noise, outliers, or "uninteresting background." For example, some newspaper stories may share a common theme, such as global warming, while other stories are more generic or one-of-a-kind. Thus, to find the important topics in last month's stories, we may want to search only for clusters of documents that are tightly related by a common theme. In other cases, a complete clustering of the objects is desired. For example, an application that uses clustering to organize documents for browsing needs to guarantee that all documents can be browsed.

3. TYPES OF CLUSTERS

Clustering aims to find useful groups of objects (clusters), where usefulness is defined by the goals of the data analysis. In order to visually illustrate the differences among these types of clusters, we use two-dimensional points, as shown in Figure 2, as our data objects. We stress, however, that the types of clusters described here are equally valid for other kinds of data.

Well Separated: A cluster is a set of objects in which each object is closer (or more similar) to every other object in the cluster than to any object not in the cluster. Sometimes a threshold is used to specify that all the objects in a cluster must be sufficiently close (or similar) to one another. This idealistic definition of a cluster is satisfied only when the data contains natural clusters that are quite far from each other. Fig. 2(a) gives an example of well-separated clusters that consists of two groups of points in a two-dimensional space. The distance between any two points in different groups is larger than the distance between any two points within a group. Well-separated clusters do not need to be globular, but can have any shape.

Prototype-Based: A cluster is a set of objects in which each object is closer (more similar) to the prototype that defines the cluster than to the prototype. of any other cluster. For data with continuous attributes, the prototype of a cluster is often a centroid, i.e., the average (mean) of all the points in the cluster. When a centroid is not meaningful, such as when the data has categorical attributes, the prototype is often a medoid, i.e., the most representative point of a cluster. For many types of data, the prototype can be regarded as the most central point, and in such instances, we commonly refer to prototype- based clusters as **center-based clusters.** Not surprisingly, such clusters tend to be globular. Figure 2(b) shows an example of center-based clusters.

Graph-Based: If the data is represented as a graph, where the nodes are objects and the links represent connections among objects. Then a cluster can be defined as a **connected component**; i.e., a group of objects that are connected to one another, but that have no connection to objects outside the group. An important example of graph-based clusters is **contiguity-based clusters**, where two objects are connected only if they are within a specified distance of each other. This implies that each object in a contiguity-based cluster is closer to some other object in the cluster than to any point in a different cluster. Figure 2(c) shows an example of such clusters for two-dimensional points. This definition of a cluster is useful when clusters are irregular or intertwined, but can have trouble when noise is present since, as illustrated by the two spherical clusters of Figure 2(c), a small bridge of points can merge two distinct clusters.

Density-Based: A cluster is a dense region of objects that is surrounded by a region of low density. Figure 8.2(d) shows some density-based clusters for data created by adding noise to the data of Figure 2(c). The two circular clusters are not merged, as in Figure 2(c), because the bridge between them fades into the noise. Likewise, the curve that is present in Figure 2(c) also fades into the noise and does not form a cluster in Figure 2(d). A density- based definition of a cluster is often employed when the clusters are irregular or intertwined, and when noise and outliers are present. By contrast, a contiguity- based definition of a cluster would not work well for the data of Figure 2(d) since the noise would tend to form bridges between clusters.

Shared-Property (Conceptual Clusters): More generally, we can define a cluster as a set of objects that share some property. This definition encompasses all the previous definitions of a cluster; e.g., objects in a center-based cluster share the property that they are all closest to the same centroid or medoid. However, the shared-property approach also includes new types of clusters. Consider the clusters shown in Figure 2(e). A triangular area (cluster) is adjacent to a rectangular one, and there are two intertwined circles (clusters). In both cases, a clustering algorithm would need a very specific concept of a cluster to successfully detect these clusters. The process of finding such clusters is called conceptual clustering. However, too sophisticated a notion of a cluster would take us into the area of pattern recognition, and thus, we only consider simpler types of clusters in this paper.

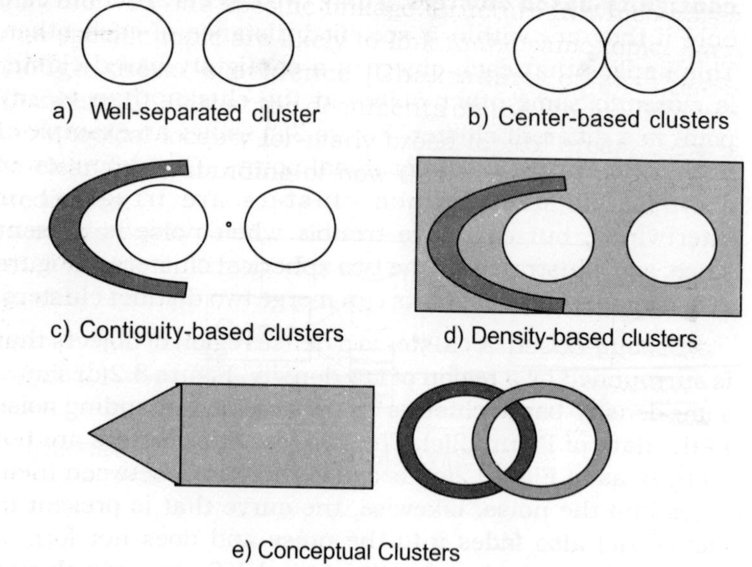

Fig. 2. Different types of clusters as illustrated by sets of two-dimensional points

4. CLUSTERING IN CENTRALIZED ROUTING

Routing in a network may involve a complex collection of functions that work more or less independently and yet support each other by exchanging services or information. The complexity arises due to maintaining a coordination between all the nodes of the subnet, coping with link and node failures, requiring redirection of traffic and an updation of databases maintained by the system, and modifying routes in case of congestions to achieve high performance.

A. NEWCLUST Algorithm: A heuristic algorithm NEWCLUST has been proposed by Dysart and Georganas[4]

for the design of multidrop teleprocessing networks with concentrators. The algorithm selects a set of candidate concentrator locations by using a clustering procedure and then obtains the final concentrator locations by a 'drop' routine. Multipoint links are then established between each of the selected terminal concentrators and their neighboring terminals. The concentrator selection depends on the number of terminals to be attached to it; the amount of traffic generated at each terminal, and the link and concentrator capacity. The terminal locations are selected on the basis of distances between the nodes.

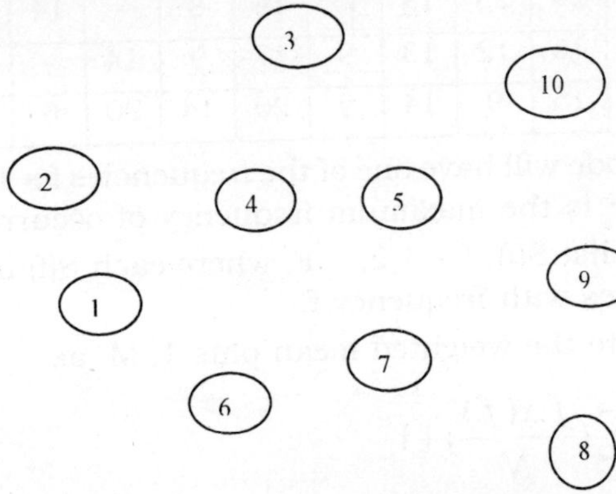

Fig. 3. Nodes in The Network

A ten-node network shown in fig.3 is taken as an example. Table 1 gives the Euclidean distances between different nodes. A heuristic algorithm is applied to partition the network into two clusters of five nodes each.

A brief description of the NEWCLUST algorithm as applied to the network of fig.3 for determining candidate NRCs is described as under;

1. Form a list of each node and its k nearest nodes where k is a design parameter that is used to specify the number of nearest nodes to be considered for each node.
2. From this list determine the frequency of occurrence, f, of each node.

Table 1: Distances Between Nodes

	1	2	3	4	5	6	7	8	9	10
1	-	11	16	10	16	11	18	25	24	24
2	11	-	6	6	8	14	16	24	16	15
3	16	6	-	8	6	16	15	23	12	9
4	10	6	8	-	6	9	10	18	13	14
5	16	8	6	6	-	12	10	17	9	9
6	11	14	16	9	12	-	9	14	17	20
7	18	16	15	10	10	9	-	8	9	14
8	25	24	23	18	17	14	8	-	14	20
9	24	16	12	13	9	17	9	14	-	6
10	24	15	9	14	9	20	14	20	6	-

3. Each node will have one of the frequencies f = 1,2, ...F, where F is the maximum frequency of occurrence.
4. Form a list S(f), f = 1,2, ...F, where each S(f) includes the nodes with frequency f.
5. Calculate the weighted mean plus 1, M, as

$$M = (\sum_{f=1}^{F} (\frac{f.x(f)}{N}) + 1$$

   Where x (f) is the number of nodes in list S (f).

   M will be truncated as trunc (M + 0.5) to approximate it to its nearest integer, since it represents the lower limit of frequency to be considered for selecting candidate NRCs and frequency is taken as an integer.
6. The initial list of nodes that are candidates for becoming NRCs is obtained by the nodes in the list S(F) where F is the maximum frequency. Further nodes are added from S (f), M < f < F

An illustration of the procedure as applied to the ten-node network of Fig 3 with k set to 3 is as follows:

The procedure specified in [4] for the NEWCLUST algorithm after the selection of initial concentrator locations does not apply to our problem as such since it follows a feasible partitioning on the basis of concentrator locations and the total traffic that can be handled by a concentrator. A drop routine is followed to attach, detach and reattach the terminals to concentrators till the traffic constraints are satisfied. In our problem under consideration, the aim is to divide the network into specified number of partitions, which may be dependent on the number of nodes in the network.

Table 2: Frequency of Occurrence of Nodes

Node N	List of the node and its k nearest neighbors	Frequency of occurrence f
1	1,2,4,6	2
2	2,3,4,5	5
3	3,2,4,5	5
4	4,2,3,5	6
5	5,2,3,4	6
6	6,1,4,7	4
7	7,6,9,8	4
8	8,6,7,9	2
9	9,5,7,10	3
10	10,3,5,9	2

Table 3: Nodes With Frequency *f*

S(f)	List of nodes with frequency f
S(1)	(0)
S(2)	(1,8,10
S(3)	(9)
S(4)	(6,7)
S(5)	(2,3)
S(6)	(4,5)

M = trunc (4.9 + 0.5) = 5

Candidate NRC's = Nodes in S (6) and nodes whose frequencies lie between 5 & 6.

S(6) = (4,5)

S(5) = (2,3)

Candidate NRCs = (2, 3,4,5)

The above procedure gives nodes (2,3,4,5) as the candidate control centers. In our problem under consideration, the aim is o divide number of nodes in the network. For example, for a network of 'n' nodes we may form n/j clusters with j being a decision parameter defining the number of nodes in a cluster. Thus suitable modifications are required to the NEWCLUST algorithm for applicability to the clustering of a network running a centralized hierarchical routing protocol.

The other observed inadequacy of the NEWCLUST algorithm for the proposed strategy is the specification of the design parameter k. The parameter specifies a definite value k, i.e. exactly k nearest neighbors of a node. There may be a possibility of having more than k nodes as nearest neighbors due to equal distances. For example, in the above illustration, if we choose k as 4, then for node 1, we have nodes 2, 4, 6, 3, 5 as 5 nearest neighbors since nodes 3 and 5 are both equidistant from node 1. Similar is the case with node 5, 7 and 10. This can lead to non-uniformity in calculating the frequency of occurrence of nodes. The NRC's that will be obtained with k = 4 are 2,6,7,9,3,4,5.

Further partitioning of the network will become a complex process as the number of initial NRC's chosen is large and we have to obtain a specific number of partitions rather than a random number as in the case of choice of concentrators in a multidrop teleprocessing network. No specific criteria have been specified in NEWCLUST algorithm for selecting the value of k.

5. PROPOSED APPROACH

Problem Statement:

Given:

1) N = { N_i ê i = 1,2,....., n} – Set of n nodes.

2) D = { d_{ij} ç i = 1,2,.....,n; j = 1,2,.....,n; i ¹ j} – distance table, where d_{ij} is the Euclidean distance between node i and node j and is specified as integer.

3) Maximum number of clusters is defined as j.

Determine:

Select j nodes to represent the NRC's and partition the network into j clusters with each cluster having one NRC.

Constraint:

1. Within each cluster, the distance between the nodes and the NRC is minimized.

Step I. Determining candidate NRC's:

1) Find the minimum, $d_{min,}$ and the maximum, d_{max}, distance between any two nodes from the distance matrix D.

2) Compute mean distance as $d_{mean} = (d_{min} + d_{max}) / 2$. (If d_{mean} is real then a truncated value of d_{mean} is taken since distance d_{ij} is specified as integer)

3) Form a list L of each node and its nearest neighbors that are within a distance d_{mean} from that node.

4) From the list L, determine the frequency of occurrence 'f' of each node.

5) The initial list of nodes that are candidates for becoming NRC's is obtained from the above list by choosing those k nodes which have maximum frequency of occurrence, where k=j, and j is a design parameter to specify the number of clusters to be formed (if k>j, then j NRC's will be chosen out of the k NRC's in Step III).

Step II. Formation of clusters:

Node i of N is associated with NRC j:

$i \in NRC_j$ if $d_{ij} < d_{ik}$ $\forall k \in C$, j k, $j \in C$

Where

N : Set of n nodes of a network {1,2,.....n}.

C : Set of k NRC's

Step III: Final clustering:

1) If $k > j$, then $(k - j)$ NRC's and their associated nodes have to be dropped out and associated with the existing NRCs if they do not already exist.

The NRCs to be dropped will be identified as:

If d_{im} is the distance of the node i from NRC m, then

$$D_m = \Sigma d_{im} \qquad \forall i \in X_m, \quad m \in C$$

X_m: Set of nodes associated with NRC m

The NRC for which D_m is the maximum is to be dropped and the dropped NRC and its associated nodes are to be associated with the other NRC's with whom they have the least distance.

2) Remove duplicate occurrences of nodes if any from overloaded NRCs.

3) If k=j but unequal number of nodes are associated to the NRCs, then, a balance can be made by shifting those nodes from the overloaded NRC which are farthest from the NRC and associating those nodes with those NRC's to which they are closest. This will be done only if we want each cluster to have equal number of nodes.

6. CONCLUSION

A clustering algorithm for clustering the nodes of a large network for optimizing centralized routing is proposed in this paper. The criterion undertaken is the proximity of nodes , i.e , nodes that are close to each other will belong to the same cluster. The clusters are formed by first identifying the nodes that can best represent the routing control centers since the consideration is of centralized routing. Sometimes the proximity of nodes within a particular region may be more than some other region. In that case, it may probably not be feasible to disassociate the nodes from the region of high density to which they belong and associate them to other regions with whom they are at longer distances.

7. FUTURE WORK

The design parameter 'j' will be chosen to partition the network into j clusters consisting of equal number of nodes. But it is not necessary to impose a constraint to have equal and exactly a specified number of nodes in each cluster. Sometimes the proximity of nodes within a particular region may be more than some other region. In that case, it may probably not be feasible to disassociate the nodes from the region of high density to which they belong and associate them to other regions with whom they are at longer distances. Considering all the aspects, the proposed strategy can be considered as efficient in terms of resource utilization and path calculation. The main stress in this study has been on the design of a routing strategy, carried out as an improvement to Centralized routing, to make routing decisions on the basis of predictions of delays on the links in a network by a central node keeping global record of the network. However, there might be some aspects that have remained unnoticed or have been ignored. Probably a more detailed investigation may reveal the unnoticed shortcomings of the strategy.

REFERENCES

[1] Anil K. Jain and Richard C. Dubes. *Algorithms for Clustering Data.* Prentice-Hall, 1988.

[2] Raza Ali (425), Usman Ghani (462), Aasim Saeed (464) *"Data Clustering and its applications".*

[3] Matthias Jarke, Maurizio Lenzerini, Yannis Vassiliou, and Panos Vassiliadis. *Fundamentals of Data Warehouses.* Springer, 1999.

[4] Hugh G. Dysart, N. D. Georganas, *"NEWCLUST: An Algorithm for the Topological Design of Two-Level, Multidrop Teleprocessing Networks",* IEEE Trans. on Communications, Vol. Com-26, No.1, Jan 1978

[5] Periklis Andritsos, *"Data Clustering Techniques Qualifying Oral Examination Paper"*University of Toronto,Mar 2002.

11

Performance Analysis of Quality of Services of 3G and 4G Networks

*Manoj Yadav**

Abstract – *Mobile communication is a need of today, globalisation demands a high speed of internet on portable devices when user in a high mobility. Research are continues to find out a solution of that problem. 3G and 4G networks are made to provide high speed of data transfer in full mobility. 4G is said to be a complete IP solution where voice, data and streamed multimedia can be given to users on an "Anytime, Anywhere and Anyhow", basis, and at higher data rates than previous generations. The paper is based on the performance analysis of both the networks and to figure out how we can increase performance of existing 3G networks.*

This paper explores standards and technology of 4G networks. It will also describe new technologies that leads path of 4G networks. With the help of Simulation experiments the

*M.Tech (C.S.E), GJUS&T, Hisar. e-mail yadmavmanoj12@gmail.com

performance of the 3G and 4G networks are analyses. The experiments are taken with the help of simulator Qualnet5.0. With the Simulation of various network setups as per requirement and performance of the both networks by taking parameters such as throughput, collisions, end to end delay and packet delivery ratio are analyses. This will surely helps in enhancing the performance of 3G networks.

Keywords – *4G, 3G, 2G, 1G, OFDMA, UMTS, PDR.*

1. INTRODUCTION

Evolution of Wireless Communication has been rapid. Demands for further development have surfaced even faster. These demands have originated innovations. From the age of pre-cellular

Mobile telephone technology, referred to as 0G in some literatures, till date wireless communication has been through remarkable changes.

First generation (1G) mobile systems, introduce in early 1980's, initiated commercial mobile voice services. 1G mobile systems offered voice and low speed data transmission and were operated in circuit switched mode. The key technology used in 1G-network system was Frequency Division Multiple Access (FDMA) schemes and operate in the 450 and 800MHz frequency bands. The major problems of 1G mobile system were internetworking between different networks and the quality was far from the standard offered by wire line telephony. These shortcomings were overcome with the advent of the Second Generation (2G) mobile systems. By using digital technology instead of analog one, 2G systems such as Global System for Mobile Communications (GSM) increased the number of supported users within a cell and enhanced voice quality significantly. In its original form, the GSM is the 900, 1800 and 1900MHz frequency bands use a Time Division Code Multiple Access (TDMA) scheme for circuit mode transmission of digitized speech and digital data at up to 9.6kb/s. Since its commercialization in 1990's, GSM has been currently upgraded, by the introduction of High Speech

Circuit Switched Data (HSCSD), General Packet Radio Services (GPRS), and Enhanced Data rates for GSM Evolution (EDGE), Enhanced Circuit Switched Data (ECSD) and Enhanced GPRS (EGPRS). [1][9]

2G's success story prompted the development of 2.5G and 3G mobile systems. 3G technology supports 144 Kbps data rate, with high-speed movement (vehicles), 384 Kbps (on campus) and 2 Mbps for stationary (in building). [2]Even before 3G networks are fully launched and utilized, various study groups are considering the shape of the next generation of cellular technology, so called 4G. There is no single global vision for 4G as yet, but the next generation of network is likely to be fully IP-based. In 4G the radio interfaces will support up to approximately 100 Mbps for high mobility and up to approximately 1Gbps for low mobility such as nomadic/local wireless access.

4 G Mobile Communications

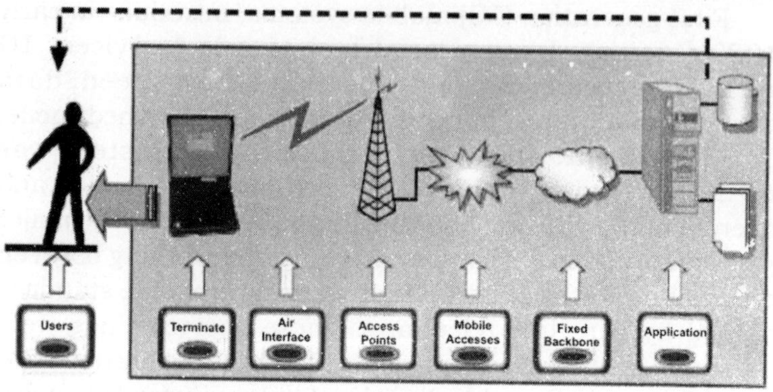

Fig. 1. 4G Network

3G is based on a wide-area concept applying circuit and packet switching for transmission with limited access technology, such as WCDMA, CDMA and TD-SOMA. However, the 4G standard will base on broadband IP-based, entirely applying packet switching method of transmission with seamlessly access convergence. 4G mobile systems will include all systems from various networks, from public to private, from operator driven broadband networks to personal areas and from cellular to ad hoc networks. One of the terms used to describe 4G is MAGIC—Mobile multimedia, anytime anywhere, Global mobility support, integrated wireless solution, and customized personal service. [2]

Standards of 3G and 4G Networks

Universal Mobile Telecommunication System i.e. UMTS is the standard of 3G networks and Mobile WiMAX is of 4G networks.

Universal Mobile Telecommunication System (UMTS): Universal Mobile Telecommunications System (UMTS) is one of the 3G mobile telecommunications standards. The first deployment of the UMTS is the release99 (R99) architecture. It is specified by 3GPP and is part of the global ITU IMT-2000 standard. The most common form of UMTS uses W-CDMA (IMT Direct Spread) as the underlying air interface but the system also covers TD-CDMA and TD-SCDMA (both IMT CDMA TDD). Being a complete network system, UMTS also covers the radio access network (UMTS Terrestrial Radio Access Network, or UTRAN) and the core network (Mobile Application Part, or MAP), as well as authentication of users via USIM cards (Subscriber Identity Module). [3][4]

Unlike EDGE (IMT Single-Carrier, based on GSM) and CDMA2000 (IMT Multi-Carrier), UMTS requires new base stations and new frequency allocations. However, it is closely related to GSM/EDGE as it borrows and builds upon concepts from GSM. Further, most UMTS handsets also support GSM, allowing seamless dual-mode operation. Therefore, UMTS is sometimes marketed as 3GSM, emphasizing the close relationship with GSM and differentiating it from competing technologies. The name UMTS, introduced by ETSI, is usually used in Europe. Outside of Europe, the system is also known by other names such as FOMA or W-CDMA. In marketing, it is often just referred to as 3G. UMTS, using 3GPP, supports maximum theoretical data transfer rates of 42 Mbit/s, although at the moment users in deployed networks can expect a transfer rate of up to 384 kbit/s for R99 handsets, and 7.2 Mbit/s for HSDPA handsets in the downlink connection.[5] This is still much greater than the 9.6 kbit/s of a single GSM error-corrected circuit switched data channel or multiple 9.6 kbit/s channels in HSCSD (14.4 kbit/s for CDMAOne), and—in competition to other network technologies such as CDMA2000, PHS or WLAN—offers access to the World Wide Web and other data services on mobile devices. Since 2006, UMTS networks in many countries have been or are in the process of being upgraded with High Speed Downlink Packet Access (HSDPA), sometimes known as 3.5G. Currently, HSDPA enables downlink transfer speeds of upto 21 Mbit/s. Work is also progressing on improving the uplink transfer speed with the High-Speed Uplink Packet Access (HSUPA). Longer term, the 3GPP Long Term Evolution project plans to move UMTS to 4G speeds of 100 Mbit/s down and 50 Mbit/s up, using a next generation air interface technology based upon Orthogonal frequency-division multiplexing. The high data speeds of UMTS are now most often utilized for Internet access: experience in Japan and elsewhere has shown that user demand for video calls is not high, and Telco provided audio/video content has declined in popularity in favor of high-speed access to the World Wide Web - either directly on a handset or connected to a computer via Wi-Fi, Bluetooth, Infrared or USB. It offers teleservices like speech or SMS and bearer services, which provide the capability for information transfer between access points. It is possible to negotiate and renegotiate the characteristics of a bearer service at session or connection establishment and during ongoing session or connection. Both connections oriented and connectionless services are offered for Point-to-Point and Point-to-Multipoint communication. Bearer services have different QoS parameters for maximum transfer delay, delay variation and bit error rate. Offered data rate targets are:

- 144 kbit/s satellite and rural outdoors
- 384 kbit/s urban outdoors
- 2048 kbit/s indoor and low range outdoor

2. MOBILE WIMAX

Mobile WiMAX was successfully adopted by ITU as one of the IMT-2000 technologies in November 2007. The main idea of Mobile WiMAX is broadband wireless communication and mobility. Mobile WiMAX offers high speed Internet service which provides various information and multimedia data with high data rate on broadband regardless of place and time. Despite the fact that the services are based on multimedia data transmission, it is difficult to transmit a large amount of data to each group of user in wireless environment because of limited bandwidth. To avoid this restriction, multicast and broadcast service (MBS) was initiated in Mobile WiMAX. The MBS concept is defined in IEEE802.16e standard [I] which supports mobility. Since then mobile WiMAX (a.k.a. IP-OFDMA) has officially become a major global cellular wireless standard along with 3GPP UMTS/HSPA and 3GPP2 CDMA/ EVDO. Mobile WiMAX is an OFDM-based technology available for deployment today, and new WIMAX devices come to market at much reduced cost than that of current 3G solutions. Currently over 260 service providers are deploying fixed, portable and mobile WiMAX networks in 110 countries [6].

3. MOBILE WIMAX EVOLUTION

The Mobile WiMAX Release 1.0 System Profile, based on 802.16e or 802.16-2005, was completed in late 2006, and the radio-level certification of products began in 2007. The certification follows a phased approach to address deployment priorities and vendor readiness. System Profile Release 1.0 includes all 802.16-2005 mandatory features, and also requires some of the optional features needed for enhanced mobility and QoS support. Since early 2007, the WiMAX Forum and the IEEE 802.16 Working Group have started separate evolution projects to improve the performance of the current release of mobile WiMAX and keep the momentum of evolving mobile WiMAX as a leading mobile broadband wireless communication solution. In the WiMAX Forum the evolution project is known as mobile WiMAX release 1.5; the current mobile WiMAX release is 1.0. The focus of this project includes adding FDD configuration to the mobile WiMAX profile, enabling MIMO/BF under FDD mobile WiMAX, adding persistent allocation to improve efficiency for VoIP data traffic, reducing MAP control message overhead, and reducing handoff latency. The target of this project is to provide performance enhancement to current mobile WiMAX systems within a short time period (targeting deployment in late 2009) and without introducing significant changes to the IEEE 802.16-2005 specification. The project that introduces more fundamental performance enhancements to mobile WiMAX is led by the IEEE 802.16 Working Group. This project and the associated future standard are known as 802.16m. The target for 802.16m is to meet the requirements of IMT Advanced, the fourth generation (4G) successor of IMT-2000. In other words, 802.16m will be the 4G mobile WiMAX evolution. [7]

Result and Analysis

Fourth Generation (4G) and Third Generation (3G) are the next generation of wireless networks. We will describe the performance of Quality of service with the help of network simulator **QUALNET**. Qualnet is the most applicable network simulator, which is a commercial spin-off from the GloMosim simulator, which is based on C++ programming. All protocol are implemented in a series of C++ files, and called by the simulation kernel. One of advantages of Qualnet is that it is more scalable. During the simulation time, it enables the user can see the all signals being transmitted and received at each node, which assists in the understanding of what is happening in a freshly manner. Qualnet simulator used the three main programs such as the analyzer and the packet tracer. When simulator runs the given simulation, analyzer displays the simulation results and packet tracer aids to realize the path of a packet through the network. There is also a protocol developer in the GUI; however, it is much more powerful to develop protocols from C++ coding [8].

Qualnet allows investigation and evaluation of fixed and mobile WiMAX devices, applications and networks. WiMAX channel model of Qualnet includes co-channel interference, urban path loss, fading, and shadowing and mobility effects. Through detailed models, unrivaled speed and scalability,

Qualnet [9] provides an environment for controlled and repeatable experimentation that leads to improved network performance and a better end-user experience. These services are intended to provide data at high speed, high capacity. The analysis has been done by several experiments that describe the performance of the system. With the help of some parameters and experiments we can analyze the performance of both the networks 4G and 3G networks on their standards. In the experiments we will change the number of nodes and mobility between them. Also we use a client\server application CBR to send packets to a particular destination. Then we will analyze the impact of changing nodes and mobility on the both services. With the help of some metrics like packet delivery ratio, throughput etc. obtained from .stat file of QUALNET. We can check out the performance. The simulation parameter are used in experiments are listed below in table.

Parameters	**Values UMTS**	**Values MOBILE WiMAX**
Frequency	3.1 GHz	2.4 GHz
Channel Bandwidth	10 MHz	20MHz
Simulation Area	1500×1500	1500×1500
Simulation Time	20M	20M
Number of Nodes	0-25	0-25
Packet Size	2048	2048
Traffic Type	CBR	CBR
Mac Protocol	802.11	MACA
Routing Protocol	AODV	AODV
IP Version	IPv4	IPv6
Mobility Speed	0-50(m/s)	0-50(m/s)

Packet Delivery Ratio (PDR): It is the ratio between the number of packets that are received and the number of packets sent. This metric only considers backward path traffic i.e. the data packets from the gateways to the mesh nodes. PDR is most important metric that we should consider in packet forwarding. We can say this is the best parameter to evaluate the performance of a network. It may affects by different criteria such as packet size, group size, action range and mobility of nodes. PDR performance with respect to mobility is plotted in figure below. From the results, we can see that the packet delivery ratio is almost same in scenarios in case of UMTS and MOBILE WiMAX. MOBILE WiMAX i.e. 4G receives more packets. This is the formula to find out the PDR.

PDR = Total Number of Packets Received/Total Number of Packets Sent×100

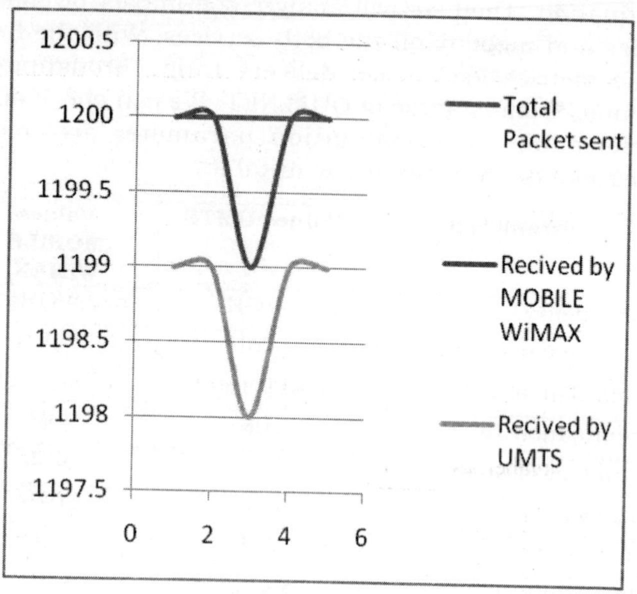

Fig. 2. Packet Delivery Ratio

Average End to End Delay: The delay is the total latency experienced by a packet to traverse the network from the source to the destination. At the network layer the end-to-end packet latency is the sum of processing delay, packetization, transmission delay, queuing delay, and propagation delay. The end-to-end delay of a path is the summation of the node delay at each node plus the link delay at each link on the path. . In wireless link, the propagation delays are very small and almost equal for each hop on the path. The queuing delay and MAC delay are considered as two main factors that accumulated the node's delay. As mobility increases links broke frequently. Figure below shows end-to-end delay for the UMTS at different node mobility. In case of MOBILE WiMAX the delay is negligible.

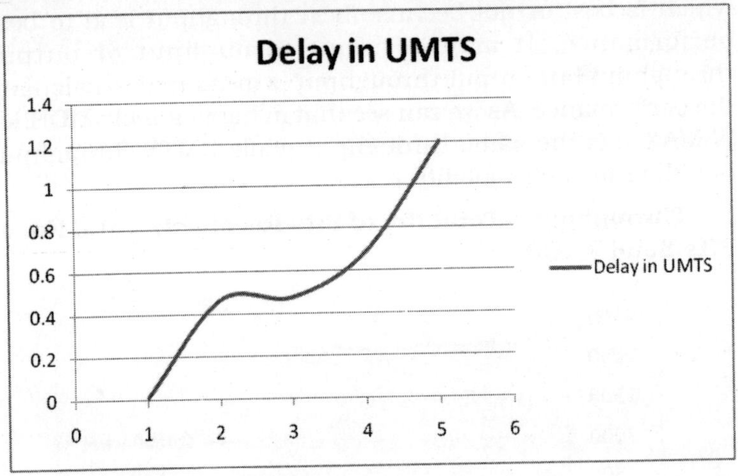

Fig. 3. End to End Delay

Collisions: When two or more nodes want to transmit data packets without sensing or listening to the transmission channel and if there is already congestion on the channel then a collision state occurs. In collision either the contents of the data packets are modified or the contents are completely lost and the data packet is of no use for the destination. So the source has to transmit those data packets again to the destination. So this metric is used to measure that how many collisions occurs during the transmission.

Collision Ratio: In networks packet collision occurs when two or more packets from different source nodes arrive at the same destination node simultaneously. The simulation measures the number of total packets (total_pkt) arriving at a specific node and calculates how many packets encounter collision (collided_pkt); the packet collision ratio is the ratio of collided_pkt to total_pkt. The metric packet loss rate measures the percentage of packets discarded at an end-node, due to either collision or corruption. It is defined as the ratio of (collided_pkt + corrupted_pkt) to total_pkt. The collision ratio is more in case of UMTS.

Throughput: It defines the total number of sent bits in per second. The matrix explain the quality of technology which is best or not because best throughput lead to best performance. It may be input throughput or output throughput but output throughput is measured to calculate the performance. As we can see that in high mobility MOBILE WiMAX has the same throughput while UMTS throughput is falling in high mobility.

Throughput = Total No. of Bits Received/ Total No. of Bits Send × 100

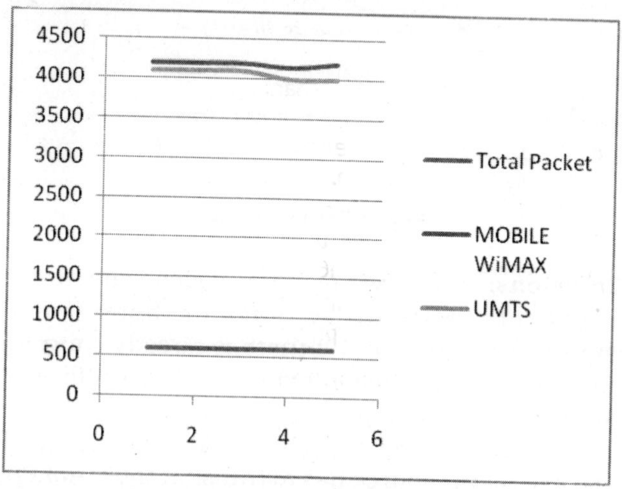

DISCUSSION AND CONCLUSION

From the results it is apparent that MOBILE WiMAX i.e. standard of 4G networks can provide an optimal solution of mobile broadband for users in high mobility rather than UMTS, standard of 3G networks. It means that user can access the data with the same speed as that of broadband service. 4G's performance is supposed to be four to ten times of 3G. In case of some ideal scenarios in Qualnet5.0 on 4G's most popular standard Mobile WiMax. We are sending fewer numbers of packets and mobility is also not too much. Yet, UMTS networks i.e. supposed to give a speed of 2Mbps in full mobility having much delay, less throughput, more collisions than MOBILE WiMAX. From the performance analysis of the Quality of Services parameters of 3G and 4G networks, we can say that 4G networks will provide better services than that of 3G. According to results the more end to end delay and collision in 3G shows that 4G provides optimal data transfer. Also speed of uplink and downlink is more in 4G than that of 3G, which makes 4G networks better than 3G networks.

REFRENCES

(1) Hui, Y., S., & Yeung, H., K. (2003) "Challenges in the Migration to 4G Mobile Systems", *Proceeding in IEEE Communications Magazine*, pp. 54-59.

(2) Khan, A.H., Qadeer, M.A., Ansari, J.A., & Waheed, S.(2009). "4G as a Next Generation Wireless Network", *Proceeding in International Conference on Future Computer and Communication, IEEE*, pp. 334-338.

(3) Eva Reguera San Josb, Fernando J. Velez (2003) "Enhanced UMTS Services and Applications: a perspective beyond 3G" *printed and published by IEEE*, pp. 146-150.

(4) http://en.wikipedia.org/wiki/Umts; 3 September 2010.

(5) M. Frodigh, S. Parkvall, C. Roobol and P. Johansson (2001) "Future Generation Wireless Networks", *IEEE Personal Communications*, Oct. 2001.

(6) Fan Wang, Amitava Ghosh, Chandy Sankaran, Philip J.Fleming, Frank Hsieh and Stanley J. Benes (2008) "Mobile WiMAX Systems: Performance and Evolution", *Proceeding of IEEE Communication Magazine, October 2008*, pp. 41-49.

(7) Kamran Etemad (2008) "Overview of Mobile WiMAX Technology and Evolution", *proceeding of IEEE Communication Magazine, October 2008*, pp. 31-40.

(8) Khishigjargal Gonchigsumlaa, Young-II Kim (2010), "The Simulation Model of Multicast and Broadcast Service in the MOBILE WiMAX for Qualnet", *proceeding of ICACT 2010, IEEE.*

(9) Jamil, M., Shaikh, S. P., Shahzad, M., & Awais, Q. "4G: The Future Mobile Technology", *Proceeding of IEEE.*

□□□

12

Emerging Smart Approach

Wireless Sensor Networks

*Rubal Chaudhry, Neha Sharma, Sourav Walia**

Abstract – *Smart environments represent the next evolutionary development step in building, utilities, industrial, home, shipboard, and transportation systems automation. Like any sentient organism, the smart environment relies first and foremost on sensory data from the real world. Sensory data comes from multiple sensors of different modalities in distributed locations. The information needed by smart environments is provided by Distributed Wireless Sensor Networks, which are responsible for sensing as well as for the first stages of the processing hierarchy. In this paper we explore the prospects and major aspects of wireless sensor networks.*

Keywords – *Smart, Environment, Wireless, Sensor, attacks, security.*

*Department of Computers, R.P. Inderaprastha Institute of Technology, Bastara, Karnal, India. E-mail: *rubal1686@gmail.com, sharmaneha29@gmail.com, sourav70walia@gmail.com*

1. INTRODUCTION

A Wireless Sensor Network typically consists of a large number of nodes which are equipped with a low end microprocessor, a radio for communication and a number of sensors depending on the physical phenomena that are to be measured [1]. These sensor nodes help to monitor natural phenomena like temperature, humidity etc. accurately in space and time or detects events of interest [2]. A few special nodes called *sinks* gathers data collected by various nodes in the network. Sinks normally are more powerful than the ordinary nodes in terms of processing power, available storage and available energy. A large number of ordinary (non-sink) nodes collect data and send the collected data to these sinks. A non-sink node can perform the following tasks -collect and process data and use a radio to communicate with other nodes. The processing capabilities of ordinary nodes are limited and high end processing is carried out at the sinks. Sinks can also act as gateways to other networks like the Internet. The sensor nodes are normally small in size and the energy available for each node is limited. Each node, once it is deployed, operates unattended till its battery drains.,

2. WHY WIRELESS SENSOR NETWORKS?

Fundamental objectives of sensor networks are reliability, accuracy, flexibility, cost effectiveness and ease of deployment. Key characteristics and benefits of WSN (Wireless Sensor Networks) are outlined below:

- *Sensing accuracy:* The utilization of a larger number and variety of sensor nodes provides potential for greater accuracy in the information gathered as compared to that obtained from a single sensor.
- *Area coverage:* This implies that fast and efficient sensor network could span a greater geographical area without adverse impact on the overall network cost.
- *Fault tolerance*: Device redundancy and consequently information redundancy can be utilized to ensure a level of fault tolerance in individual sensors.

- *Connectivity:* Multiple sensor networks may be connected through sink nodes, along with existing wired networks (e.g. Internet). The clustering of networks enables each individual network to focus on specific areas or events and share only relevant information.
- *Minimal human interaction:* Having minimum human interaction makes the possibility of having less interruption of the system.
- *Operability in harsh environments:* Sensor nodes, consisting of robust sensor design, integrated with high levels of fault tolerance can be deployed in harsh environments that make the sensor networks more effective.
- *Dynamic sensor scheduling:* Implying some scheduling scheme, sensor network is capable of setting priority for data transmission.

3. SMART SENSORS AND WIRELESS SENSOR NETWORK – A BACKGROUND

Sensor nodes are of the combination of sensing and special-purpose computing devices tied with wireless communications. When networked, such sensor nodes would build up the part of larger systems, providing data, as well as performing and controlling multitude of tasks and functions. Small size and cost of individual sensor nodes would be the key ingredient for a large number of applications both in ordinary as well as harsh environments. Sensor networks can be used in support of preparation and prevention during various phases of pre-event, rapid response during the event, and post recovery along with analysis after the event. To benefit the environment, in practical, these large number of miniaturized commodity sensor nodes could be installed, for example in buildings, on roads, in vehicles, at the riverbanks, or at coastal areas etc.

A smart sensor node is a combination of sensing, processing and communication technologies. Figure 1 shows the basic architectural components of a sensor node. The sensing unit senses the change of parameters, signal conditioning circuitry prepares the electrical signals to convert to the digital domain, the sensed analog signal is converted and is used as the input to the application algorithms or processing unit, the memory helps processing of tasks and the transceiver is used for communicating with other sensors or the base stations or sinks in WSN.

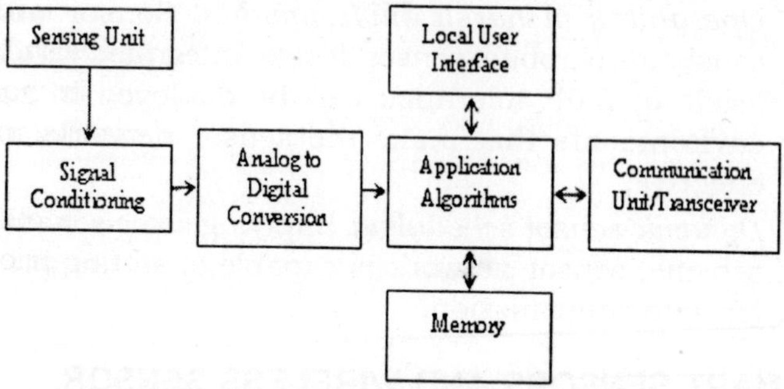

Fig. 1. Basic architectural components of a smart sensor

Sensors can monitor temperature, pressure, humidity, soil makeup, vehicular movement, noise levels, lighting conditions, the presence or absence of certain kinds of objects or substances, mechanical stress levels on attached objects, and other properties [3]. Their mechanism may be seismic, magnetic, thermal, visual, infrared, acoustic, or radar [4]. A smart sensor is also capable of self-identification and self-diagnosis. The mechanisms of smart sensors work in one of three ways: by a line of sight to the target (such as visual sensors), by proximity to target (such as seismic sensors), and by propagation like a wave with possible bending (such as acoustic sensors).

Sensor networks are predominantly data-centric rather than address-centric. In such a network, queries are directed to a region containing a cluster of sensor nodes rather than specific sensor addresses. Given the similarity in the data obtained by sensors in a dense cluster, aggregation of the data is performed locally. That is, a summary or analysis of the local data is prepared by an aggregator node within the cluster, thus reducing the communication bandwidth requirements.

4. ARCHITECTURE

Selecting the optimum sensors and wireless communications link requires knowledge of the application and problem definition. Battery life, sensor update rates, and size are all major design considerations. Examples of low data rate sensors include temperature, humidity, and peak strain captured passively. Examples of high data rate sensors include strain, acceleration, and vibration. Recent advances have resulted in the ability to integrate sensors, radio communications, and digital electronics into a single integrated circuit (IC) package. This capability is enabling networks of very low cost sensors that are able to communicate with each other using low power wireless data routing protocols. A wireless sensor network (WSN) generally consists of a base station (or "gateway") that can communicate with a number of wireless sensors via a radio link. Data is collected at the wireless sensor node, compressed, and transmitted to the gateway directly or, if required, uses other wireless sensor nodes to forward data to the gateway. The transmitted data is then presented to the system by the gateway connection.

A. Individual Wireless Sensor Node Architecture: A functional block diagram of a versatile wireless sensing node is provided in Fig. 2. A modular design approach provides a flexible and versatile platform to address the needs of a wide variety of applications [5]. For example, depending on the sensors to be deployed, the signal conditioning block can be re-programmed or replaced. This allows for a wide variety of different sensors to be used with the wireless sensing node. The use of flash memory allows the remote nodes to acquire data on command from a base station, or by an event sensed by one or more inputs to the node. Furthermore, embedded firmware can be upgraded through the wireless network in the field.

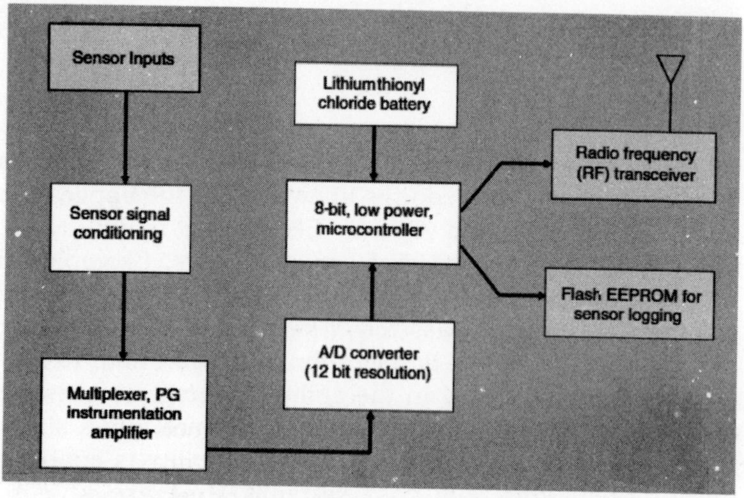

Fig. 2. Wireless Sensor Node Functional Block Diagram

The microprocessor has a number of functions including:

- Managing data collection from the sensors.
- Performing power management functions.
- Interfacing the sensor data to the physical radio layer.
- Managing the radio network protocol.

A key feature of any wireless sensing node is to minimize the power consumed by the system. Generally, the radio subsystem requires the largest amount of power. Therefore, it is advantageous to send data over the radio network only when required. This sensor event-driven data collection model requires an algorithm to be loaded into the node to determine when to send data based on the sensed event. Additionally, it is important to minimize the power consumed by the sensor itself. Therefore, the hardware should be designed to allow the microprocessor to judiciously control power to the radio, sensor, and sensor signal conditioner.

B. Network Topology: A communication network is composed of nodes, each of which has computing power and can transmit and receive messages over communication links, wireless or cabled. The basic network topologies are shown in the figure 3 and include fully connected, mesh, star, ring, tree, bus. A single network may consist of several interconnected subnets of different topologies. Networks are further classified as Local Area Networks (LAN), e.g. inside one building, or Wide Area Networks (WAN), e.g. between buildings.. Therefore, for large networks, the routing problem is computationally intractable even with the availability of large amounts of computing power.

Mesh networks are regularly distributed networks that generally allow transmission only to a node's nearest neighbors. The nodes in these networks are generally identical, so that mesh nets are also referred to as peer-to-peer (see below) nets. Mesh nets can be good models for large-scale networks of wireless sensors that are distributed over a geographic region, e.g. personnel or vehicle security surveillance systems.

An advantage of mesh nets is that, although all nodes may be identical and have the same computing and transmission capabilities, certain nodes can be designated as 'group leaders' that take on additional functions. If a group leader is disabled, another node can then take over these duties.

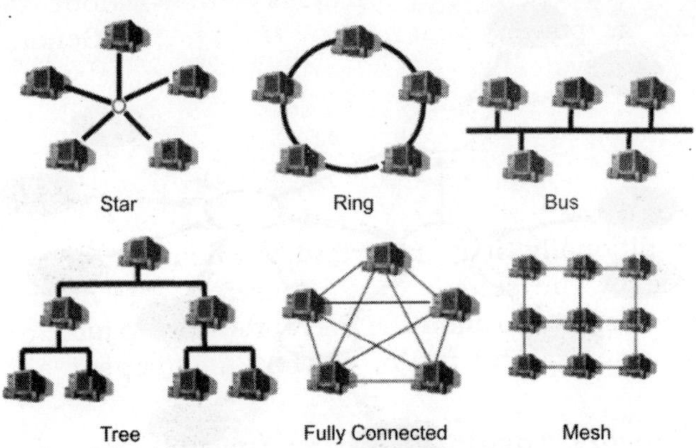

Fig. 3. Network Topologies

All nodes of the **Star Topology** are connected to a single hub node. The hub requires greater message handling, routing, and decision-making capabilities than the other nodes.

If a communication link is cut, it only affects one node. However, if the hub is incapacitated the network is destroyed.

In the **Ring Topology** all nodes perform the same function and there is no leader node. Messages generally travel around the ring in a single direction. However, if the ring is cut, all communication is lost.

A **Hybrid** between the star and mesh network provides for a robust and versatile communications network, while maintaining the ability to keep the wireless sensor nodes power consumption to a minimum. In this network topology, the lowest power sensor nodes are not enabled with the ability to forward messages. This allows for minimal power consumption to be maintained. However, other nodes on the network are enabled with multihop capability, allowing them to forward messages from the low power nodes to other nodes on the network. This is the topology implemented by the up and coming mesh networking standard known as ZigBee.

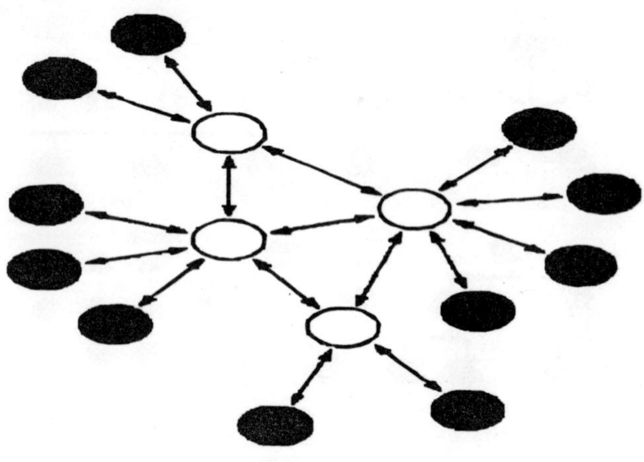

Fig. 4. Hybrid star-mesh network topology

The **Self-Healing Ring Network** (SHR) shown has two rings and is more fault tolerant.

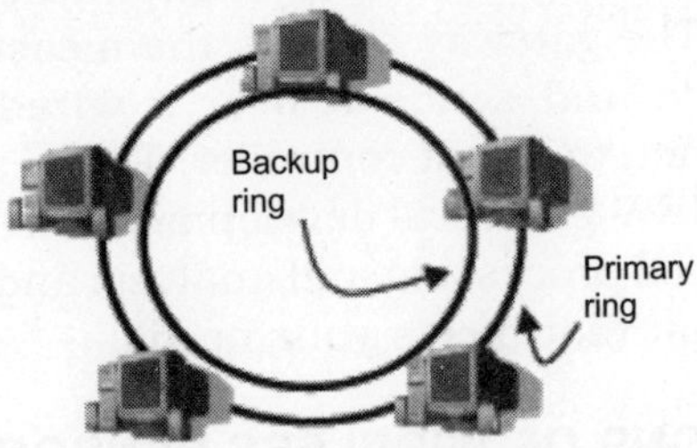

Fig. 5. Self-Healing Ring Network

In the bus topology, messages are broadcast on the bus to all nodes. Each node checks the destination address in the message header, and processes the messages addressed to it. The bus topology is passive in that each node simply listens for messages and is not responsible for retransmitting any messages.

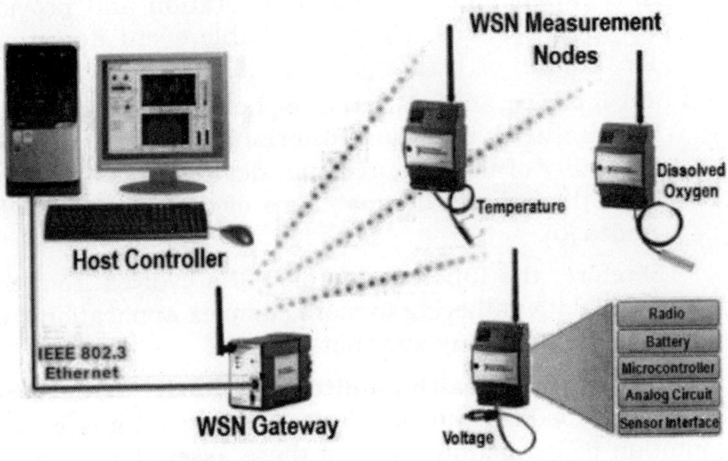

Fig. 6. Architecture of Wireless sensor Networks

C. Common Wireless Sensor Network Architecture: In a common WSN architecture, the measurement nodes are deployed to acquire measurements such as temperature, voltage, or even dissolved oxygen. The nodes are part of a wireless network administered by the gateway, which governs network aspects such as client authentication and data security. The gateway collects the measurement data from each node and sends it over a wired connection, typically Ethernet, to a host controller. There, software such as the NI LabVIEW graphical development environment can perform advanced processing and analysis and present your data in a fashion that meets your needs.

5. APPLICATIONS OF WIRELESS SENSOR NETWORKS

The range of WSNs applications has extended considerably, mainly due to the following reasons:

- The processing capabilities of the nodes have evolved up to a point that enables them to execute complex tasks and to make decisions autonomously;
- A group of sensor nodes can combine their resources and capabilities through collaboration and provide complex services, such as reliable event detection, localization or tracking.
- An interoperable collection of heterogeneous devices can achieve superior functionality by using the flexibility of the resource-lean devices in conjunction with the enhanced capabilities of the more endowed nodes [6].

Therefore, the functionality of WSNs evolves from the traditional data gathering to more complex applications, as shown by the following succinct review:

A. Structural Health Monitoring – Smart Structures: Sensors embedded into machines and structures enable condition-based maintenance of these assets [3].Typically, structures or machines are inspected at regular time intervals, and components may be repaired or replaced based on their hours in service, rather than on their working conditions.Wireless sensing will allow assets to be inspected when the sensors indicate that there may be a problem, reducing the cost of maintenance and preventing catastrophic failure in the event that damage is detected.

B. Industrial Automation: In addition to being expensive, leadwires can be constraining, especially when moving parts are involved. The use of wireless sensors allows for rapid installation of sensing equipment and allows access to locations that would not be practical if cables were attached.

C. Environmental monitoring: Environmental monitoring is the traditional WSN application, where a static array of sensors is randomly or uniformly deployed over an area to gather sensor readings and to transmit them at a central point for processing. Typical settings include precision agriculture [7], habitat monitoring or ocean water monitoring [8].

D. Animal monitoring: Different from the environmental monitoring applications by introducing mobility within WSNs, this scenario assumes that nodes are attached to animals for the purpose of studying their behaviour, locating or confining them within an area. Examples include wild life monitoring [9] and cattle herding.

E. Emergency: Emergency applications have as main objective the rescue of people in danger. For this purpose, people at risk carry a sensor node that permits localization in case of disaster. Example applications include rescue of avalanche victims [10] and fire fighting and rescue.

F. Military: WSN represents a promising technology for military applications because low-cost, disposable sensor nodes can be deployed in these destructive environments. Some of the military applications of sensor networks are: battlefield surveillance, mapping opposing terrain, nuclear, biological and chemical attack detection and reconnaissance, target tracking.

G. Transport and logistics: Transport and logistics represent an important market for WSNs. The goal is to monitor the storage conditions of products, to verify the loads, and to real-time localize the goods at production sites, distribution centres or stores.

6. BASIC SECURITY SCHEMES IN WIRELESS SENSOR NETWORKS

Security is a broadly used term encompassing the characteristics of authentication, integrity, privacy, non repudiation, and anti- playback [11]. The more the dependency on the information provided by the networks has been increased, the more the risk of secure transmission of information over the networks has increased.. In this section, we discuss the network security fundamentals and how the techniques are meant for wireless sensor networks.

A. Security Schemes: 1) *Cryptography*: WSNs consist of tiny sensors which really suffer from the lack of processing, memory and battery power [12][13]. Applying any encryption scheme requires transmission of extra bits, hence extra processing, memory and battery power which are very important resources for the sensors' longevity. Applying the security mechanisms such as encryption could also increase delay, jitter and packet loss in wireless sensor networks [14]. Moreover, some critical questions arise when applying encryption schemes to WSNs like, how the keys are generated and how keys are managed, revoked, assigned to a new sensor added to the network or renewed for ensuring robust security for the network.

2) *Steganography:* Steganography is the art of covert communication by embedding a message into the multimedia data (image, sound, video, etc.). The main objective of steganography is to modify the carrier in a way that is not perceptible and hence, it looks just like ordinary. It hides the existence of the covert channel, and furthermore, in the case that we want to send a secret data without sender information or when we want to distribute secret data publicly, it is very useful.

3) *Physical Layer Secure Access*: Physical layer secure access in wireless sensor networks could be provided by using frequency hopping. A dynamic combination of the parameters like hopping set (available frequencies for hopping), dwell time (time interval per hop) and hopping

pattern (the sequence in which the frequencies from the available hopping set is used) could be used with a little expense of memory, processing and energy resources.

B. Threats and Issues: Most of the threats and attacks against security in wireless networks are almost similar to their wired counterparts while some are exacerbated with the inclusion of wireless connectivity.

The security mechanisms devised for wireless ad hoc networks could not be applied directly for wireless sensor networks because of the architectural disparity of the two networks. While ad hoc networks are self-organizing, dynamic topology, peer to peer networks formed by a collection of mobile nodes and the centralized entity is absent; the wireless sensor networks could have a command node or a base station (centralized entity, sometimes termed as sink). The architectural aspect of wireless sensor network could make the employment of a security schemes little bit easier as the base stations or the centralized entities could be used extensively in this case. Nevertheless, the major challenge is induced by the constraint of resources of the tiny sensors. In many cases, sensors are expected to be deployed arbitrarily in the enemy territory (especially in military reconnaissance scenario) or over dangerous or hazardous areas.

C. Attacks in Wireless Sensor Networks: Attacks against wireless sensor networks could be broadly considered from two different levels of views. One is the attack against the security mechanisms and another is against the basic mechanisms (like routing mechanisms). Here we point out the major attacks in wireless sensor networks.

Denial of Service: Denial of Service (DoS) [15] is produced by the unintentional failure of nodes or malicious action. The simplest DoS attack tries to exhaust the resources available to the victim node, by sending extra unnecessary packets and thus prevents legitimate network users from accessing services or resources to which they are entitled. DoS attack is meant not only for the adversary's attempt to subvert, disrupt, or destroy a network, but also for any event that diminishes a network's capability to provide a service. In wireless sensor networks, several types of DoS attacks in different layers might be performed. The mechanisms to prevent DoS attacks include payment for network resources, pushback, strong authentication and identification of traffic.

Attacks on Information in transit: In a sensor network, sensors monitor the changes of specific parameters or valus and report to the sink according to the requirement. As wireless communication is vulnerable to eavesdropping, any attacker can monitor the traffic flow and get into action to interrupt, intercept, modify or fabricate packets thus, provide wrong information to the base stations or sinks. As sensor nodes typically have short range of transmission and scarce resource, an attacker with high processing power and larger communication range could attack several sensors at the same time to modify the actual information during transmission.

Sybil Attack: In many cases, the sensors in a wireless sensor network might need to work together to accomplish a task, hence they can use distribution of subtasks and redundancy of information. In such a situation, a node can pretend to be more than one node using the identities of other legitimate nodes.This type of attack where a node forges the identities of more than one node is the Sybil attack [15].

Sybil attack tries to degrade the integrity of data, security and resource utilization that the distributed algorithm attempts to achieve. Sybil attack can be performed for attacking the distributed storage, routing mechanism, data aggregation voting, fair resource allocation and misbehavior detection [15]. Basically, any peer-to-peer network (especially wireless ad hoc networks) is vulnerable to sybil attack. However, as WSNs can have some sort of base stations or gateways, this attack could be prevented using efficient protocols. Douceur showed that, without a logically centralized authority, sybil attacks are always possible except under extreme and unrealistic assumptions of resource parity and coordination among entities. However, detection of sybil nodes in a network is no so easy. Newsome et. al. [15] used radio resource testing to detect the presence of sybil node(s) in sensor network and showed that the probability to detect the existence of a sybil node is:

$$\Pr(\text{detection}) = 1 - \left(1 - \sum_{allS,M,G} \frac{\binom{s}{S}\binom{m}{M}\binom{g}{G}}{\binom{n}{c}} \frac{S-(m-M)}{c}\right)^r$$

Where, n is the number of nodes in a neighbor set, s is the number of sybil nodes, m malicious nodes, g number of good nodes, c is the number of nodes that can be tested at a time by a node, of which S are sybil nodes, M are malicious (faulty) nodes, G are good (correct) nodes and r is the number of rounds to iterate the test.

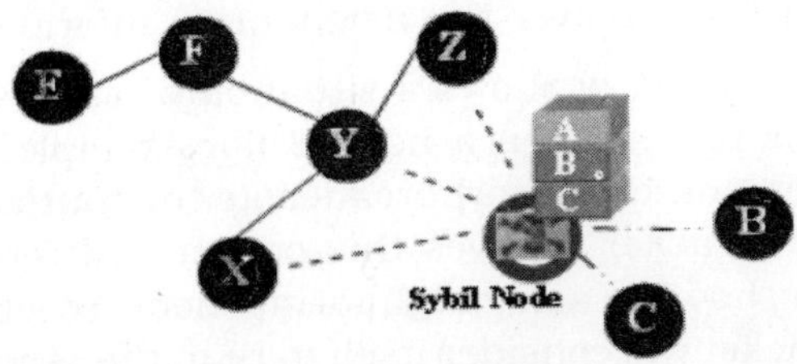

Fig. 7. Sybil Attack

Blackhole/Sinkhole Attack: In this attack, a malicious node acts as a blackhole [15] to attract all the traffic in the sensor network. Especially in a flooding based protocol, the attacker listens to requests for routes then replies to the target nodes that it contains the high quality or shortest path to the base station. Once the malicious device has been able to insert itself between the communicating nodes (for example, sink and sensor node), it is able to do anything with the packets passing between them. In fact, this attack can affect even the nodes those are considerably far from the base stations. Fig. 8 shows the conceptual view of a blackhole/sinkhole attack.

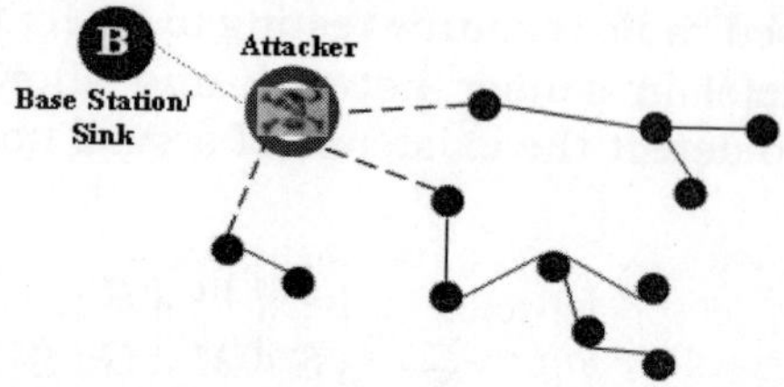

Fig. 8. Conceptual view of Blackhole Attack

Wormhole Attack: Wormhole attack [15] is a critical attack in which the attacker records the packets (or bits) at one location in the network and tunnels those to another location. The tunneling or retransmitting of bits could be done selectively. Wormhole attack is a significant threat to wireless sensor networks, because; this sort of attack does not require compromising a sensor in the network rather, it could be performed even at the initial phase when the sensors start to discover the neighboring information.

Figure 9 (a and b) shows a situation where a wormhole attack takes place. When a node B (for example, the base station or any other sensor) broadcasts the routing request packet, the attacker receives this packet and replays it in its neighborhood. Each neighboring node receiving this replayed packet will consider itself to be in the range of Node B, and will mark this node as its parent. Hence, even if the victim nodes are multihop apart from B, attacker in this case convinces them that B is only a single hop away from them, thus creates a wormhole.

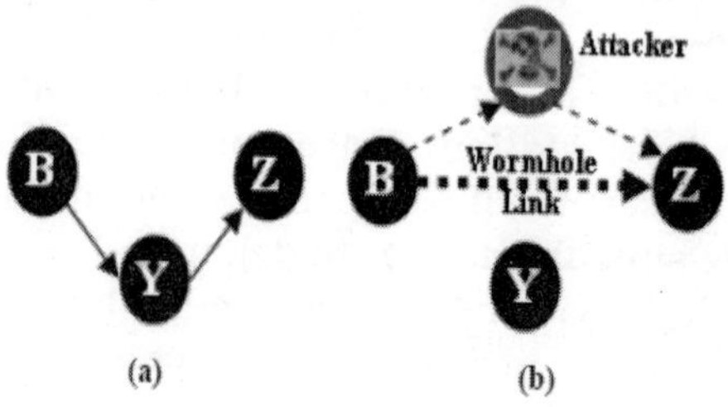

Fig. 9. Wormhole Attack

REFERENCES

[1] C. Chong and S. Kumar, "Sensor networks: evolution, opportunities, and challenges," *Proceedings of the IEEE*, vol. 91, no. 8, pp. 1247–1256, 2003.

[2] A. Mainwaring, D. Culler, J. Polastre, R. Szewczyk, and J. Anderson, "Wireless sensor networks for habitat monitoring," *Proceedings of the 1st ACM international workshop on Wireless sensor networks and applications*, pp. 88–97, 2002.

[3] Estrin, D., Govindan, R., Heidemann, J., and Kumar, S., "Next Century Challenges: Scalable Coordination in Sensor Networks", Proc. ACM MobiCom, 1999, pp. 263-270.

[4] Akyildiz, I. F., Su, W., Sankarasubramaniam, Y, and Cayirci, E.,"Wireless Sensor Networks: A Survey", Computer Networks, 38, 2002, pp. 393-422.

[5] Townsend C.P, Hamel M.J., Arms S.W. (2001): Telemetered Sensors for Dynamic Activity &Structural Performance Monitoring, SPIE's 8th Annual Int'l Conference on Smart Structures and Materials, Newport Beach, CA.

[6] A. Cerpa, J. Elson, D. Estrin, L. Girod, M. Hamilton, and J. Zhao. Habitat monitoring: application driver for wireless communications technology. *SIGCOMM Computer Communication Review*, 31(2 supplement):20–41, 2001.

[7] A. Baggio. Wireless sensor networks in precision agriculture. In *Workshop on Real-World Wireless Sensor Networks (REALWSN 2005)*, Stockholm, Sweden, June 2005.

[8] S. Chatterjea, T. Nieberg, N. Meratnia, and P. J. M. Havinga. A distributed and self-organizing scheduling algorithm for energy-efficient data aggregation in wireless sensor networks. Technical Report TR-CTIT-07-10, Enschede, February 2007.

[9] P. Juang, H. Oki, Y.Wang, M. Martonosi, L. S. Peh, and D. Rubenstein. Energyefficient computing for wildlife tracking: design tradeoffs and early experiences with zebranet. *SIGPLAN Not.*, 37(10):96–107, 2002.

[10] F.Michahelles, P.Matter, A. Schmidt, and B. Schiele. Applying wearable sensors to avalanche rescue. *Computers and Graphics*, 27(6):839–847, 2003.

[11] Undercoffer, J., Avancha, S., Joshi, A., and Pinkston, J., "Security for Sensor Networks", CADIP Research Symposium, 2002, http://www.cs.sfu.ca/~angiez/personal/paper/sensor-ids.pdf

[12] Perrig, A., Szewczyk, R., Wen, V., Culler, D., and Tygar, J. D., "SPINS: Security Protocols for Sensor Networks", Wireless Networks, vol. 8, no.5, 2002, pp. 521-534.

[13] Hollar, S, "COTS Dust", Master's Thesis, Electrical Engineering and Computer Science Department, UC Berkeley, 2000

[14] Saleh, M. and Khatib, I. A., "Throughput Analysis of WEP Security in Ad Hoc Sensor Networks", Proc. The Second International Conference on Innovations in Information technology (IIT'05), September 26-28, Dubai, 2005

[15] Al-sakeeb, Woo-lee, Seon Hong"security in wiresee sensor networks:issues & challenges" Kyung Hee University, Korea.

❑❑❑

13

Indexing Web Documents for Computing on Web

Dr. Pushpa R. Suri, Harmunish Taneja***

Abstract – *The information on WWW is growing day by day. The primary function of current Web search engines is to efficiently search for the results at the document level. However, countless structured information about real-world objects is embedded in static Web pages and online Web databases. Users usually search for information of a certain 'object', rather than a web page containing the query terms. Document-level information retrieval can unfortunately lead to inaccurate results in answering object-oriented queries. The use of an object-oriented design paradigm greatly reduces the complexity of the system while improving reusability and manageability. The most distinguishing requirement of today's search result through*

*Department of Computer Science and Applications, Kurukshetra University, Kurukshetra- 136119, Haryana, India. *ushpa.suri@yahoo.com*

**Department of Information Technology, Maharishi Markendeshwar University, Mullana, Haryana- 133203, India. *harmunish.taneja@gmail.com*

information computing systems for complex heterogeneous systems is to dynamically adapt to vigorously changing conditions. Guaranteeing timeliness has become a decisive aspect of quality of service for many important applications. Object oriented approach may improve performance for non-conventional applications that manipulate large volumes of data. This is addressed by removing irrelevant data accessed by queries and transactions and by reducing the data exchange among sites. Vector-space approaches to information retrieval rank the results of the search according to their relative similarity to the query. One vector-space approach, Latent Semantic Indexing (LSI), has achieved better retrieval performance than lexical searching techniques. In this paper, technique for web object indexing using latent semantic indexing and Inverted indexes are discussed by discovering inherent structure information with domain knowledge that catalogues the documents efficiently.

Keywords – *Latent Semantic Indexing (LSI), Inverted Index, Web Objects, Information Retrieval, World Wide Web (WWW)*

1. INTRODUCTION

Conventional lexical (or Boolean) information computing and retrieval techniques often return too much information to the user. Sometimes valuable information is not found in the document collection as the terms used in the query differ from the terms used in the document. Due to this, the ability to search that information and derive useful facts is declining. With the increase in the redundant storage and the same at the less expense, the amount of information retained by the organizations is expected to enhance. Searching the information to inference for the important decisions has become more cumbersome. Information retrieval tools on the web like search engines, download web pages, texts, images etc. from WWW [1]. New techniques are developed to automatically partition the data into sets small enough for a human to understand. A classic search engine comprises of the following components:

- **Crawler:** it scrutinizes the pages on the web and gathers the required information for the search engine from given set of URL's.

- **Indexer:** An indexer optimizes speed and performance for finding relevant documents for a search query. Besides indexing, The Indexing process collects, parses and stores data in order to facilitate fast and accurate information retrieval.
- **Page Repository :** Web crawler collects the information from WWW and the same is stored in a database called page repository. The indexer indexes the various documents contained in repository. The documents are identified by doc ID, length and URL.

The point of using an index is to increase the speed and efficiency of searches of the document collection. Without some sort of index, a user's query must sequentially scan the document collection, finding those documents containing the search terms. With only a few thousand files on a typical laptop, a typical "find" operation takes a minute or longer. As the users want the results at the earliest, hence a sequential scan is not feasible. To overcome this problem, Inverted indexes and LSI helps user to search the information on WWW in the fast manner and with the optimality. In this paper these two approaches are discussed for computing the information on WWW. The general architecture of the search engines on the web is as shown in fig 1.

Indexing is used to increase the speed and efficiency of computing for the documents collection on WWW. Latent Semantic Indexing [7], is a vector-space approach to conceptual information retrieval and is useful in situations where traditional lexical information retrieval approaches fail. LSI estimates the semantic content of the documents in a collection, and uses that estimate to rank the documents in order of decreasing relevance to a user's query. Since the search is based on the concepts contained in the documents rather than the document's constituent terms, LSI can retrieve documents related to a user's query even when the query and the documents do not share any common terms. LSI ranks the documents according to their relevance to the user's query, therefore the system helps the user decide which information may be more specific to the user's interests. Although LSI is competent of achieving significant retrieval performance over standard lexical retrieval techniques [8], the complexity of the LSI model often causes its execution efficiency to lag far behind the execution efficiency of the simpler, Boolean models, especially on large data sets. By carefully examining the LSI model and noting the various optimizations that can be applied to its underlying implementation, though, both the retrieval benefits of the LSI model and execution efficiency near that of the Boolean retrieval techniques can be attained.

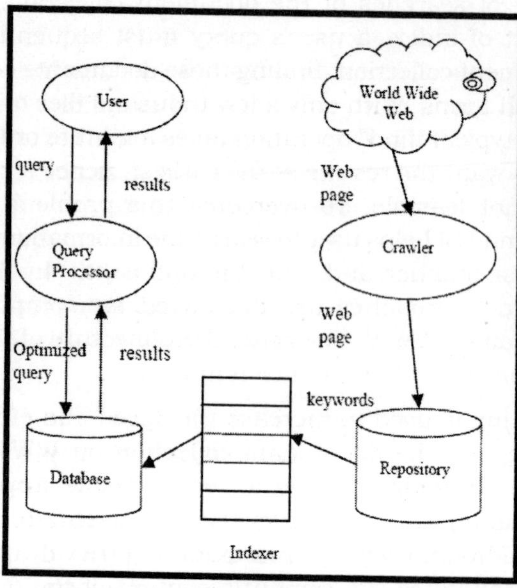

Fig. 1. General architecture of the Search Engine

Using LSI model, users can quickly search large data sets without understanding any details of the LSI model. The Latent Semantic Indexing information retrieval model builds upon the prior research in information retrieval and, using the singular value decomposition [16] to reduce the dimensions of the term-document space. LSI clearly represents terms and documents in a prosperous, high-dimensional space, allowing the underlying ("latent"), semantic relationships between terms and documents to be exploited during searching. LSI model views the terms in a document as erratic indicators of the concepts contained in the document. It assumes that the variability of word choice partially obscures the semantic structure of the document. By reducing the dimensionality of the term-document space, the underlying, semantic relationships between documents are revealed, and much of the "noise" is eliminated. LSI statistically analyses the patterns of word usage across the entire document collection, placing documents with similar word usage patterns near each other in the term-document space, and allowing semantically related documents to be near each other even though they may not share terms [8]. Indexing the information is an off line process. Associating the inverted indexes with the LSI, efficient search results can be expected. Section 2 elaborates key technologies of web objects. Challenges in web computing are discussed in Section 3. In section 4 the related work is discussed. Section 5 explores latent semantic indexing used in Information computing. In Section 6, discusses Inverted Indexes for documents and finally section 7 concludes the paper.

2. WEB OBJECTS: KEY TECHNOLOGIES

Web Objects: These are identifiable concepts to facilitate significance to the application domain. Web object is an object-oriented environment for developing and deploying web applications. Web Object scan can be defined as the principle data units about which Web information is to be collected, indexed and ranked [15,17]. The time and cost benefits of rapid, object-oriented development attracted major corporations to WebObjects in the early days of web computing. WebObjects has a number of key technologies that differentiate it from some application servers:

- *Streamlined Database Access:* Database tables are represented in WebObjects as collections of classes called Enterprise Objects. The high level of abstraction relieves developers from the hard work of writing inflexible, database-specific code.

- *Separation of Presentation, Logic, and Data:* WebObjects enforces a clean separation of presentation (Web pages), logic (Code) and data (data store).
- *State Management:* WebObjects provides objects that allow maintaining information for the life of a particular user session.
- *Scalability and Performance:* Administrators run multiple instances of an application, either on one or on multiple application servers.
- *Cost:* The tools and frameworks required to develop and deploy WebObjects applications are available on open source and can easily be downloaded from WWW.

3. CHALLENGES IN WEB COMPUTING

For Information computing on WWW, user can store the web pages and index them to make future searches faster and request query evaluation to identify and retrieve pages most closely related to the subject matter of a user query [4]. Following are the challenges of object oriented approach of computing the web information [15]:

- Objects of the same type are distributed in diverse Web sources, whose structure is highly heterogeneous.
- Assigning weights to the links of different types of relationships on web pages to make the popularity ranking reasonable is extremely challenging.
- Dynamic queries are equivalent to the direct manipulation interaction style, combining rapid feedback and visual controls to "sculpt" searches on the fly.
- Faceted metadata search may sound fancy, but it is simply the ability to query simultaneously along multiple attributes or dimensions.
- Collaborative filtering uses the input (ratings) of other users to offer suggestions to another user — frequently

used for recommending text, products, music, or movies.

- Multilingual searches involve documents in different languages, including translation services as appropriate.
- Visual searches represent query parameters in a non textual format where applicable, for example with airline seats or calendar displays.

4. RELATED WORK

Study in web information computing and retrieval has followed a number of matching developmental paths. Latent Semantic Indexing (LSI) represents terms and documents in a term-document space and is considered a vector-space information computing and retrieval model. The vector-space model for information retrieval is one of the information computing and retrieval techniques that are studied in current era of web computing. Although the vector-space techniques share common characteristics with other techniques in the information retrieval hierarchy, they all share a core set of similarities that justify their own class. Query is represented as a vector where term is a nonnegative value denoting the number of occurrences in the query [18]. Both the document vectors and the query vector provide the locations of the objects in the term-document space. By computing the distance between the query and other objects in the space, objects with similar semantic content to the query apparently will be mined [11]. Vector-space models that do not attempt to collapse the dimensions of the space treat each term independently, essentially imitating an inverted index [13]. By applying different similarity measures to compare queries to terms and documents, properties of the document collection can be emphasized or deemphasized. [6] Provides various commercial and scientific applications require analysis of user behaviour in the internet using LSI and Inverted Indexing. LSI differs from previous attempts at using reduced-space models for information retrieval in several ways. Most notably, LSI represents documents in a high-dimensional space. [18] Used seven dimensions to represent his semantic space. Both terms and documents are explicitly represented in the same space. According to [6], no attempt is made to interpret the meaning of each dimension. Each dimension is merely assumed to represent one or more semantic relationships in the term-document space. LSI is able to represent and manipulate large data sets, making it viable for real-world applications [5,7]. Compared to other information retrieval techniques, LSI performs surprisingly well. [8] Found that LSI provided 30% more related documents than standard word-based retrieval techniques when searching the WWW. Over five standard document collections, the same study indicated that LSI performed an average of 20% better than lexical retrieval techniques. LSI is fully automatic, easy to use, requires no complex expressions or syntax to represent queries, and can be used to index extremely large text corpora [9,10]. Because terms and documents are explicitly represented in the space, relevance feedback [7] can be seamlessly integrated with the LSI model, providing even better overall retrieval performance.

On the other hand an inverted index is an optimized structure that is built primarily for retrieval, with update being only a secondary consideration. The basic structure *inverts* the text so that instead of the view obtained from scanning documents where a document is found and then its terms are seen, an index is built that maps terms to documents (pretty much like the index found in the back of this book that maps terms to page numbers). Instead of listing each *document* once, inverted index lists each *term* in the collection only once and then show a list of all the documents that contain the given term. Each document identifier is repeated for each term that is found in the document.

5. LATENT SEMANTIC INDEXING

There are two phases in the LSI model: a pre processing phase and the query phase. In pre processing phase the term-document space is built and in the query phase queries are projected into that space and a similarity measure is applied to find terms and documents near the query. The pre processing phase is a one-time cost and is independent of the number of queries posed to the database in the second phase. As the users interact with the query processing phase, the functionality, execution efficiency and the interface of this phase is very important. In LSI, six-tuples are taken as input [18] i.e. q = (b, r, n, t, d, f), where b is the number of the document collection to search, r indicates whether the query engine should return a ranked list of terms, documents, or both terms and documents, n is the number of terms, documents, or both to return to the user, t is a set of words (terms) used to describe the query, d is a set of documents whose corresponding text is used to refine the query through relevance feedback, and f is the current number of factors used to represent the query, terms, and documents.

For a particular query, b, r, n, f, and at least one of t and d are required. Both the term (t) and the document (d) cannot be empty. For a given value of q, the LSI server performs the following tasks [18]:

1. Eliminate the terms considered common in the document collection from term (t). Typically, when the documents are assembled, the frequency of each word in the collection is analysed, and words that occur most often in the collection are not indexed, but instead are added to the stop list of the collection. A stop list for a given document collection is a list of words generally not worth indexing in the collection [2,13]. Words that occur frequently in the collection are not valuable in the index since they make it difficult to distinguish documents from one another, increase the amount of space required to store the index, and increase the time required to process a query. When a search is performed, terms that appear on the stop list are removed from the query since they are not indexed in the document collection.

2. Eliminate the terms that do not occur in the document collection from t. Words that do not occur in the document collection cannot be used to project the query into the term-document space.

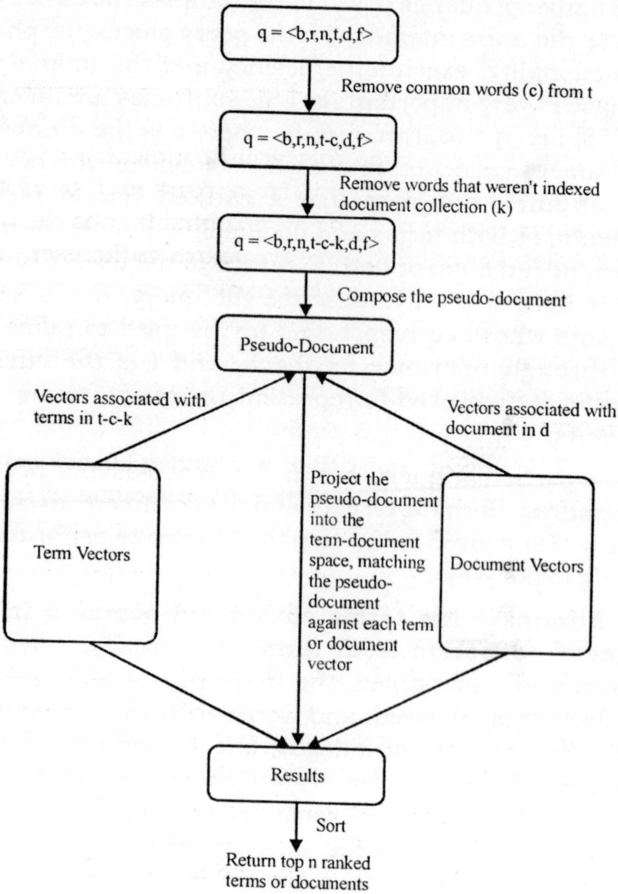

Fig. 2. The query phase of the LSI model

3. By composing the pseudo-documents that represents the query. Each term in the document collection (excluding too common to the index) occupies a particular position in the term-document space. The position of a particular term in the space is given by a vector, called its term vector. Similarly, each document in the collection is represented by a document vector that specifies the document's position in the term document space. In the LSI model, a document is placed at the centroid of the terms that comprise the document. The pseudo-document that represents a query consists of the weighted sums of the term vectors associated with the terms in t combined with the sums of the document vectors associated with the documents in d.

4. Project the pseudo-document into the term-document space and find the n highest ranking terms, documents, or both. Although several different similarity measures can be used to determine the highest ranking terms and documents for a given query, the cosine similarity measure is most often used to find terms and documents near the pseudo-document in the term-document space. The cosine similarity measure computes the angle between the vector representing the pseudo-document and each term or document vector. The higher the cosine between the pseudo-document and a term or document, the closer the term or document is to the pseudo-document, in spite of Euclidean distance. When computing the cosine, only the first "f" elements of the term and document vectors are used. This allows the user to adjust a more conceptual match (which corresponds to smaller values of f) or a more literal match (corresponding to larger values of f). Then, the results of each cosine are sorted, and the top n ranking terms or documents are returned to the user. Typically, the results returned to the user include the similarity of the pseudo-document to each of the top n ranked terms or documents and the corresponding terms or document titles.

6. THE INVERTED INDEX

Within the search engine domain, data are searched far more frequently than they are updated [3]. Certainly, users make changes to documents, but it is not clear that a searcher requires the latest change to satisfy most search requests. Given this situation a data structure called an *inverted index* is commonly used by search engines. An inverted index is able to do many accesses in O(1) time at a price of significantly longer time to do an update, in the worst case O(*n*). Index construction time is longer as well, but query time is generally faster. Since index construction is an off- line process, shorter query processing times at the expense of lengthier index construction times is an appropriate tradeoff.

Inverted index storage structures can exceed the storage demands of the document collection itself. The inverted index can also be compressed to around ten percent of the original document collection. Given the alternative (of twenty minute searches), search engine developers are happy to trade index construction time and storage for query efficiency. An inverted index contains two parts: an *index of terms,* (generally called simply the *term index, lexicon,* or *term dictionary*) which stores a distinct list of terms found in the collection and, for each term, a *posting list,* a list of documents that contain the term.

Consider the following two documents:

D1: The GDP increased 2 percent this quarter.

D2: The spring economic slowdown continued to spring downwards this quarter.

An inverted index for these two documents is given below:

2 → [D1]

continued → [D2]

downwards → [D2]

economic → [D2]

GDP → [D1]

increased → [D1]

percent → [D1]

quarter → [D1] → [D2]

slowdown → [D2]

spring → [D2]

the → [D1] → [D2]

this → [D1] → [D2]

to → [D2]

D1	
documentID	1
distinctTerms	
term	**tf**
spring	1
quarter	1
2	1
gdp	1
percent	1

D2	
documentID	2
distinctTerms	
term	**tf**
spring	2
quarter	1
economic	1
slowdown	1
continued	1

The inverted index for the same will look as

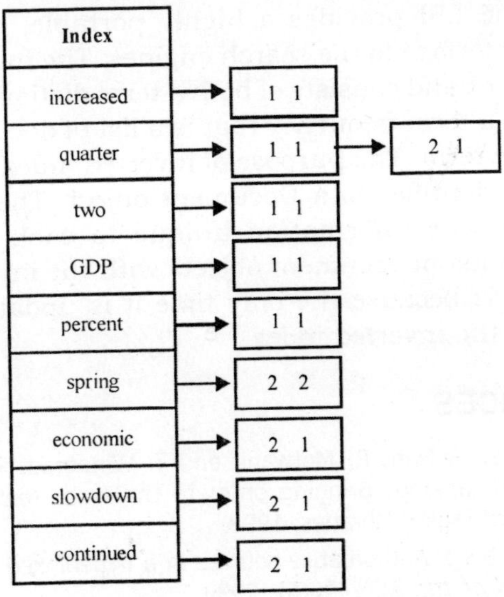

As shown above the terms *continued, economic, slowdown, spring,* and *to* appear in only the second document, the terms *GDP, increased,* and *percent* appear in only the first document, and the terms *quarter, the,* and *this* appear in both documents. Essentially, after parsing, documents are added in an inverted index. The inverted index only needs a term dictionary, namely the index, and the corresponding posting lists. The document List is simply an Array List of Document objects

7. CONCLUSIONS

Latent Semantic Indexing is a novel information computing and retrieval model that can be treated as valuable with the increase in the amount of information. It has been used effectively in a variety of applications, including information filtering and cross-language information retrieval. LSI has the potential to become the information computing retrieval method of choice by those who desire an alternative to keyword searching. LSI is an efficient, flexible, and extensible method of indexing the. Its object-oriented design makes it easy to maintain and modify. The LSI provides a highly portable, simple, and powerful interface to the search engines. The inverted index on the other hand consists of both a term dictionary and, for each term, a term frequency that is a list of documents that contain the term. The purpose of inverted index is to map a document identifier to a Document object. The Document object contains information unique to each document. Storing the list of document objects with the inverted index makes sense because the only time it is updated is when we update the inverted index.

REFERENCES

[1] L. Page, S. Brin, R. Motwani, and T. Winograd. The pagerank citation ranking: Bringing order to the web. Technical report, Stanford Digital Libraries, 1998.

[2] J. Kleinberg. Authoritative sources in a hyperlinked environment. *Journal of the ACM*, 46(5), 1999.

[3] Sheila Tejada, Craig A. Knoblock, and Steven Minton. Learning domain-independent string transformation weights for high accuracy object identification. In *Knowledge Discovery and Data Mining (KDD)*, 2002.

[4] Andrey Balmin, Vagelis Hristidis, and Yannis Papakonstantinou. Authority-based keyword queries in databases using objectrank. In *Very Large DataBases (VLDB)*, 2004.

[5] J. Lafferty, A. McCallum, and F. Pereira. Conditional random fields: Probabilistic models for segmenting and labeling sequence data. In *ICML*, 2001.

[6] N. Ashish and C. Knoblock. Wrapper generation for semi-structured internet sources. In *Proc. Workshop on Management of Semistructured Data*, Tucson, 1997.

[7] Andrey Balmin, Vagelis Hristidis, and Yannis Papakonstantinou. Authority-based keyword queries in databases using objectrank. In *Very Large Data Bases (VLDB)*, 2004.

[8] Deng Cai, Xiaofei He, Ji-Rong Wen, and Wei-Ying Ma. Block-level link analysis. In *ACM SIGIR Conference (SIGIR)*, 2004.

[9] Bin He, Kevin Chen chuan Chang, and Jiawei Han. Discovering complex matchings across web query interfaces: a correlation mining approach. In *Knowledge Discovery and Data Mining (KDD)*, 2004.

[10] Nickolas Kushmerick, Daniel S. Weld, and Robert B. Doorenbos. Wrapper induction for information extraction. In *Intl. Joint Conference on Artificial Intelligence (IJCAI)*, pages 729,737, 1997.

[11] Bing Liu, Robert Grossman, and Yanhong Zhai. Mining data records in web pages. In *ACM SIGKDD International Conference on Knowledge Discovery and Data Mining (KDD)*, 2003.

[12] Ruihua Song, Haifeng Liu, Ji-Rong Wen, and Wei-Ying Ma. Learning block importance models for web pages. In *World Wide Web conference (WWW)*, 2004.

[13] Jiying Wang, Ji-Rong Wen, Frederick H. Lochovsky, and Wei-Ying Ma. Instance-based schema matching for web databases by domain-specific query probing. In *Very Large Data Bases (VLDB)*, 2004.

[14] Wensi Xi, Benyu Zhang, Yizhou Lu, Zheng Chen, Shuicheng Yan, Huajun Zeng, Wei-Ying Ma, and Edward A. Fox. Link fusion: A unified link analysis framework for multi-type interrelated data objects. In *WWW*, 2004.

[15] Zaiqing Nie, Yuanzhi Zhang, Ji Rong Wen, WeiYing Ma ObjectLevel Ranking: Bringing Order to Web Objects in International World Wide Web Conference *WWW 2005*, May 10-14, 2005, Chiba, Japan.

[16] N. Belkin and W. Croft, Retrieval techniques, in: M. Williams (Ed.), *Annual Review of Information Science and Technology (ARIST)*, Vol. 22, Elsevier Science Publishers B.V., 1987, Chap. 4, pp. 109-145.

[17] Muyuan Wang, Zhiwei Li, Lie Lu, Wei-Ying Ma, Naiyao Zhang, Web Object Indexing Using Domain Knowledge in the proceeding of ACM Conference'05, Month 1-2,2005, pp 1-10.

[18] Letsche, Toward large-scale information retrieval using latent semantic indexing, Master's Thesis, University of Tennessee, Knoxville, Aug. 1996.

14

Faster and Efficient Linguistic Analysis Based Mobile Crawler

*Rubal Chaudhry, Neha Sharma, Sourav Walia**

Abstract – *The traditional crawling methods are no longer able to catch up with constantly updating and growing web. Realizing the problems an alternative distributed crawling scheme with the use of mobile crawlers is needed which will minimize network utilization and also keeps up with document changes. There should be a way so that people can improve the way they find information on the Web by resolving ambiguities present in natural language text. This is achieved by linguistic processing which gives two main advantages. First, a gain of deeper understanding of the content of Web pages so it can better match users' queries with indexed documents Second, we can organize and present the results to the user in more intuitive ways. This paper explains some of NLP techniques*

*Department of Computers, R.P. Inderaprastha Institute of Technology, Bastara, Karnal, India. email: *rubal1686@gmail.com, sharmaneha29@gmail.com*

and how they can be implemented in order to find right information on the web.

Keywords – *Search engine, Crawler, NLP, Stationary & mobile agents*

1. INTRODUCTION

The **World Wide Web** (commonly shortened to **the Web**) is a system of interlinked hypertext documents accessed via the Internet. With a Web browser, a user views Web pages by entering a URL that may result in text, images, videos, and other multimedia and navigates between them using hyperlinks. The World Wide Web was created in 1989 by Sir Tim Berners-Lee, working at the European Organization for Nuclear Research (CERN) in Geneva, Switzerland and released in 1992. A **Web search engine** is a search engine designed to search for information on the World Wide Web. Information may consist of web pages, images and other types of files. Some search engines also mine data available in newsgroups, databases, or open directories. Unlike Web directories, which are maintained by human editors, search engines operate algorithmically or are a mixture of algorithmic and human input.There are differences in the ways various search engines [4,2] work, but they all perform three basic tasks:

- They search the Internet based on important words.
- They keep an index of the words they find, and where they find them.
- They allow users to look for words or combinations of words found in that index.

2. WEB CRAWLER

A crawler is a program that downloads and stores Web pages, often for a Web search engine. Roughly, it starts off by placing an initial set of URLs, in a queue, where all URLs to be retrieved are kept and prioritized. From this queue, the crawler gets a URL (in some order), downloads the page, extracts any URLs in the downloaded page, and puts the new

URLs in the queue. This process is repeated. Collected pages are later used for other applications, such as a Web search engine or a Web cache. Roughly a spider follows the following algorithm:

Spider ()

Begin

While (URL set is not empty)

Begin

Take a URL from the set of seed URLs;

Determine the IP address for the host name;

Download the Robot.txt file, which carries downloading permissions and also specifies the files to be excluded by the spider;

Determine the protocol of underlying host like http, ftp, gopher etc.;

Based on the protocol of the host, download the document;

Identify the document format like doc, html, or pdf etc.;

Check whether the document has already been downloaded or not;

If the document is fresh one

Then

Read it and extract the links or references to the other cites from that documents;

Else

Continue;

Convert the URL links into their absolute URL equivalents;

Add the URLs to set of seed URLs;

End;

End;

Most crawler follow the Robots Exclusion Principle. A main idea behind any crawler design is to leave the actual crawler doing as little processing as possible, thus leaving it free to download documents faster. So URL resolution is left to mapper processes and the spider processes use the resolved IP addresses.

3. RELATED WORK

Due to the current size, increasing rate, and high change frequency of the web, no web crawling schema is able to pace with the web. While current web crawlers managed to index more than 3 billion documents [3], it is estimated that the maximum web coverage of each search engine is around 16% of the estimated web size. Distributed crawling was proposed to improve this situation. However, all the previous work was not taking full advantage of the distributed nature of the application. While some of the previously suggested systems were fully distributed over the Internet (many different locations), each web document was not necessarily crawled from the most near crawler but from a randomly selected crawler. While the distribution of the crawling function was efficiently reducing the network bottleneck from the search engine's site and significantly improving the quality of the results, the previous proposals were not at all optimized. Then proposed an optimal, for the distributed crawlers, URL delegation methodology, so that each URL is crawled from the nearest crawler. The approach,called IPMicra, facilitates crawling of each URL from the nearest crawler (where nearness is defined in terms of network latency) without creating excessive load to the Internet infrastructure. In addition to location aware crawling, IPMicra, provides load balancing taking into consideration the crawler's capacity and configuration. Furthermore, it dynamically adjusts to the changing nature of the Internet infrastructure itself. This short introduction is followed by a brief description on related work, giving emphasis to UCYMicra, a distributed crawling infrastructure which we extend to perform location aware web crawling. Then we have summarized the use of NLP with the mobile crawlers so that the web services can be used efficiently.

Sergey Brin and Lawrence Page [5] explained the prototype of a large-scale Google search engine, which makes heavy use of the structure present in hypertext to crawl and index the Web efficiently and produce much more satisfying search results. Google answer tens of millions of queries every day. Apart from the problems of scaling traditional search techniques to data of this magnitude, there were new technical challenges involved with using the additional information present in hypertext to produce better search results also how to effectively deal with uncontrolled hypertext collections. Their next goals were to improve search efficiency and to scale to approximately 100 million web pages, scalable architecture and a research tool.

Jan Fiedler and Joachim Hammer [7] proposed crawlers are transferred to the source(s) where the data resides in order to filter out any unwanted data locally before transferring it back to the search engine. This reduces network load and speeds up the indexing phase inside the search engine. This approach to Web crawling is particularly well suited for implementing so-called "smart" crawling algorithms which determine an efficient crawling path based on the contents of Web pages that have been visited so far. In order to demonstrate the viability of our approach we have built a prototype for mobile Web crawling that uses the University of Florida Intranet as its testbed. Based on this experimental prototype, they provide a cost-benefit analysis that outlines the advantages of mobile Web crawling.

Alexandros Ntoulas, Gerald Chao, Junghoo Cho[1] proposed various NLP techniques that can be used to remove ambiguities. Their goal was to improve the way people find information on the Web by resolving ambiguities present in natural language text. This is achieved by performing linguistic analysis on the content of the Web pages we index, which is a departure from existing Web search engines that return results mainly based on keyword matching. This additional step of linguistic processing gives Infocious two main advantages. First, It gains *deeper understanding* of the content of Web pages so it can better match users' queries with indexed documents and therefore can improve relevancy of the returned results. Second, based on its linguistic processing, so that it can *organize* and *present* the results to the user in more intuitive ways.

Zornitsa Kozareva [6] explored two aspects: the automatic generation of gazetteer lists from unlabeled data; and the building of a Named Entity Recognition system with labeled and unlabeled data. NER consists in detecting the most silent and informative elements in a text such as names of people, company names, location, monetary currencies, and dates. Early NER systems (Fisher et al., 1997),(Black et al., 1998) etc., participating in Message Understanding Conferences (MUC), used linguistic tools and gazetteer lists.

Scott M. Thede and Mary P. Harper [8] proposed the extension to the hidden Markov model for part-of-speech tagging using second-order approximations for both contextual and lexical probabilities. This model increases the accuracy of the tagger to state of the art levels. These approximations make use of more contextual information than standard statistical systems. New methods of smoothing the estimated probabilities are also introduced to address the sparse data problem.

4. THE PROBLEM

A critical look at the available literature indicates the following issues to be addressed towards design of an efficient crawler.

- Wastage of network bandwidth in maintaining the connection every time for each internal URL.
- Unnecessary burden on the web crawler.
- Ambiguity present in the web text.
- Basic keyword matching scheme does not work well where we have queries that have different meanings in different context.
- When user ask for something than crawl manager send the query to all mobile agent.

5. LINGUISTIC PROCESSING

The linguistic analysis resolves language ambiguities, appends the linguistic information to the content of a Web page, and sends documents to other modules for processing.

A. Part of Speech Tagging: The *POS* tagging is treated as a probabilistic classification task using Markov model, i.e.

$$T = T_{best}(S) = \text{argmax}_T\ P(T \mid S);$$

Where S is the input sentence and T is the set of POS tags assigned to each word of the sentence. In this formulation, the POS assignment for each word w_i in the sentence is treated as a random variable T_i. Each variable can take on the values $\{1,\ldots, |N|\}$, where $|N|$ is the number of different POS tags. Therefore, the task is to determine the instantiations of T such that $P(T \mid S)$ is maximized. POS tagging is one of the most well studied problems in NLP and is also one of the most accurate.POS tagging is the first step in the linguistic analysis of every Web page. A pre-compiled dictionary is used to improve efficiency. If a word does not appear in the dictionary, we calculate its POS tags based on its prefix or suffix.

B. Word sense disambiguation: *Word sense disambiguation* is the problem of selecting a sense for a word from a set of predefined possibilities. For example, the word *jaguar* may refer to a car brand-name, an operating system1 or an animal. The task of distinguishing between the meanings of a polysemous word is called *word sense disambiguation (WSD).* Having the word senses disambiguated would allow the users to search for a specific sense of a word, thus eliminating documents containing the same keyword but that are semantically irrelevant.

Hence we calculate that given observed features, what is most likely sense (category/class) of a word? This can be calculated as:

$$\text{Sense (Category)} = \underset{\text{sense?S}}{\text{argmax}}\ P(S \mid F1, F2, F3 \ldots\ldots Fn)$$

C. Named Entity Recognition [6]: NER is largely a classification task of labeling the noun phrases in a document. This task is again modeled as a statistical tagging problem, calculating P(E | p), where E is the entity tag given a phrase p. A gazette, which is an entity dictionary that maps a phrase to its entity type E, is compiled from the Web and is used to simplify the NER task. For each proper noun and noun phrase in a document, the NER classifier computes this probability and the class with the maximum probability is chosen as the correct named entity tag.

D. Classification of text: The classification task is used as a way to organize results and hide the complexities involved with various ambiguities. That is, instead of prompting the user with a list of definitions, this method simply organizes the results into categories. Therefore, in the example case of the *jaguar* query, pages about Jaguar cars would fall under the *Automobile* category, whereas pages about the software would be under the *Computers* category. The users can then choose one of these categories to narrow their search. This feature is made possible by classifying every page downloaded index into categories prior to querying.

Classification is done by Automatic Classification using training data using Naïve Bayes classification technique.

The probability of a class c given a document d_j is calculated by Bayes' theorem as follows:

$$P(c \mid d_j) = \frac{P(d_j \mid c)p(c)}{P(d_j)}$$

E. Text Quality calculation: As the linguistic processing module processes the text probabilistically, the resulting probabilities are combined and saved for each sentence. These probabilities are then factored into an overall score for the entire document, which we refer to as the textual quality (or *Text Quality*) of the page. This probability is used during ranking to promote pages with high-quality textual content, as well as during indexing to weigh the relative importance of anchor texts.

F. Page summaries: The module takes as input the data from the linguistic processing modules and stores the pages in a compressed format. Upon returning a document as a search result, the document's summary is retrieved from this module to display the context around the query words.

Additionally, this module stores and retrieves the list of concepts extracted by the NLP module for every document. These concepts are used as navigational aids for users, as well as for improving text categorization

6. PROPOSED SOLUTION

In all of the current major Web search engines, the process of identifying the relevant documents typically involves matching the keywords present in the user's query with the documents in the local repository. That is, for a Web page to be considered relevant to a query it simply has to contain the query keywords. Until now this particular approach has worked very well in serving most of the users' needs. However, there are queries for which simple keyword matching will not suffice.

The main goal of the Natural Language Processing (NLP) field is to understand the process of information exchange between humans when they communicate using natural languages. A better understanding of this process would allow computers to extract and operate on information and knowledge represented using natural languages in a more reliable fashion. The field of NLP has a long and rich history, encompassing linguistics, computer science, psychology and even neuroscience. Over the years, a variety of approaches and methodologies have been used to better resolve ambiguities so to extract the semantics within natural language text.

The most common types of language ambiguities have been discussed, and a statistical NLP approach can be used in resolving each.

The benefits from resolving such ambiguities are defined as follows:

1. User can get deeper understanding of the content of Web pages so it can better match users' queries with indexed documents and therefore can improve relevancy of the returned results.
2. Various types of ambiguities present in the text can be removed.
3. Classification of web pages can be done in an easier way.
4. Based on its linguistic processing, search engine can organize and present the results to the user in more intuitive ways.

A. Components of proposed Solution: This method uses a distributed architecture, stationary and mobile agents through the web. This research is basically proposed to make several mobile agents. They find the needed information by moving among different sites simultaneously.

The architecture consists of following major components.

- Mobile Crawlers
- Crawl Manager
- Linguistic Processing
- Link Database
- Central Repository

(1) Mobile Crawlers: The cawler is the part of a search engine that handles the task of retrieving pages from the Web and storing them locally for processing. This distributed crawler behaves like other typical crawlers in the sense that it discovers and follows the links inside a Web page in order to download other Web pages. However, there is an extension in this crawler with mobile crawlers accessing the web in parallel such that it can provide us with a fresh subset of the Web with a minimal overhead. There are two type of agents used for providing and controlling the mobility. These are stationary agents and mobile agents.

(2) Crawl Manager: Crawl manager is responsible for creation and maintenance of the central queue. The user enters the query that first of all goes to the Crawl manager component. Crawl Manager feeds the central queue with the seed URL initially. It is also responsible for creation and maintenance of stationary agents. The algorithm for assigning the stationary agent is attached with this module. In the algorithm Stationary agent keeps WAIT condition at the central queue data structure which when SIGNALS the value of semaphore, stationary agent gets created. The various active stationary agents after collecting the data from respective mobile agent gives the data to Crawl Manager for further processing. Once a web page comes to crawl manager it saves that in to centralized repository which along with saving the content of web page does two tasks. First it extracts all the links from the page and sends them to the link database, described below. Second, it hands the page off to the linguistic analysis component.

(3) Linguistic Processing: It resolves ambiguities present in text. The various techniques used are

- Word Sense Disambiguation.
- Part of Speech Tagging.
- Named Entity Recognition.

It also annotates Web Pages by applying following techniques after Linguistic Processing

- Classification of Text
- Text Quality Calculation
- Page Summaries.

(4) Link Database: The link database performs two functions.

First it manages the task of assigning a globally unique ID for every link that the crawler has identified. The second functionality is to store some information with URLs which will come after linguistic processing of the web text. This information will contain the class or category associated with the text and also various POS's tags associated with it like noun, verb etc. This information is attached with each URL and its ID after all the linguistic processing is being done on the document and is used during the ranking of results, as well as for rescheduling crawls.

Suppose a user fires a single word query that is ambiguous in nature then the system will prompt to the user various categories under which the query word may fall. These categories are predefined by the system from the training data or the previous similar query by applying NLP to the text which was previously downloaded.

(5) Central Repository: This is the main database used by the system. The whole data fetched and downloaded by the system is stored in this database. This database can be compressed by some compressing technique to reduce storage capacity. The special indexer module is maintain to access the database in a fast manner the indexer store.

B. Basic Working: Initially the Crawl Manager gets the user request as query (that gets converted into URL), and then after putting the corresponding URL (seed URL) in the central queue, it assigns a stationary agent to that URL; then stationary agent creates the mobile agents and sends that to the web site. The mobile agent becomes stationary there, and performs high bandwidth local index searching. Each stationary agent is associated with a mobile agent and maintains a local queue which will contain URLs which were assigned to it by the crawl manager from the central queue. Each mobile agent is associated with a particular web site and remains there for fetching the internal links further. The links that are present outside the website are sent back to Central Queue and those links will be given to other stationary agents which were waiting for the URL (whose local queue is empty). The mobile agents after downloading the pages compress them and send the compressed information back to the stationary agents. These stationary agents submit the retrieved information to the Crawl Manager.

Algorithms

For Crawl Manager

```
Begin
do forever
   Begin
            Pickup URL from Central Queue;
```

```
            SIGNAL(Something to Crawl);
    End;
End;
```

For Stationary Agent

```
Begin
do forever
            Begin
                for each stationary agent i
                    if Local queue_i is not full
                        WAIT(Something to Crawl);
                            Store the URL in i_th Local queue;
                                SIGNAL(Something to
                                download);
break;
            End;
End;
```

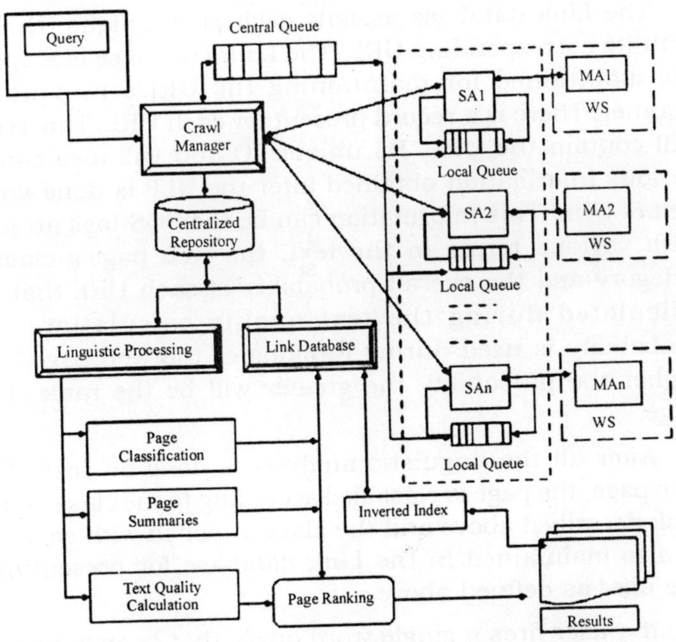

Figure 1. Architecture of a linguistic analysis based mobile crawler

For Mobile Agent

Begin

WAIT(Something to download);

Read Robot.txt

Download document;

Segregate internal and external links;

For internal links download the documents further;

Send the external links back to the Stationary Agent;

End;

The Crawl Manager stores the whole content in Centralized Repository which is the main database of the system. Then each downloaded page is sent for linguistic processing to the Linguistic Processing module and all the links present in a page are sent to Link Database.

The Link database assigns each page unique ID along with its corresponding URL. The Link Database is a special file maintained for maintaining the URL's in a unique manner. There is a record present for each URL. This record will contain the URL, Its unique ID and will also contain various information obtained after the NLP is done on the text of URL. This information can be the POS tags attached with various terms in the text, the web page's class or category and the overall probability of each URL that was calculated during the text quality calculation. This probability is used during Ranking of the web pages. The higher the probability the greater will be the rank of the page.

After all the linguistic analysis is done on text of the web page, the page is classified according to the classification task described above and the class attached with each URL is also maintained in the Link database for presenting to the user as defined above.

If a user fires a single word query that is ambiguous in nature that is there can be more than one context in which that word can be used; disambiguation task can be done on the query term itself and presenting the user more than one concept or classes which can be associated with the term. Then the user can select among different classes presented by the system. The system sends the query text and associated class to inverted index which stores the URL's id indexed from the class or category name.

After getting the URL's ID the system goes back to link manager and gets the full URL and its content's index from the link database file. The full text can be fetched from the centralized repository which maintains the database of pages in a compressed format.

For the queries that contain more than one word the AND rule is applied for fetching the document.

7. CONCLUSION

Building an effective web crawler to solve our purpose is not a difficult task, but choosing the right strategies and building an effective architecture will lead to implementation of highly efficient web crawler application. In this work, an extension of migrating web crawler has been proposed in which once the coordinator receive the data from the mobile crawler it stored the information in it's database and analysis the data by using the existing analyzing technique once the analysis is done the crawler. The use of mobile agents improves the performance of web search engines. The performance gains translate to improved web coverage and freshness of search results. In conclusion, adoption of the proposed scheme could bring advantages for both crawlers and websites.

8. FUTURE WORK

The proposal is a Web search system designed to help users find information more easily and precisely by resolving ambiguities in natural language text. In realizing this, analysis of current natural language technologies (e.g. POS tagging, concept extraction, etc.) for their benefits and trade-offs in applying them to Web-scale information retrieval has been done. Equally important are the considerations for enabling the user to exploit the power of these technologies intuitively and transparently.

Robustness to disambiguation errors: Even with humans, natural language disambiguation is not perfect. Hence, systems that utilize NLP information need to be robust against errors. We have taken initial steps by maintaining probabilities from the NLP disambiguation, but more work is needed to study the impact of NLP errors on search quality, and better ways to cope with them.Many more possibilities exist for applying our NLP annotated repository to improve other NLP tasks, such as machine translation, text summarization, and question answering.

REFERENCES

[1] Alexandros Ntoulas, Gerald Chao, Junghoo Cho (2005)" Improving Web Searching Through Linguistic Analysis" International World Wide Web Conference Committee (IW3C2).

[2] Infospace Inc. Metacrawler search engine.

[3] A. K. Sharma, J. P. Gupta, D. P. Agarwal, "A novel approach towards efficient Volatile Information Management", Proc. Of National Conference on Quantum Computing, 5-6 Oct.' 2002, Gwalior.

[4] B.Kahle, "Archiving the Internet" , Scientific American 1996.

[5] Sergey Brin and Lawrence Page, "The anatomy of large scale hyper textual web search engine", Proc. of 7th International World Wide Web Conference, volume 30, Computer Networks and ISDN Systems, pp 107-117, April 1998.

[6] Bootstrapping Named Entity Recognition with Automatically Generated Gazetteer Lists, Zornitsa Kozareva, Dept. de Lenguajesy Sistemas Inform´aticos, University of Alicante, Alicante, Spain

[7] Using Mobile Crawlers to Search web efficiently, "Jan Fiedler, Joachim hammer" , 2000.

[8] S. M. Thede and M. P. Harper. A second-order hidden markov model for part-of-speech tagging. In Proceedings of ACL-99, 1999.

15

Mounting Learning Management Systems in the Academe

Dr. S. N. Panda, Gaurav Kumar**, Shant Kaushik****

Abstract – *The use of web based learning management systems is getting pace in the academia in the last few years. The education world is making use of immense features developed and deployed in hundreds of available virtual learning environments. The higher education institutes and universities throughout the globe are giving more emphasis on launching the academic activities using learning management systems. As per the report of Bersin et al. 2009, the LMS (Learning Management System) industry represents an $860 million market which is made up of more than 60 different*

*Professor and Principal, Regional Institute of Management and Technology, Mandi Gobindgarh, Punjab, India, E-mail : panda.india@gmail.com

**Research Scholar, Computer Science, Manav Bharti University, Solan, Himachal Pradesh, E-mail : kumargaurav.in@gmail.com

***Lecturer, Computer Science, D.A.V. College, Ambala City, Haryana, India

providers. Number of packages and software suite are available in the software industry to implement virtual learning in the academia which includes open source as well as licensed software products to be embedded within these products for the delivery and management of instructor-led synchronous and asynchronous online training based on learning object methodology. This paper typifies the use of web based learning technologies for the enhancement of academic activities in the academia. The paper expresses the study and experiments that can be conducted on an eminent learning management system MOODLE.

Keywords – *Web Based Learning Technologies, Learning Management Systems, Virtual Learning Environment, Asynchronous Learning, E-Learning, Open Source Technology, Virtual Learning Environment, Performance Evaluation, E-Learning Products.*

1. INTRODUCTION

The academe all through the orb is making use of the excellent features in virtual learning environments (VLE) and Learning Management Systems (LMS) to intensify the existing system of traditional learning. The LMS products are escalating the development of virtual classrooms, learning environments as well as mobile learning establishments. The academia is focusing on the Anytime-Anywhere-Availability (AAA) rather than classical Chalk and Talk (CAT) theory of faculty members to the learners. The LMS products are replacing the conventional face-to-face classroom teaching and makes use of technology. To achieve this goal, LMS or VLE Products are used in the administration, documentation, tracking, reporting of training programs, classroom events, online events, e-learning programs, and training content. Hundreds of software applications and suite are available in the market which enables the mentors to deploy these features to implement e-learning. MOODLE is one of the e-learning platform or learning management system which is excellent in performance in all parameters.

Till now MOODLE has 36,421,666 users and hosted in 212 countries throughout the global education industry. The following statistics typifies the increasing use of MOODLE in the academia—

Registered validated sites	50,127
Number of countries	212
Courses	3,705,107
Users	36,421,666
Teachers	1,161,764
Enrolments	18,347,280
Forum posts	61,422,679
Resources	31,959,359
Quiz questions	54,885,538
[Source - MOODLE Statistics as on Sept. 12, 2010]	

The Learning Management Systems typically provides a number of features including -

- User Management and Administration
- Lessons Management
- Courses, Curriculum and Categories management
- Files management and Recovery Remedies
- Exam and Quiz builders
- Assignments builders and evaluation modules
- Communication tools (Forum, Chat, Calendar, Glossary)
- Progress tracking and reporting
- Authentication methods
- Enrollment methods
- Certifications and Reports generators
- Extensibility via Modules
- Payments integration (through Paypal and other Payment Gateways)
- Social tools (Lesson & system history, user wall, user status, Facebook interconnection, twitter)
- Customizable notification system through email
- Skins, Themes and Templates

MOODLE also possess several features needed in an enterprise environment:

- Organization structure management
- Skills management
- Job positions management
- Automatic assignment of courses to specific job descriptions
- Skills gap tests management
- User card with training history
- LDAP support

Moreover, developers can broaden Moodle's modular construction by creating plugins for specific new functionality. Moodle's infrastructure supports many types of plug-ins:

- Activities (including word and math games)
- Resource types
- Question types (multiple choice, true and false, fill in the blank, etc)
- Data field types (for the database activity)
- Graphical themes
- Authentication methods (can require username and password accessibility)
- Enrollment methods
- Content filters

Here is the description of major network based learning platforms as well as comparative analysis in terms of performance and accessibility.

2. GLOBAL MARKET AND FUTURE OF E-LEARNING

As per the report in 2009 by American Society for Training and Development (ASTD), 91 percent of respondents are using LMS's in their organizations. E-Learning is experiencing exceptional growth and will continue to do so for the anticipated future. The analysis and forecast released by research firm Ambient Insight bolstered previous research in this area, showing that electronic learning, by dollar volume, reached $27.1 billion in 2009 and predicting this figure to be double by 2014, with academic institutions leading the way.

Table 1: Top E-Learning Management Systems

LMS	Architecture Model - Development Language	Developers
MOODLE	PHP	Dr. Martin Dougiamas Australia
OLAT	Java	University of Zurich in association with the community
eFront	PHP	Epignosis Ltd
ATutor	PHP	Adaptive Technology Resource Centre, University of Toronto
Sakai	J2EE	University of Michigan, Stanford University, Indiana University
Claroline	PHP	University of Leuven, Belgium
Dokeos	PHP	Belgium based Community

As per the reports, "The Worldwide Market for Self-paced e-Learning Products and Services: 2009-2014 Forecast and Analysis," by 2014, e-learning will reach a dollar volume of $49.6 billion, representing a compound annual growth rate (CAGR) of 12.8 percent over five years. The dollar figures in the research included expenditures in five categories of electronic learning technologies, or "self-paced e-learning products." These included: packaged content, custom content development services, learning platform and tool hosting services, authoring software and tools, and installed learning platforms.

3. MOODLE - AN EXCELLENT VIRTUAL LEARNING ENVIRONMENT

The educational institutes are searching for a secure platform as well a product with all the features which includes

Institution	2009 Online Enrollment Totals	Online Enrollment Growth from 2008 to 2009
University of Phoenix Online	310,400	22%
Kaplan University	68,200	47%
DeVry	56,300	26%
Strayer University	54,300	25%
American Public Education	53,600	49%
Bridgepoint Education	45,500	101%
Walden University	40,500	17%
UMassOnline	40,000	18%
Liberty University	36,200	15%
Education Management	34,800	54%
Capella Education	33,900	26%
Grand Canyon Education	32,600	53%
University of Maryland University College	30,400	17%
Source: The Worldwide Market for Self-paced E-Learning Products and Services: 2009-2014 Forecast and Analysis, Ambient Insight, February 2010.		

all the components that are required in the academia. These components include Online Exams., Quiz, Forums, Chat, Wiki, Blog, Newsletter, Bulletin Board, Content/Course Management System. Hundreds of e-learning products are available in the global learning industry, but the academic establishments are concentrating on open source technologies because of flexibility and efficiency of these products.

Moodle was developed by Martin Dougiamas as part of his research thesis and to help educators create online courses with a focus on interaction and collaborative construction of content.

Top 5 sites by users

Site	Users	Courses
Moodle.org	979,328	65
OU online	651,727	5,332

Site	Users	Courses
Hocmai.vn - Ngôi trư?ng chung c?a h?c trò Vi?t	573,752	132
MyLinE - Online Resources for Learning in English	204,166	46
Christian Courses	181,457	177
[Source - MOODLE Statistics as on Sept. 12, 2010]		

Top 10 sites by courses

Site	Users	Courses
VDU Moodle	3,566	59,920
Minha UFMG	62,887	56,385
Universidade Presbiteriana Mackenzie	64,627	26,288
Ming Chuan University portal	66,443	25,119
Concordia Course Web Sites	114,801	24,545
[Source - MOODLE Statistics as on Sept. 12, 2010]		

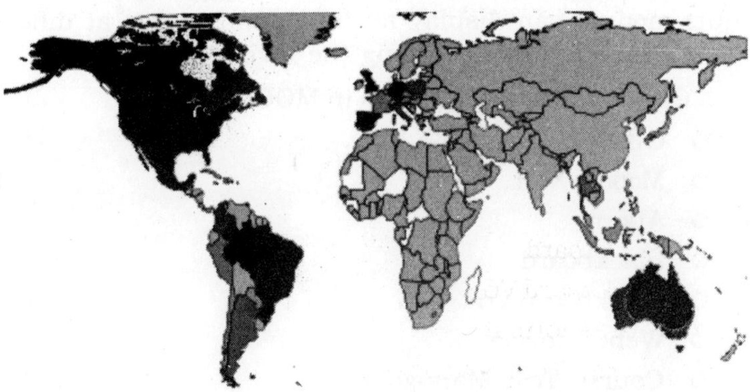

Country	Registrations
United States	9,307
Spain	4,352
Brazil	3,352
United Kingdom	3,155
Germany	2,312
Mexico	1,885

Country	Registrations
Portugal	1,801
Australia	1,325
Colombia	1,262
Italy	1,203
Top 10 from registered sites in 212 countries	
[Source - MOODLE Statistics as on Sept. 12, 2010]	

The screenshots of LMS deployment cited here is with reference to the configuration and deployment of a leading Open Source Solution, Moodle™ [Modular Object Oriented Dynamic Learning Environment] in the academic institutions.

Moodle has number of excellent features and modules. The Quiz Activity Module in Moodle LMS is one of the modules capable to design and set quizzes consisting of a large variety of question types, including multiple choices, true-false, and short answer questions. The questions are kept in the Question bank and can be re-used in multiple tests. The quiz module can display feedback and scores at different times during the quiz, using the review options.

Question Import Formats in MOODLE

- GIFT
- Moodle XML
- Aiken
- Blackboard
- Blackboard V6+
- WebCT format
- Course Test Manager
- Embedded Answers (Cloze)
- Examview
- Diploma 6

Here are the examples of the Aiken Format available in MOODLE LMS:

This is my Question ?

A. First Option

B. Second Option

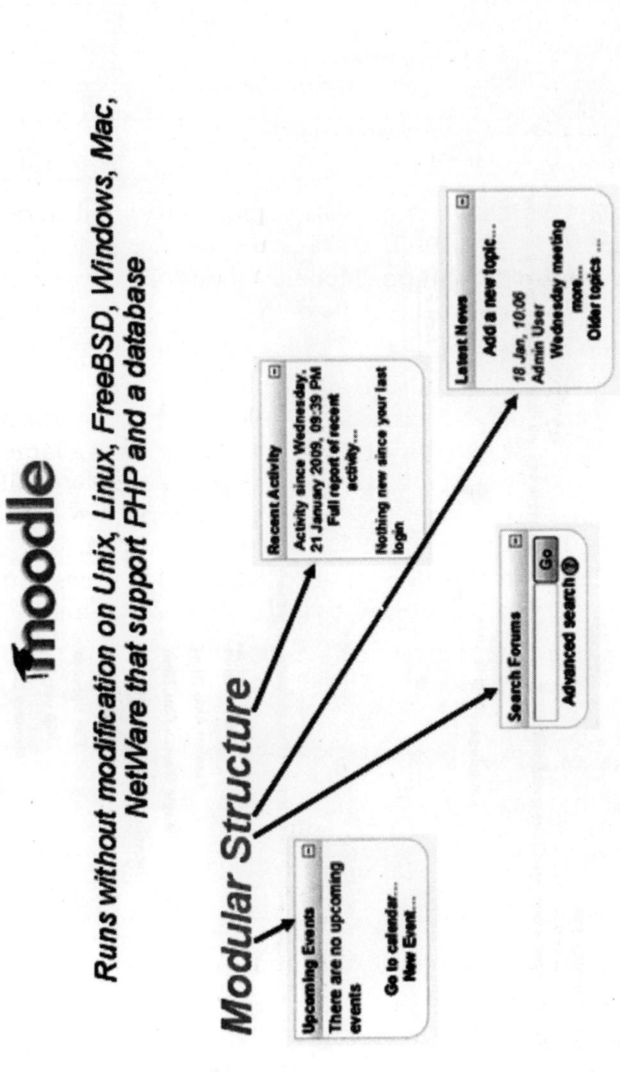
moodle
Runs without modification on Unix, Linux, FreeBSD, Windows, Mac, NetWare that support PHP and a database
Modular Structure
Upcoming Events
There are no upcoming events
Go to calendar...
New Event...
Recent Activity
Activity since Wednesday, 21 January 2009, 09:39 PM
Full report of recent activity...
Nothing new since your last login
Search Forums
Go
Advanced search
Latest News
Add a new topic...
18 Jan, 10:06
Admin User
Wednesday meeting
more...
Older topics ...

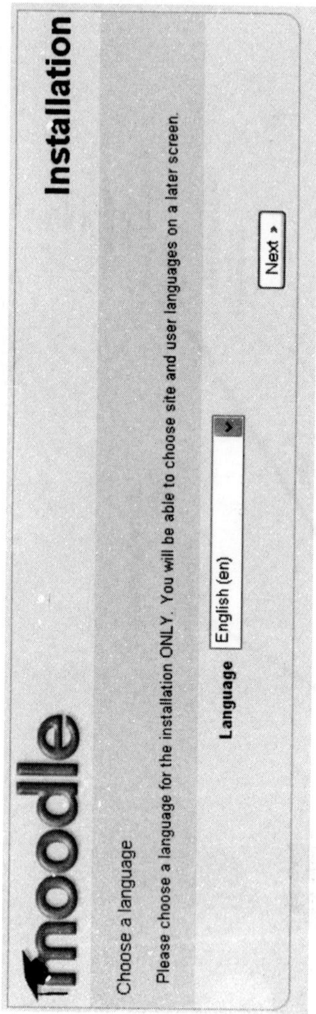
moodle
Installation
Choose a language
Please choose a language for the installation ONLY. You will be able to choose site and user languages on a later screen.
Language
English (en)
Next »

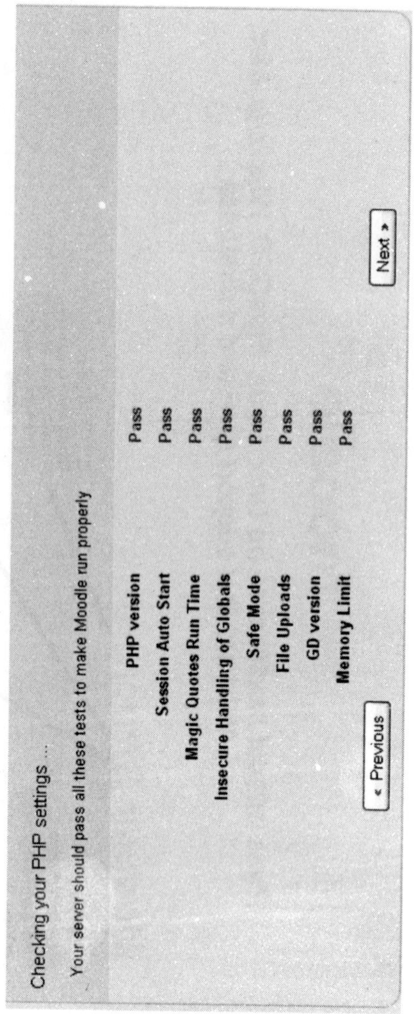
Checking your PHP settings ...
Your server should pass all these tests to make Moodle run properly
PHP version Pass
Session Auto Start Pass
Magic Quotes Run Time Pass
Insecure Handling of Globals Pass
Safe Mode Pass
File Uploads Pass
GD version Pass
Memory Limit Pass
« Previous
Next »

[MOODLE SCREENSHOT - SUCCESSFUL INSTALLATION]

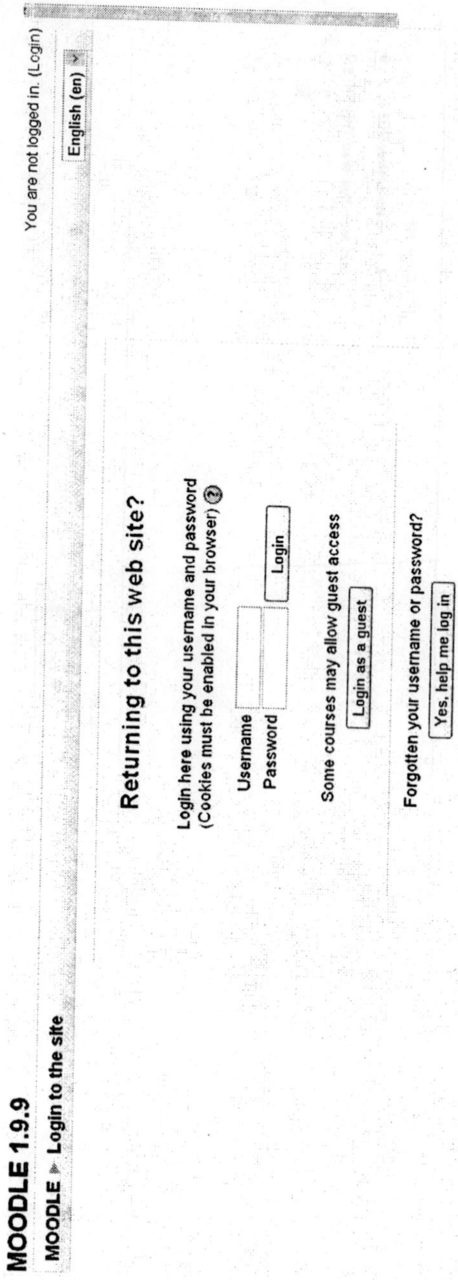

[MOODLE SCREENSHOT – LOGIN PAGE]

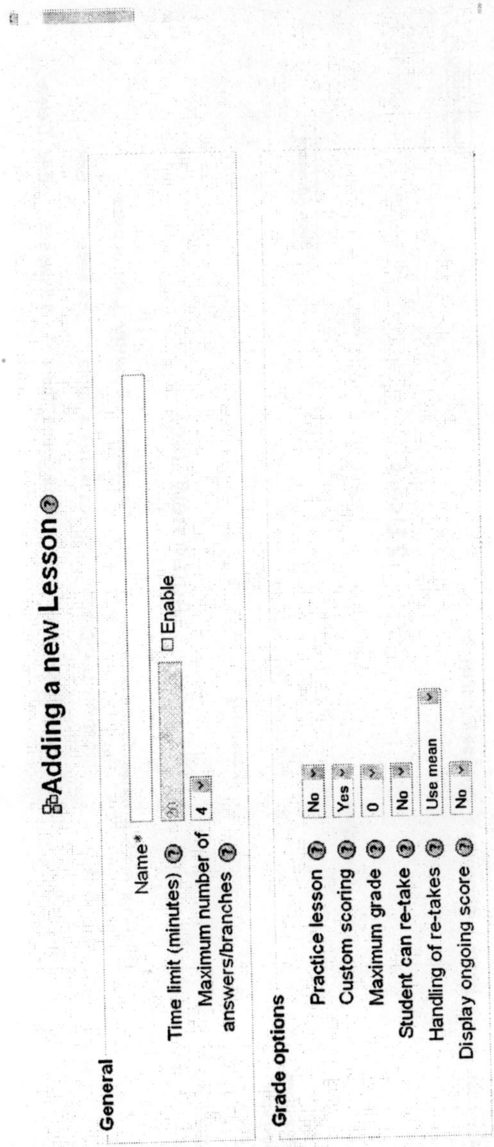
Adding a new Lesson
General
Name*
Time limit (minutes)
Enable
Maximum number of answers/branches
4
Grade options
Practice lesson
No
Custom scoring
Yes
Maximum grade
0
Student can re-take
No
Handling of re-takes
Use mean
Display ongoing score
No

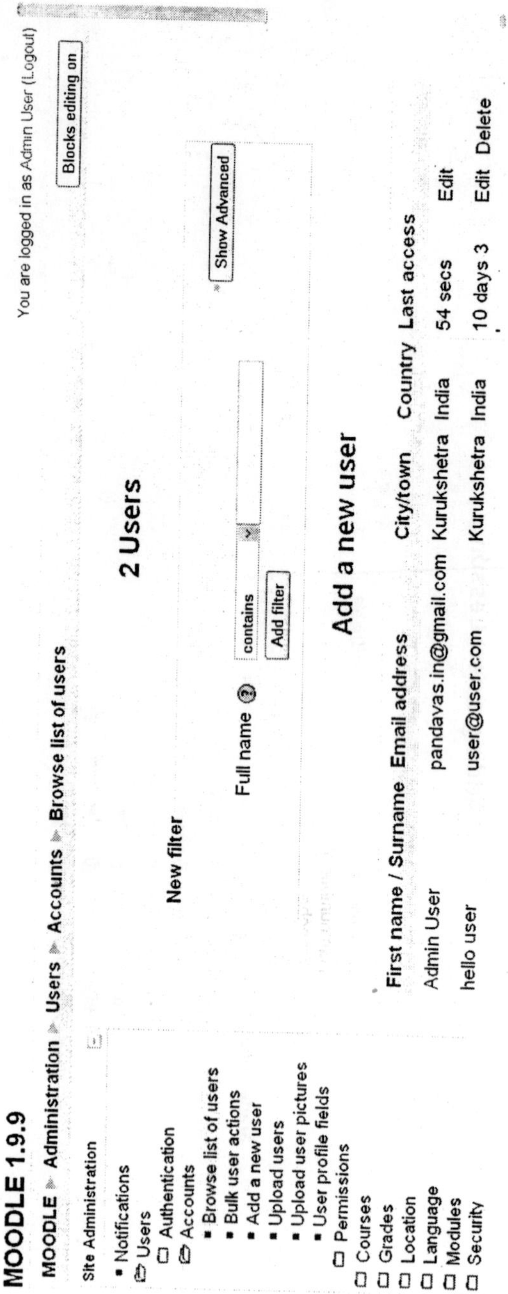

[MOODLE SCREENSHOT – USER MANAGEMENT]

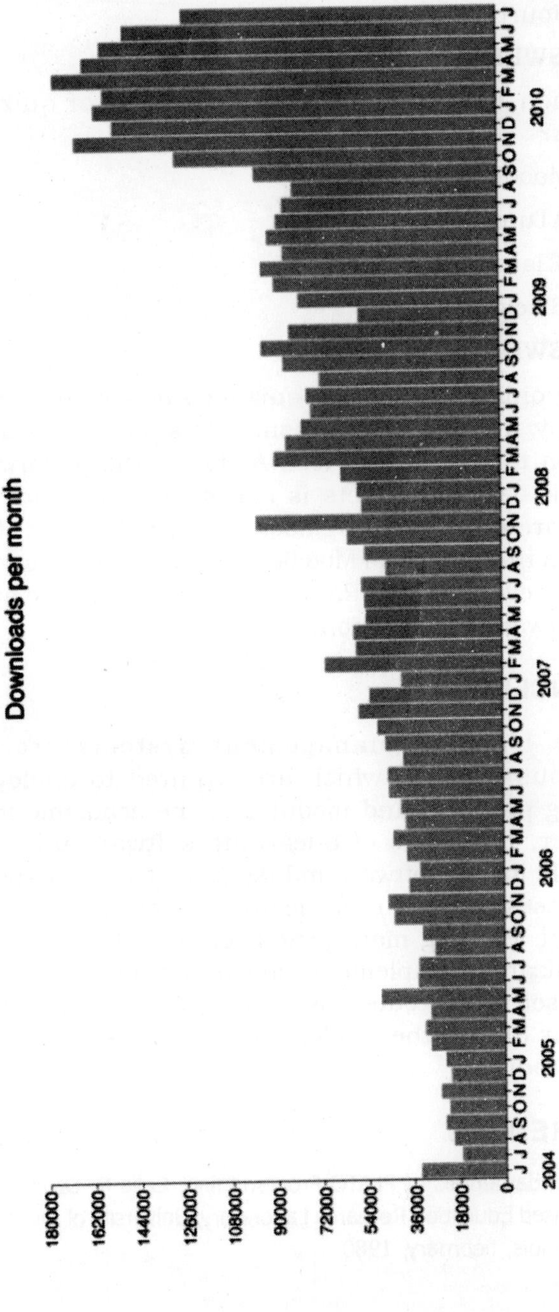

[Source - MOODLE Statistics as on Sept. 12, 2010]

C. Third Option

D. Fourth Option

ANSWER: A

Which LMS has the largest number of quiz import formats?

A) Moodle

B) ATutor

C) Claroline

D) Blackboard

ANSWER: A

The online tests using quiz module can be configured with any number of questions per subject and any time duration to attempt the test. As far as the performance of network based products is concerned, the concurrency issues are discussed foremost. As per the rule of thumb stated in the manual of Moodle, it can support 50 concurrent users for every 1 GB of RAM depending on specific hardware and software combination.

4. CONCLUSION

The learning management systems are having numerous features which are required to deploy the e-learning products and modules in the academic institute. However, hundreds of e-learning software products are available in the software industry, MOODLE is still on top and possess almost every feature which is required in an excellent learning management system. The development, customization, implementation and deployment of open-source software products is a promptly growing route and in the near future, the academe will get great premium from these products.

REFERENCES

[1] Fundamentals of PLATO Programming, Celia R. Davis, Computer-based Education Research Laboratory, University of Illinois, Urbana, Illinois, February, 1980

[2] Bersin, Josh; Howara, Chris; O'Leonard, Karen; Mallon, David (2009), Learning Management Systems 2009, Bersin & Associates

[3] Matt Asay, CNET News, May 15, 2008, "The Open-Source Industry is Worth $60 billion"

[4] E. M Knorr, "Course Management System (CMS) Evaluation and Strategy at UBC: A Viewpoint from the Faculty of Science", Department of Computer Science, University of British Columbia

[5] Current Moodle Statistics http://moodle.org/stats/ Last Accessed: Feb. 18, 2010

[6] H. R. Wang and B. L. Liu, "A Comparison of Moodle and Sakai: Implications for Public Service Teaching Platforms," Distance Education in China(chinese), vol. 6, pp.67–69, June 2008.

[7] J. Papastergiou, "Use of a Course Management System Based on Claroline to Support a Social Constructivist Inspired Course: A Greek case study," Marina Educational Media International, vo44. 1, pp.43–60, January 2007.

[8] G. Leurs and J. Roland, "Dokeos," Linux Magazine - Haarlem, vol. 1, pp.56-78, January 2009.

[9] An Open Source Platform for Educators, Cheng-chao Su National Taiwan Junior College of Performing Arts su@ntjcpa.edu.tw

[10] Official Documentation of Moodle, Moodle Installation Guide, http://docs.moodle.org/en/Installing_Moodle

[11] K. Robinson and C. Kathleen, "Encouraging Presence and a Sense of Community in a Virtual Residential School," Open Learning, vo24. 2, pp.127-140, February 2009.

[12] David Nagel, "The Future of E-Learning Is More Growth", 2010

[13] Ellis, Ryann K. (2009), Field Guide to Learning Management Systems, ASTD Learning Circuits, http://www.astd.org/NR/rdonlyres/12ECDB99-3B91-403E-9B15-7E597444645D/23395/LMS_fieldguide_20091.pdf

[14] Expertus; TrainingOutsourcing (August 30, 2006), Survey 1: Channel Partner Training, Training Challenges Survey Series, conducted by Expertus and TrainingOutsourcing.com, http://www.trainingindustry.com/uploadedFiles/Our_Community/List_of_Sponsors/Elite_Sponsors/Expertus-%20Channel%20Partner%20Training%20Survey%20Results.pdf

[15] URL : http://en.wikipedia.org/wiki/Moodle Last Accessed : September 12, 2010

[16] MOODLE Statistics as on Sept. 12, 2010

[17] Levensaler, Leighanne; Laurano, Madeline (2009), Talent Management Systems 2010, Bersin & Associates.

□□□

16

"A Multi Agent Approach Using Stigmergy as a New Model for Optimizing Supply Chain Networks"

*Deepika Chaudhary**

Abstract – *In today highly competitive, global market place the pressure on organizations to find new ways to create and deliver value to customers grows ever stronger. Gradually in emerging economies as well as mature markets the power of buyer has overtaken that of the customer. It is against this backdrop that the discipline and philosophy of Logistics and supply chain management has moved to the center stage over the last two decades. Furthermore the role becomes more critical in current scenario when the companies are focusing on core competencies and outsourcing thus creating a large supply networks.*

*Chitkara Institute of Engg & Technology Jhansla, Teh. Rajpura, Distt Patiala-140401, Punjab. email: deepika.chaudhary@chitkara.edu.in

Computational or Nature Inspired Intelligence has emerged as a rapid growing field in the past few years. Its variety of intelligent techniques emulate human intelligence and processes found in Natural systems such as adaptation and learning , planning under large uncertainty , coping with large amount of data etc. Successful industrial applications of intelligent systems usually deal with several of these aspects and its therefore natural to combine various technologies with different capabilities within an integrated decision support system.

The objective of this paper is to discuss various methodologies of Nature Inspired Intelligence such as swarm intelligence , ant colony optimization , bee algorithms to explore and exploit the search space in a much more smarter manner so that they can provide effective solution to complex supply chain problems . This paper also emphasize and describes an multi agent approach using stigmergy (A class of mechanism which simulates the interaction behavior of social insects) as a way to optimize various function in supply chain management.

1. INTRODUCTION

The supply chain is a worldwide network of suppliers, factories, warehouses, distribution centers, and retailers through which raw materials are acquired, transformed, and delivered to customers. In recent years, a new software architecture for managing the supply chain at the tactical and operational levels has emerged. It views the supply chain as composed of a set of intelligent software agents, each responsible for one or more activities in the supply chain and each interacting with other agents in the planning and execution of their responsibilities. Global markets have made the supply chain more complex than ever to manage . So in order to remain competitive , companies must place greater attention on improving and optimizing their supply chain. Supply chain optimization is the application of processes and tools to ensure the optimal operation of a manufacturing & distribution of supply chain. This includes the optimal placement of inventory within supply chain , minimizing , operating cost (including manufacturing cost

, transportation cost & distribution cost) this often involves the application of mathematical modeling techniques using computer software. In this paper a new approach to the supply chain has been discussed which is called as multi agent approach using stigmergy. The supply chain management in a company now a days is viewed either as a competitive weapon or as a corporate milestone. The old strategy of mass production derived from notions of economics of scale is no longer seen as valid and is being discarded in favour of strategy that facilitates flexibility reduced design cycle times, reduced time to market for the customer. These situation creates the need for a novel design of a systems that is able o manage such situations effectively & efficiently. Traditional centralized systems, hierarchical manufacturing control architectures & their top down development cannot cope with the increased rate of changes in the system. Currently the changes are tackled on a case by case basis by introducing expensive, time consuming ad-hoc solutions. Where as solutions are not rigorous enough to face other changes that appear afterwards. The concept of multi agent system offers a solution consisting of a set of non-centralized , mutually co-operating elements called agents each of which acts autonomously. These multi agent systems are suited to the distributed manufacturing environment, since the manufacturing applications presents characteristics like modularity, decentralized activities, frequent changes, ill-structure complex tasks for what the agent solutions are best suited. In such systems agents exchange information and knowledge in order to achieve the desired kind of collaboration.

2. MULTI AGENT SYSTEMS

This section focuses on the field i.e. multiagent systems and then discusses the concept of stigmergy and how this can be implemented in multi agent systems.

2.1 The Concept of Agents

Intelligent agents are a new paradigm of software system development. They are used in a broad and increasing variety of applications. For a long time, there was no single definition of agent and multiagent system. Now a days it seems that researchers agree on the following definition proposed by Wooldridge and Jennings : the term "agent" denotes a hardware or software based computer system, that has the following characteristics:

Autonomy : Agents operate without the direct intervention of humans or others and has some kind of control over its actions and internal state;

Social ability : agents interact with other agents (possibly human) via some kind of agent communication language;

Reactivity : agents perceive their environment , (which may be physical world , a user , a collection of other agents, the internet or perhaps all combined) and respond in a limely fashion to changes that occur in it;

Pro-activeness : agents do not simply act in response to their environment they are able to exhibit goal directed behavior by taking the initiative.

Concerning supply chains, Dodd and Kumara [79] think that Mark Fox was probably the first to organize the supply chain as a network of intelligent agents . Indeed supply chains are made up of heterogeneous production subsystem gathered in vast dynamic and virtual coalitions. Intelligent subsystems e.g. multiagent system, enables increased autonomy of each member in supply chain. Each partner pursues individual goals while satisfying both local and external constraints. Therefore one or several agents can be used to represent each partner in supply chain. Moreover the agent paradigm is a natural metaphor for network organizations, since companies prefer maximizing their own profits that the profit of supply chain. Infact the distributed manufacturing units also have the same characteristics as agents.

2.2 Stigmergy In Ant Colonies & Multi Agent Systems

Stigmergy is a class of mechanisms that mediates animal interactions. The term stigmergy is derived from two Greek words, stigma which means sign and erg on which means work. A sign in the environment triggers an action(erg on) within the insect society. An insect observes its local environment and is motivated to certain action because of current state of environment. For instance ants are able to find shortest paths between nests and food sources sort there brood and build nests.

There are two concepts for changing the environment resulting in two flavors of stigmergy, i.e. sematectonic- and sign-based stigmergy [8]. With sematectonic stig-mergy, a change in the physical characteristics of theenvironment stimulates further activities of the insects (agents). Activities like the piling-up of mud by termites. Stimulate other termites to add material to such a structure. Nest cleaning behavior of ants illustrates very well this form of stigmergy: as ants clean the nest, they change their environment (the nest becomes cleaner), therefore other ants stop engaging in this activity and the cleaning eventually stops. It will start again when dirt accumulates again. Brood sorting or the piling of dead ants uses this mechanism as well. In sign-based stigmergy, a signaling mechanism is used to coordinate the insects (agents). Here, the animals are not stimulated by an evolving result of their activities, but use an extra task-independent mechanism. Investigations of biological insect societies show that these animals coordinate themselves by producing a dissipative field in their environment. Ants interact by spreading a smelling chemical substance—pheromones (stigma)—into their neighborhood during their activities. Such a deposition of scentor pheromones modifies the environment for other ants and determines their activities in a certain way [9]. The pheromone concentration and distribution reflects facts about the current problem the ants are working on. This insect behavior has inspired a new field of research, which is known as ant algorithms [6]. An application of this algorithm is the "ant system" (AS)[2,4]. The original AS was applied to the traveling salesman problem and inspired a range of applications and extensions like scheduling, vehicle routing, and routing in telecommunication networks. From this work the "ant colony optimization" meta-heuristic was derived [3]. In ACO, algorithms are instances of this meta-heuristic, in which a colony of ants builds solutions concurrently, asynchronously, and incrementally [4]. Another example is AntNet [2], an application of ACO algorithms for routing in tele-communication networks. In the ongoing work, ant colony optimization fits the framework well and is streamlining the software by applying it where appropriate. However, as stated earlier, the research discussed in this paper only shares the inspiration but not the goals of ACO research. Moreover, discussing ant colony optimization as a meta-heuristic is irrelevant for the research presented in this paper. In contrast to longer-established coordination mechanisms, stigmergy has some important advantages: It is a lightweight mechanism in comparison to direct negotiation (implying a rendezvous) between agents. Direct negotiation operates in a manner analogous to people buying a house. Stigmergy is analogous to one person buying 1 kg of apples in a supermarket. The display of the apples and their price constitute the signs in the environment. The signs (pheromones) can have an information content determined by the designer. For instance, an ant may insert the smell of the food itself as part of the information, allowing other ants to prefer the trails that indicate the most suitable food source in the prevailing situation. In contrast, market-based coordination mechanisms reduce the dissipative field to a single dimension (i.e. money). Stigmergy is a system design/engineering approach that brings a much-enhanced separation of concerns and modularity. It brings a skeleton in which optimizing elements can be placed, but also other concerns can be addressed like feasibility, trace- ability, and so on. However, stigmergy has some potential disadvantages. First of all, decisions are taken without synchronization—apples are sold for a fixed price on a first-come-first-served basis. Therefore, direct negotiation probably is better suited for infrequent decisions with profound implications; stigmergy can nevertheless be used to guide such negotiations by providing useful decision-supporting information in the environment, on which negotiators can base their offers and bids such that more optimal contracts are made in less time and less iterations. Furthermore, in sign-based stigmergy, the signs reflect facts with some delay. Proper measures to cope with this property may be necessary. The research here is based on the sign-based stigmergy of food foraging ants. Recall that sign-based stigmergy exhibits an interesting property: the signs that are locally available in the environment allow agents to learn about global properties of the system. Food foraging ants execute a simple procedure:

In absence of any signs in the environment (consisting of scents from a pheromone), ants perform a randomized search for food. When an ant discovers a food source, it drops a smelling chemical substance, i.e. pheromone—on its way back to the nest while carrying some of the food. Thus, it creates a pheromone trail between nest and food source. An important property of such pheromone trail is that it will evaporate if none of the ants deposes fresh pheromones. When an ant senses a pheromone trail, it will be urged by its instinct to follow this trail to the food source. Note that a scent strength gradient indicates the direction toward the food. When this ant arrives at the food source, it will return with food, while deposing more pheromones. In this manner, the strength of the pheromone trail is maintained and even reinforced. When the ant finds an exhausted food source, it starts a randomized search for a new food source and the trail disappears because of the evaporation. The above scheme results in an emergent overall behavior for the colony that is highly ordered and very effective at foraging food. At the same time, it is robust against the uncertainty and complexity posed by the environment. An important capability of this type of stigmergy is that global information (i.e. where to find food in a remote location) is made available locally (i.e. in which direction must the ant move to get to this food).The main achievement is that individual ants are not exposed to the complexity and dynamics of the situation.

The system copes with the complexity of the environment by incorporating the environment itself into the solution; no ant needs a mental map of the environment. Similarly, the evaporation and refreshing of the pheromone trails allows the ants to cope with the dynamics of the environment; there is no information in the head of the ants that must be kept in sync with reality. Derived from the described principles and properties, pheromone based coordination of ants shows the following benefits:

- Simple Coordination Mechanism: ants interact with the environment in a standard and simple way and not with each other.
- Automatic guidance to optimized solutions: the exploration of the ants guarantees that the society shows robust behavior. The spreading of the global information (trails to food sources) and the feedback on the behavior of the ant society guides the system towards a solution which is optimized but not necessarily optimal.
- Capability to handle dynamic situations : Ants uses a simple interfacing to their pheromone environment, so that an ant joining or leaving a society does not effect the society in its acting as whole. Together with a permanently changing environment, the ant society has the ability to adapt to changing situations, using mechanisms like exploration and evaporation of information.

These attractive system-engineering characteristics prompted this research on ant-colony inspired multi-agent systems. The remainder of this paper illustrates how the above mechanisms are translated in the setting of multi-agent approach. Note that it is important to apply the insights rather than to attempt to mimic nature's solution In the beginning of the 20th century, people have built aircraft flapping their wings, rather unsuccessfully.

3. SOFTWARE ARCHITECTURE FOR PROPOSED MULTI AGENT STIGMERGIC SYSTEM

The following sections describe how ant colony mechanisms can be implemented in supply chain management systems. To capture the Real world situations accurately three models are proposed for software development process:

- The "Essential Model" is used to create an understanding about the application domain. It describes the objects and events that occur in application domain; the Essential model provides the structure of the "Concept Model", the central data structure that resides within the software system.
- The "Specification Model" describes the architecture and abstract stimulus-response behavior of the software system
- The "Implementation model " is concerned with the control flow with in the software.

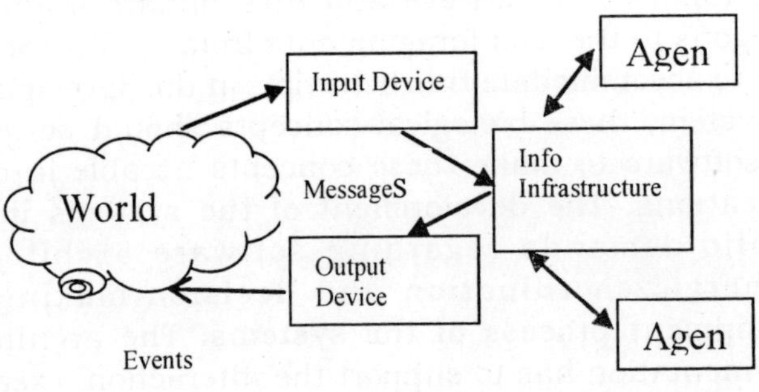

Fig. 1. Software Architecture for Stigmergic Systems

Using this approach of "Essential Modeling" provides a different form of software structure for control systems. The central data pool separates a world representation from application functionality. Independent from the real world needs of any current and future control functionality information about the real process is available within the software boundaries as complete as possible. For E.g the multi-agent system which deals with some kind of manufacturing control can be built around three kind of agents product, resource and order agents. Where a product agent corresponds to an agent that has all the know-how of products that can be produced on the shop floor. A resource agent corresponds either to a processing unit or a transport unit. Each order agent corresponds to a single order that was ordered by customer. Pheromones are used as communication mediator. A pheromone is a chemical substance that is dropped by animal species in the environment as guidance for their follower. Since those agents are not able to perform a direct communication, agents need to lay down pheromones in the environment to let other agents interpret, and take them into consideration during decision-making. In order to spread pheromones, physical agents (product, resource and order agents) create ant agents, which are part of the overall aggregated agent. These ants travel virtually across the plant topology to retrieve and disseminate information analogous to the food foraging ants from an ant colony. In order to accommodate this behavior, in the development of the system, these biological concepts should be mapped into software to make these concepts useable in control applications. The development of the systems imposes specific demands regarding software architecture, stigmergic coordination and decision-making, and development process of the systems. The architecture implementation has to support the interaction, execution, and decision-making of "ant-like" mechanism to enable a "stigmergic management" of a production process. There are three concepts that must be reflected within the architecture:

1. An artificial ant agent as the acting individual.
2. An artificial pheromone as the information carrier.
3. The environment as a display and distribution mechanism for information.

These three elements must be accounted for in the architecture.

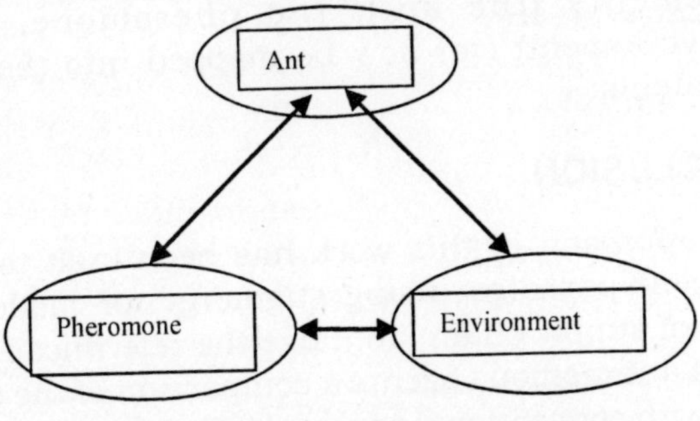

Fig. 2. Elements of a Stigmergic System

To implement this system, a typical environment should be built in order to provide mechanisms for artificial ants to move through the distributed control system and to maintain pheromone information within the control system. If artificial ant agents should roam a production environment (with resources, crossings, and transport facilities) to depose artificial pheromones as a routing advice within the transport system, the whole structure of the production system must be strictly resembled in software. The environment there fore has to provide following architectural concepts:

1. "Locations", where agents can reside and retrieve or contribute information (sense, create, or maintain pheromone objects).
2. A management mechanism for storing and maintaining artificial pheromone objects at these locations.
3. A propagation mechanism to allow the agents the movement within such a topology of locations for the purpose of deposing or sensing information (e.g. dropping pheromone objects at a specific location and building trails during the agent's traveling through the environment). The benefit of this approach is the decoupling of system and application level. All application specific documents are situated the central blackboard. The content of this blackboard reflects the

current situation of "the application". The three main elements (the ant), the pheromone, and the environment) can now be mapped into the software systems.

3. CONCLUSION

The approach in this work has been built to utilize a multi agent paradigm using stigmergy for modeling and analysis of supply chain. To judge the relevance for supply chains of autonomous agents a comparison of the same can be done with conventional approach. To this end, multi agent systems are identified as biological (ecosystem) and economical (markets) models where as traditional approaches are compared with military pattern of hierarchical approach. In this research we also tried to implement the inherent properties of ants like massive system scalability and emergent intelligent behavior. However to realize these promises a careful design of the overall system including the concept for distribution and updating stigmergic information is necessary. Thus much work remains to be done.

REFERENCES

(1) Sascha Ossowski , J. Siekmann , J. G. Carbonell, Co-Ordination in Artificial Agent Societies: Social Structures and Its Implications for Autonomous Problem-Solving Agents, Springer-Verlag New York, Inc., Secaucus, NJ, 1999

(2) Parunak, H.V.D., Go to the Ant: Engineering Principles from Natural Multi-Agent Systems, Annals of Operations Research (1997)

(3) H. Van Dyke Parunak , Albert D. Baker , Steven J. Clark, The AARIA agent architecture: an example of requirements-driven agent-based system design, Proceedings of the first international conference on Autonomous agents, p.482-483, February 05-08, 1997, Marina del Rey, California, United States

(4) Albert D. Baker, Metaphor or reality: a case study where agents BID with actual costs to schedule a factory, Market-based control: a paradigm for distributed resource allocation, World Scientific Publishing Co., Inc., River Edge, NJ, 1996

(5) Peeters, P. Van Brussel, H., Valckenaers, P., Wyns, J., Bongaerts, L., Kollingbaum, M., Heikkilae, T., Pheromone-based Emergent

Shop Floor Control Systems for flexible Flow Shops, IWES'99, Kobe (1999).

(6) Di Caro, G., Dorigo, M., AntNet: Distributed Stigmergic Control for Communication Networks, Journal of Artificial Intelligence Research 9(1998).

(7) Marco Dorigo , Eric Bonabeau , Guy Theraulaz, Ant algorithms and stigmergy, Future Generation Computer Systems, v.16 n.9, p.851-871, June 2000

(8) Marco Dorigo , Gianni Di Caro, The ant colony optimization meta-heuristic, New ideas in optimization, McGraw-Hill Ltd., UK, Maidenhead, UK, 1999

(9) Kollingbaum. M., Heikkil, T., Peeters, P., Matson, J,, Valckenaers, P., McFarlane, 0., Bluemink, G-J., Emergent Flow Shop Control based on MASCADA Agents, MIM 2000, Paints, Greece (2000)

(10) Peppard, Benchmarking Business Processes: a Framework and Classification Scheme, Proc. Esprit-Copernicus Symposium, Wroclaw, Poland, 23-24 April 1998, pp. 213-240.

(11) Valckenaers P., Van Brussels H., Brueckner S., Wyns J., Peeters P., Deadlock Avoidance in Flexible Flow Shops with Loops. 6th IFACWorkshop on Intelligent Manufacturing Systems, 2426 April 2001. Poznan. Poland (2001).

❑❑❑

17

Signed Approach for Mining Web Content Outliers

Kusum Sharma, Arvind Selwal***

Absract - *The emergence of the Internet has brewed the revolution of information storage and retrieval. As most of the data in the web is unstructured, and contains a mix of text, video, audio etc, there is a need to mine information to cater to the specific needs of the users without loss of important hidden information. Thus developing user friendly and automated tools for providing relevant information quickly becomes a major challenge in web mining research . Web Mining is the application of Data Mining Technique to discover Patterns from the Web. According to analysis targets, web mining is divided into three different types, which are web usage mining, web content mining and web structure. Web Content mining aims to mine useful information or Knowledge from web page content. Most of the*

* Student ,Final Year, CSE, email: Kusummudgil08@gmail.com

** Asstt Profesor & Head Depratment of CSE Ambala College of Engineering, Devsthali, Ambala, email: arv_*selwal@gmail.com,*

existing web mining algorithms have concentrated on finding frequent patterns while neglecting the less frequent ones that are likely to contain outlying data such as noise, irrelevant and redundant data. This paper mainly focuses on Signed approach and full word matching on the organize domain dictionary for mining web content outliers. Using this approach searching and retrieval of documents takes less time and less space. Most successful application of web mining is Personalized Shopping, Web search, Web-Wide Tracking, On-line communities, personalized portal.

Keywords – *Outliers, Relevant document, Signed Approach, Web content mining, Web documents.*

1. INTRODUCTION

With the exponential growth of information available on the internet, updating incoming data and retrieving relevant information from the web quickly and efficiently is a growing concern. Most of the web search engines typically employ conventional data retrieval and data mining techniques to discover automatically useful and previously unknown information from web content. as most of the data in the web is unstructured, and contains a mix of text, video, audio etc, there is a need to mine information to cater to the specific needs of the users.

Efforts are being made to make such data available, usually in some structured form as in matrix form for further manipulation. Web mining is an emerging research area focused on resolving these problems. The proposed work in web mining aims to develop new methodology to effectively mine useful information from web document quickly. Web mining is the application of Data mining technique to discover patterns from Web. In general, web mining tasks can be classified into three major categories, web structure mining, web usage mining and web content mining. Web structure mining tries to discover useful knowledge from the structure of hyperlinks. Web usage mining refers to the discovery of user access patterns from web usage logs. Web content mining aims to extract/mine useful information from the web pages based on their contents. Two groups of web content mining are those that directly mine the content of documents and those that improve on the content search of other tools like search engine. For Web content mining data can be image, audio, text and video. Earlier web mining algorithm do not consider documents having varying contents within same category called web content outliers. Outliers are the data that obviously deviate from others, disobey the general mode or behavior of data and disaccord with other existing data. Outliers may also reflect the true properties of data, such as the rare disastrous weather recorded in meteorological database, which often contains one or more properties whose values seriously deviate from the normal values. However, these data may contain more valuable information than normal data. Outlier detection methods broadly fall into following categories:

A. Distribution based Outlier Detection method: These are conducted by the statistics community. These methods deploy some known distribution model and detect as outliers points that deviate from the model.

B. Depth based Outlier Detection method: In this algorithm objects are organized in convex hull layers n data space according to peeling depth and outliers expected to be with shallow depth values.

C. Deviation based outlier Detection method: This techniques detect outliers by checking the characteristics of objects and identify an object as that deviates these features as outlier.

D. Distance based Outlier Detection method: In this technique a rank to all points is given, using distance of point from *k*-th nearest neighbor, and orders points by this rank. The top *n* points in ranked list identified as outliers. Alternative approaches compute the outlier factor as sum of distances from *k* nearest neighbors.

E. Density based Outlier Detection method: This method rely on local outlier factor of each point, which depend on local density of neighborhood.

Unlike Traditional outlier mining Algorithm designed for numeric data only, sets, web outliers mining algorithm should be applicable to various types of data including text, hypertext, image, video etc. Web pages that have different contents from the category in which they were taken constitute web content outlier. Web content outliers mining concentrates on finding outliers such as noise, irrelevant and redundant pages from the web documents. Also, web content outliers mining can be used to determine pages with entirely different contents from their parent sites.

In the proposed system, web documents are extracted from the search engines by giving query by the user to the web. Then the obtained web documents D is preprocessed, i.e., stop words, stem words and except text other data such as Hyperlinks, image etc. are removed .The Output is a set of documents with white-spaced separated words and it is indexed in two dimensional format (i, j), where 'i' represent web pages and 'j' represent words. Therefore, first word from first web page is indexed as (1,1), second word from the first page is indexed as (1,2) etc,. The domain dictionary is arranged in such a way that, all 1-letter word will be indexed first, followed by 2-letter words, then 3-letter words similarly up to 15-letters word which is a very reasonable upper bounds for number of characters in a word.

2. SIGNED APPROACH FOR RELEVANCY COMPUTATION

The proposed algorithm explores the advantages of full word matching and signed approach using organized domain dictionary where the indexing is done based on the length of the word. First, the input web document is preprocessed and separated into white spaced words. The full word profile for the document is generated in matrix form (i.e., W1,4 - represents 4th word in 1st page). Then the jth word from ith page is taken and its length is calculated (i.e., | Wji |) and depending on the number of characters, the respective index on the domain dictionary is searched. If the word (Wji) is found in the dictionary, then positive count is incremented by one else negative count is incremented by one. This process is carried out for all words in that web page. Finally, positive count is compared with the negative count to check the relevancy of that web page. If the positive count is less than the negative count, then that page is irrelevant, otherwise it is considered as more relevant.

3. ARCHITECTURE OF THE PROPOSED SYSTEM

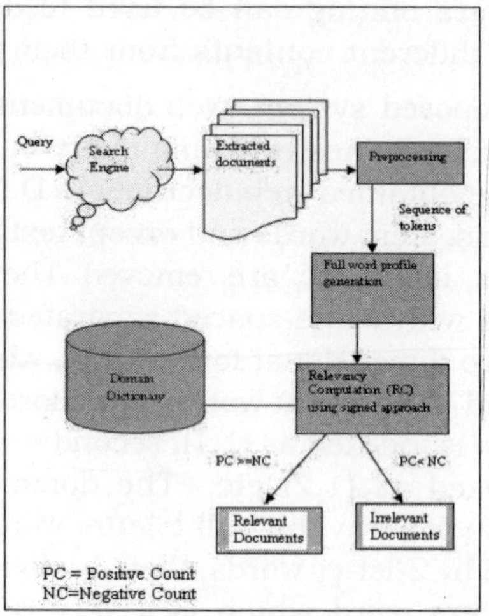

Fig. 1. Architectural Design of the proposed System

1 Letter Words	2 Letter Words	3 Letter Words	----	8 Letter Words	9 Letter Words
a	AC	ADC		Bookmark	Affiliate
C	Cc	ADF		Compiler	Algorithm
U	CD	AGP		Computer	Bandwidth
	GB	AIX		Database	Bluetooth
	IM	API		Debugger	Broadband
	IO	ARP		Digitize	Character
	IP	ASP		Direct3D	Clipboard
	IT	ATA		Download	Component
	KB	ATM		Emulation	Controller
	MB	Bcc		Exbibyte	Dashboard
	MP	Bit		Extranet	Directory
	OS	BMP		Facebook	Ethernet
	PC	Bot		Filename	Flowchart
	PS	bps		Firewall	Gigaflops
	SD	Bug		Firewire	Gigahertz
	T1	Bus		Firmware	Heuristic
	T3	CAD		Freeware	Hibernate
	XP	CGI		Gibibyte	Hyperlink
		CPA		⋮	⋮
		CPC			
		CPL			
		CPM			
		⋮			
1.txt	2.txt	3.txt	----	8.txt	9.txt

Fig. 2. Domain Dictionary for computer terms

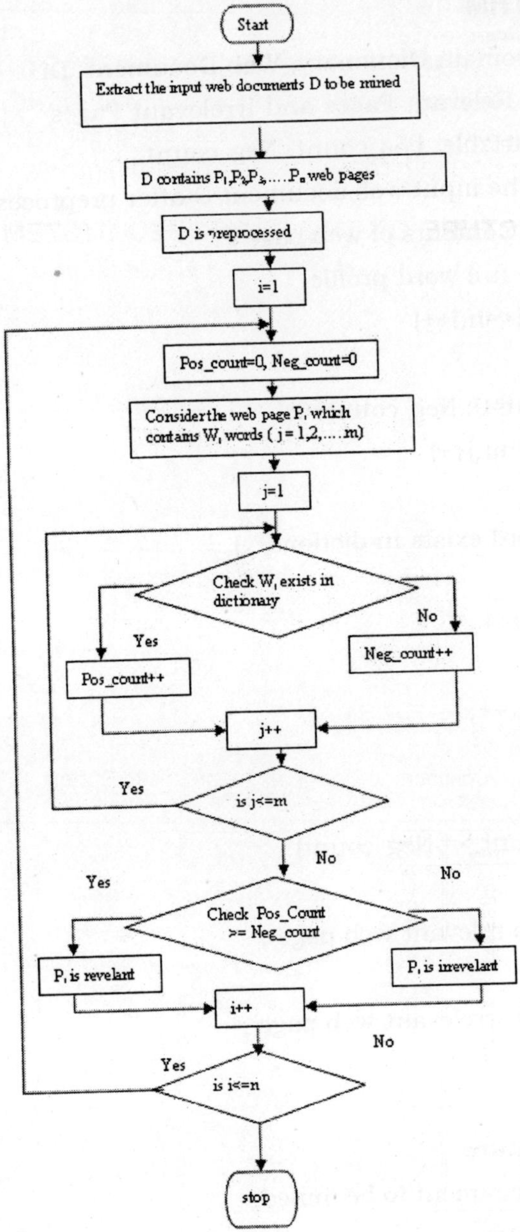
Start
Extract the input web documents D to be mined
D contains P1,P2,P3,....Pn web pages
D is preprocessed
i=1
Pos_count=0, Neg_count=0
Consider the web page Pi which contains Wj words (j = 1,2,....m)
j=1
Check Wj exists in dictionary
Yes
No
Pos_count++
Neg_count++
j++
Yes
is j<=m
No
Yes
No
Check Pos_Count >= Neg_count
Pi is revelant
Pi is irrevelant
i++
Yes
No
is i<=n
stop

4. ALGORITHM

```
Input: Domain Dictionary, Web Document Di
Output: Relevant Pages and Irrelevant Pages
Other Variable: Pos_count, Neg_count
Extract the input web document D after preprocessing.
Read the contents of web page Pi
Generate full word profile.
for ( i=1;i<=n;i++)
{
Pos_count=0; Neg_count=0;
for(j=1;j<=m;j++)
{
if ( jth word exists in dictionary)
{
Pos_count++;
else
Neg_count++;
}
}
if (Pos_count >= Neg_count)
{
Print Pi as relevant web page ;
else
Print Pi as irrelevant web page ;
}
}
```

Nomenclature

D – Web document to be mined.

Pi – Web page

Wj,i - jth word in ith web page

5. OBSERVATIONS

Experimental results ensure that the memory space, search time and run time gets reduced by using organized domain dictionary than normal indexed dictionary for checking the relevancy of the web documents. As the efficiency of web content is increased, the quality of the search engines also gets increased. This method is very simple to implement. The proposed algorithm is used by business personals to keep track of all the positive and negatives aspects related to their business

Table 1: Documents Retrieved Originally With Respect To Computer Domain

File name	Positive count	Negative count	status
File1.html	52	39	Relevant
File2.html	100	145	Not relevant
File3.html	127	107	Relevant
File4.html	13	49	Not relevant
File5.html	68	140	Not relevant
File6.html	184	113	Relevant
File7.html	169	120	Relevant
File8.html	36	75	Not relevant
File9.html	87	200	Not relevant

Table 2: Documents Retrieved After Relevancy Computation

File name	Positive count	Negative count	status
File1.html	52	39	Relevant
File3.html	127	107	Relevant
File6.html	184	113	Relevant
File7.html	169	120	Relevant

A. Precision: It is the ratio between the number of relevant documents returned originally and the total number of retrieved documents returned after eliminating irrelevant documents. Here the relevant documents indicate the required documents which satisfy the user needs.

B. Time Taken: The time taken by the entire process is the sum of the initial time taken by the general purpose search engines plus the time taken by the refinement algorithm to process the results. As the searching time to match the word with the dictionary is reduced, the overall time taken to refine the documents also gets reduced drastically.

6. CONCLUSION

Web mining is a growing research area in the mining community because of the great patronage the web continues to enjoy. Retrieving relevant content from the web is a very common task. However, the results produced by most of the search engine do not necessarily produce result that is best possible catering to the user needs. This paper proposes a new algorithm using signed approach for improving the results of web content mining by detecting both relevant and irrelevant web documents. Future work aims at experimental evaluation of web content mining in terms of reliability and to explore other mathematical tools for mining the web content. Also, a comparative study of this algorithm with existing algorithms is to be done

REFERENCES

[1] Bing Liu, Kevin Chen- Chuan Chang , Editorial: Special issue on Web Content Mining , SIGKDD Explorations, Volume 6, Issue 2. Publication Date: Aug. 2006.

[2] Cheng Wang, Ying Liu, Liheng Jian, Peng Zhang, A Utility based Web Content Sensitivity Mining Approach, International Conference on Web Intelligent and Intelligent Agent Technology (WIIAT), IEEE/WIC/ACM 2008.

[3] Hongqi li, Zhuang Wu, Xiaogang Ji, Research on the techniques for Effectively Searching and Retrieving Information from Internet, International Symposium on Electronic Commerce and Security, IEEE 2008

[4] Jaroslav Pokorny, Jozef Smizansky, Page Content Rank: An approach to the Web Content Mining

[5] Jiang Yiyong, Zhang Jifu,Cai Jainghui, Zhang Sulan, Hu Lihua , The Outliers Mining Algorithm Based On Constrained Concept Lattice, Internal Symposium on Data Privacy and E.commerce , IEEE 2007.

[6] kshitija Pol, Nita Patil, Shreya Patankar, Chhaya Das, A Survey on Web Content Mining and Extraction of Structured and Semistructured data,First International Conference on Emerging trends in Engineering and Technology, 2008

[7] Malik Agyemang, Ken Barker, Rada S. Alhajj, Framework for Mining Web Content Outliers, 2004 ACM Symposiumon Applied Computing.

[8] Peng Yang, Biao Huang, A modified Density Based Outliers Mining Algorithm for large Dataset, 2008 IEEE, International Seminar on Future Information technology and Management Engineering.

[9] Peng Yang, Biao Huang, Density Based Outliers Mining Algorithm with Application to Intrusion Detection, 2008 IEEE, Pacific asia workshop on computational Intelligence and Industrial Application.

[10] Raymond Kosala, Hendrik Blockeel, Web Mining Research: A Survey, ACM SIGKDD, July 2000.

□□□

18

SLA and Security Issues in Cloud Computing

Rajender Nath, Dinesh Verma***

Abstract – *The buzzword of 2009 seems to be "cloud computing" which is a futuristic platform to provides dynamic resource pools, virtualization, and high availability and enables the sharing, selection and aggregation of geographically distributed heterogeneous resources for solving large-scale problems in science and engineering. We are in the midst of a computing revolution. As the cost of provisioning hardware and software stacks grows, and the cost of securing and administering these complex systems grows even faster, Companies are now offering services such as storage and compute cycles, enabling higher-level services to be built on top. When we look at the security of data in the cloud computing, the*

*Department of Computer Science and Applications, Kurukshetra University. Email: rnath_2k3@rediffmail.com

**Department of Computer Science & Applications N.C. Institute of Computer science, Israna(Panipat) Email: me.dinesh17@gmail.com

vendor has to provide some assurance in service level agreements (SLA) to convince the customer on security issues. Yet, guaranteeing the security of corporate data in the "cloud" is difficult, if not impossible, as they provide different services like Software as a service (SaaS), Platform as a service (PaaS), and Infrastructure as a service (IaaS). This paper will discuss vision of cloud computing, and describe some of the key initiatives, highlighting the technical challenges involved in designing hosted, multi-tenanted data management systems & related security issues.

Keywords – *Distributed heterogeneous resources, SaaS, PaaS, IaaS.*

1. INTRODUCTION

Cloud computing is Internet-based computing, whereby shared resources, software and information are provided to computers and other devices on-demand, like electricity. On-demand self-service Internet infrastructure where you pay-as-you-go and use only what you need, all managed by a browser, application or API. Cloud computing is broken up into multiple segments including: Cloud Infrastructure, Cloud Platforms and Cloud Applications. Cloud computing describes a data-processing infrastructure in which the application software—and often the data itself—is stored permanently not on your PC but rather a remote server that's connected to the Internet. When you need to use the application or access the data, your computer connects to the server through the Internet and some of that information is cached temporarily on your client machine.

As the name suggests, the function of the cloud is to provide individuals and small and mid-sized Businesses access to an array of powerful applications and services through the internet and not concerned about the basic underlying complexities involved in delivering services. Cloud is accessible through any digital device—be a laptop, a cell phone or a smart phone that are capable to connect to internet, cloud based services like webmail, social networking, photo sharing, and video viewing are already interwoven into fabric of our daily lives. The clouds have different architecture based on the services they provide. The data is stored on to centralized location called data centers having a large size of data storage. The data as well as processing is somewhere on servers. So, the clients have to trust the provider on the availability as well as data security. The SLA is the only legal agreement between the service provider and client. The only means the provider can gain trust of client is through the SLA, so it has to be standardize.

2. CHARACTERISTICS OF CLOUD COMPUTING

Virtual – Physical location and underlying infrastructure details are transparent to users.

Scalable – Able to break complex workloads into pieces to be served across an incrementally expandable infrastructure.

Efficient – Services Oriented Architecture for dynamic provisioning of shared compute resources.

Flexible – Can serve a variety of workload types both consumer and commercial.

3. THE SERVICE LEVEL AGREEMENT

A service level agreement is a document which defines the relationship between two parties: the provider and the recipient. This is clearly an extremely important item of documentation for both parties. If used properly it should:

- Identify and define the customer's needs
- Provide a framework for understanding
- Simplify complex issues
- Reduce areas of conflict
- Encourage dialog in the event of disputes
- Eliminate unrealistic expectations

Specifically it should embrace a wide range of issues. Amongst these are usually the following: Services to be delivered Performance, Tracking and Reporting Problem

Management Legal Compliance and Resolution of Disputes Customer Duties and Responsibilities Security IPR and Confidential Information Termination.

4. SLA HAS TO DISCUSS HOW THE FOLLOWING SECURITY RISKS

The past SLA's declares waivers if the promises are not met but do this really help the customer's in fulfilling their losses. The SLA's also have to discuss about how the security is maintained, what are the methods used in maintaining security and how customer complaints are taken care? The following are the security issues that SLA has to discuss:

4.1 Privileged user access

Sensitive data processed outside the enterprise brings with it an inherent level of risk, because outsourced services bypass the "physical, logical and personnel controls" IT shops exert over in-house programs. Get as much information about the people who manage our data. Ask providers to supply specific information on the hiring and oversight of privileged administrators, and the controls over their access.

4.2 Regulatory compliance

Customers are ultimately responsible for the security and integrity of their own data, even when it is held by a service provider. Traditional service providers are subjected to external audits and security certifications. Cloud computing providers who refuse to undergo this scrutiny are signaling that customers can only use them for the most trivial functions.

4.3 Data location

When we use the cloud, we probably won't know exactly where our data is hosted. In fact, we might not even know what country it will be stored in. Ask providers if they will commit to storing and processing data in specific jurisdictions, and whether they will make a contractual commitment to obey local privacy requirements on behalf of their customers.

4.4 Data segregation

Data in the cloud is typically in a shared environment alongside data from other customers. Encryption is effective but isn't a cure-all. The cloud provider should provide evidence that encryption schemes were designed and tested by experienced specialists.

4.5 Recovery

Even if we don't know where your data is, a cloud provider should tell us what will happen to our data and service in case of a disaster. Any offering that does not replicate the data and application infrastructure across multiple sites is vulnerable to a total failure.

4.6 Investigative support

Investigating inappropriate or illegal activity may be impossible in cloud computing. Cloud services are especially difficult to investigate, because logging and data for multiple customers may be co-located and may also be spread across an ever-changing set of hosts and data centers. If we cannot get a contractual commitment to support specific forms of investigation, along with evidence that the vendor has already successfully supported such activities, then our safe assumption is that investigation and discovery requests will be impossible.

4.7 Long-term viability

Ideally, cloud computing provider will never go broke or get acquired and swallowed up by a larger company. But must be sure about the data will remain available even after such an event.

5. DATA STORAGE IN CLOUD

The lead topic of every IT conversation today is cloud computing. The key point within each of those conversations is inevitably cloud computing security. While protecting data from corruption, loss, unauthorized access, etc. are all still required characteristics of any IT infrastructure, cloud computing changes the game in a much more profound way.

Moving data into the cloud offers great convenience to users since they don't have to care about the complexities of direct hardware management. The pioneer of Cloud Computing vendors, Amazon Simple Storage Service (S3) and Amazon Elastic Compute Cloud (EC2) are both well known examples [1]. While these internet-based online services do provide huge amounts of storage space and customizable computing resources, this computing platform shift, however, is eliminating the responsibility of local machines for data maintenance at the same time. As a result, users are at the mercy of their cloud service providers for the availability and integrity of their data. Recent downtime of Amazon's S3 is such an example.

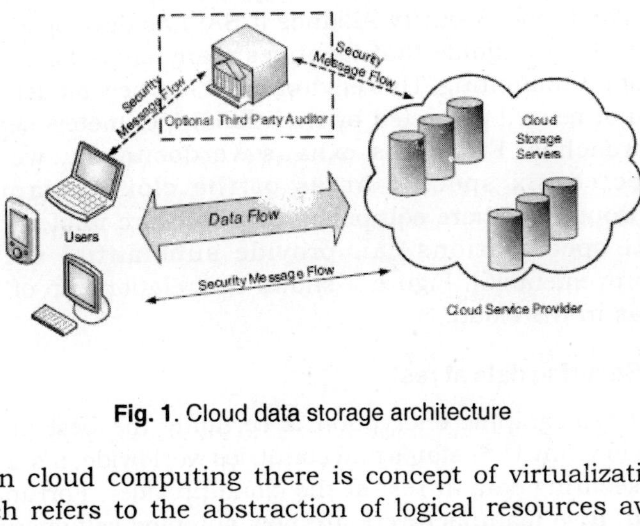

Fig. 1. Cloud data storage architecture

In cloud computing there is concept of virtualization, which refers to the abstraction of logical resources away from their underlying physical resources in order to improve agility and flexibility, reduce costs and thus enhance business value. In a virtualized environment, computing environments can be dynamically created, expanded, shrunk or moved as demand varies.

Virtual worlds require significant amounts of computing power, especially as those virtual spaces become large or as more and more users log in. Massively multiplayer online games (MMPOG) are a good example of significantly large virtual worlds. Several commercial virtual worlds have as many as nine million registered users and hundreds and thousands of servers supporting these environments [2].

Intrusion Detection System is installed on the virtual switch which logs the network traffic in-bound and out-bound into the database for auditing. The packets are examined in real-time by the intrusion detection system for a particular type of attack based on predefined rules. The rules are defined based on well known attack strategies by the intruders. The IDS could determine the nature of attack and is capable of notifying virtual server the amount security risks involved [3].

6. CRITICAL AREAS FOR CLOUD COMPUTING

The Cloud Security Alliance (CSA) has developed a 76-page security guide that identifies many areas for concern in cloud computing. This environment is a new model which cannot be well protected by traditional "perimeter" security approaches. From this exhaustive document, we have selected six specific areas of the cloud computing environment where equipment and software implementing TCG specifications can provide substantial security improvements[6]. Figure 2 shows the relationship of these areas in the cloud.

6.1 Securing data at rest

Cryptographic encryption is certainly the best practice and in many U.S. states and countries worldwide, it's the law for securing data at rest at the cloud provider. Fortunately, hard drive manufacturers are now shipping self encrypting drives that implement the TCG's Trusted Storage standards [5][6]. Self-encrypting drives build encryption hardware into the drive, providing automated encryption with minimal cost or performance impact. Software encryption can also be used, but it is slower and less secure since the encryption key can be copied off the machine without detection.

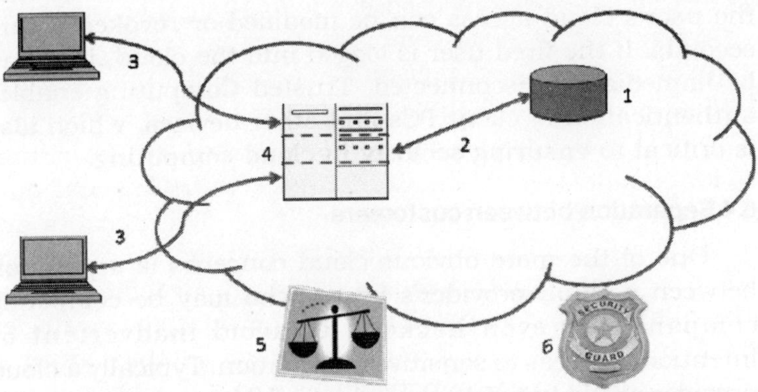

Fig. 2. Areas for security concerns in cloud computing: (1) data at rest, (2) data in transit, (3) authentication, (4) separation between customers, (5) cloud legal and regulatory issues and (6) incident response.

6.2 Securing data in transit

Encryption techniques should also be used for data in transit. In addition, authentication and integrity protection ensure that data only goes where the customer wants it to go and is not modified in transit. Well-established protocols such as SSL/TLS should be used here. The tricky part is strong authentication, as described next.

6.3 Authentication

User authentication is often the primary basis for access control, keeping the bad guys out while allowing authorized users in with a minimum of fuss. In the cloud environment, authentication and access control are more important than ever since the cloud and all of its data are accessible to anyone over the Internet. The TPM can easily provide stronger authentication than username and passwords. TCG's IF-MAP standard allows for real-time communication between the cloud provider and the customer about authorized users and other security issues. When a user is fired or reassigned, the customer's identity management system can notify the cloud provider in real-time so that the user's cloud access can be modified or revoked within seconds. If the fired user is logged into the cloud, they can be immediately disconnected. Trusted Computing enables authentication of client PCs and other devices, which also is critical to ensuring security in cloud computing.

6.4 Separation between customers

One of the more obvious cloud concerns is separation between a cloud provider's users (who may be competing companies or even hackers) to avoid inadvertent or intentional access to sensitive information. Typically a cloud provider would use virtual machines (VMs) and a hypervisor to separate customers. TCG technologies can provide significant security improvements for VM and virtual network separation [8]. In addition, the TPM can provide hardware-based verification of hypervisor and VM integrity. The TNC architecture and standards can provide strong network separation and security.

6.5 Cloud legal and regulatory issues

To verify that a cloud provider has strong policies and practices that address legal and regulatory issues, each customer must have its legal and regulatory experts inspect cloud provider policies and practices to ensure their adequacy. The issues to be considered include data security and export, compliance, auditing, data retention and destruction, and legal discovery. In the areas of data retention and deletion, Trusted Storage and TPM access techniques can play a key role in limiting access to data.

6.6 Incident response

As part of expecting the unexpected, customers need to plan for the possibility of cloud provider security breaches or user misbehavior. An automated response or at least automated notification is the best solution. TCG's IF-MAP (Metadata Access Protocol) specification enables the integration of different security systems and provides real-time notification of incidents

7. CONCLUSION

Today's IT realities make cloud computing a good fit for meeting the needs of both IT providers who demand unprecedented flexibility and efficiency, lower costs and complexity and support for varied and huge workloads and Internet users who expect exceptionally high availability, function and speed. . Overall, cloud computing security is an untapped field. Once cloud computing gains some more traction rest assured that it will be a big target for hackers. There would be a lot of glory and financial gain by bringing down a cloud or two. We believe that data storage security in Cloud Computing, an area full of challenges and of paramount importance, is still in its infancy now, and many research problems are yet to be identified.

REFERENCE

[1] Amazon.com, "Amazon Web Services (AWS)," Online at http://aws.amazon.com, 2008.

[2] N. Gohring, "Amazon's S3 down for several hours," Online at http://www.pcworld.com/

[3] Y Kobayashi,"Intrusion Detection Systems: technology and development".

[4] A. Juels and J. Burton S. Kaliski, "PORs: Proofs of Retrievability for Large Files," Proc. of CCS '07, pp. 584–597, 2007.

[5] H. Shacham and B. Waters, "Compact Proofs of Retrievability," Proc. of Asiacrypt '08, Dec. 2008.

[6] Cloud Security Alliance (CSA): http://cloudsecurityalliance.org/

[7] A Security Analysis of Cloud Computing:http://cloudcomputing.sys-con.com/node/1203943

[8] Y Kobayashi,"Intrusion Detection Systems: technology and development".

□□□

19

The Current Scenario of Web Based Travel Services

A Case Study of Indian Online Travel Sgencies (OTA's)

Vineet Kumar Gupta, Sonu Gupta**, Rohit Sharma****

Abstract – *If the advent of air travel can be termed as the major mile stone in the growth of tourism industry, then the arrival of World Wide Web can certainly be called as the turning point in the fastest growing service industry of the world. Internet has dramatically changed the whole approach of doing tourism business from the service provider's point of view and has started a new era of information access for the customers. It has also added a new dimension to the travel and tourism industry. This*

* Lecturer, CT Institute of Hotel Management & Catering Technology, Jalandhar City, Punjab, India

** Lecturer, Dept. of Computer Science, Lyallpur Khalsa College, Jalandhar City, Punjab, India.

*** Lecturer, CT Institute of Hotel Management & Catering Technology, Jalandhar City, Punjab, India

paper attempts to highlight the current scenario of web based travel services, associated with Indian OTA's. E-tourism has benefited all the players involved in tourism, from suppliers to intermediaries, from travel destinations to the ultimate consumer i.e. the tourist. E-tourism is electronic tourism and can be termed as tourism powered by internet i.e. use of web by the tourists to find out the ultimate information about the destination, selecting destinations, booking hotels, flights, etc. and use of internet by service providers in travel sector for marketing, promotion of their travel services to reach out their customers. The applications of E-tourism have become an integral part and parcel of our daily life.

Key words – *OTA, E-tourism.*

1. INTRODUCTION

E-tourism has become a new mantra of success for the Indian and foreign Online travel agencies/agents (OTA's). The number of internet users is growing tremendously in India over the years. With a mere of 5.5 million users in year 2000, the figure in year 2009 stands at 81 million users in the country. Internet penetration in India has also crossed 7% mark. This is a positive sign for the growth of web based services, particularly the travel services. More and more players like make my trip, yatra, ezeego, travel guru, bookmytrip etc. have successfully built their niche in this lucrative on line market of India. On line travel contributes 70% of all e-commerce activities globally and it is one of the most stimulating segments of India's internet sector.

Indian online travel sector which currently stands at around USD 4 billions is expected to reach around USD 8.9 billion by 2012. Fig. 1 illustrates all the major players involved in e-tourism. These all are reaping benefits of e-tourism. These include suppliers, intermediaries, destinations and the ultimate tourist as well. The laudable aspect of e-tourism is its contribution towards environment also, as majority of transactions are paperless.

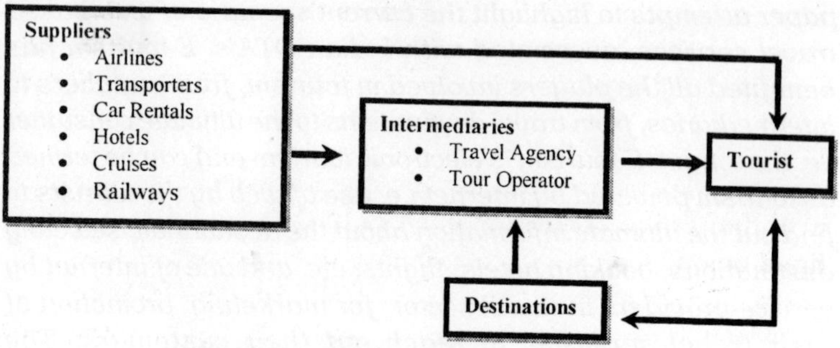

Fig. 1. Major Players in E-Tourism System

Major web based travel services:

These includes air tickets, hotel rooms, tour packages, bus ticket, travel information, car rentals, FOREX, sight seeing, cruise booking, insurance, etc.

Benefits of web based travel services to customers:

- 24×7 access to customer
- Effortless and hassle free service
- Save time and money
- Offers e-brochure facility to customers
- videos of travel destinations
- Interactive maps
- Chat options
- Blogs
- Ticket printing facility
- Voucher printing facility
- Customer services like fight directory, hotel directory

Benefits of e-tourism for service providers:

- Easy and fast dissemination of information to potential clientele
- Cost reduction in tourism marketing
- Increases sales and profit of the organization
- Offers B2B and B2C solutions
- Can obtain feed back of customers instantly

- Direct contact with customers through the application of chatting and blogging
- Global reach

Major OTA's operating in India:

More and more web based travel services are emerging in India. Some of the key players in this field are shown in fig. 2 below.

Fig. 2. Major OTA's operating in India

Objectives of the study:

- To know the impact of internet on travel business and in general tourism
- To get insight knowledge about the services provided by travel agencies on their web sites
- To know changing trends about the travel services surfed on the web by the customers
- To know the various players involved in e-tourism system
- To analyze the major services provided by OTA's.

Research Methodology:

The present research is based on web related library research, as historical records available on different websites were analyzed and presented in the forms of graphs.

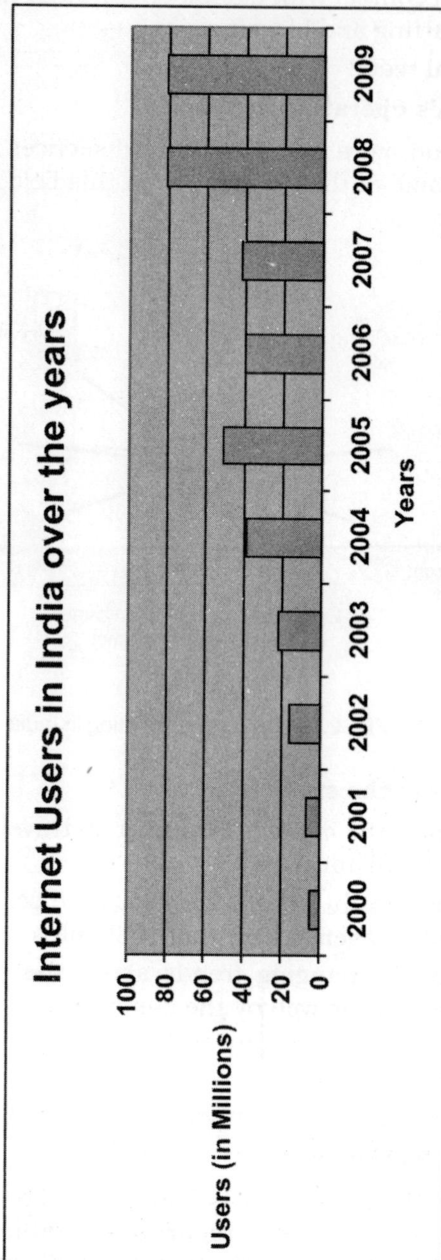

Fig. 3. Internet users in India over the years

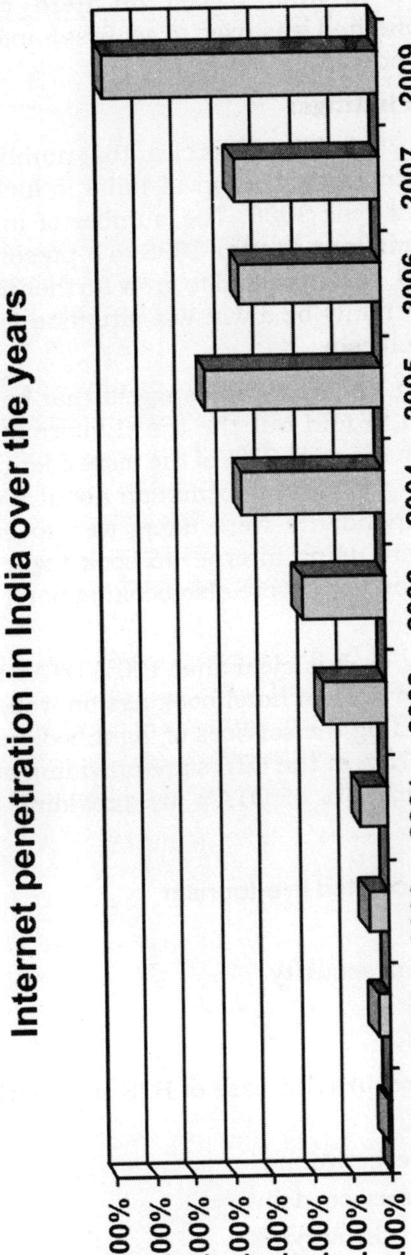

Fig. 4. Internet penetration in India over the years

This research is also based on field research as questionnaire method was used to get first hand information from the respondents.

Analysis and Findings:

From the fig. 3 and fig. 4 it is clear that number of internet users and internet penetration in India is increasing with the exception of year 2006. The number of internet users grew from 1.4 millions in year 1998 to a present level of 81 millions in 2009. It is expected to grow further in the coming years. It will certainly be a win-win situation for all players involved in e-tourism.

From the fig. 5, key trends suggest that customers are most interested to find out the travel information about a destination from the web. 93% of the respondents were using the web just to get travel information about a destination. 70% of the respondents were using web to book railway tickets, 50% were using internet to book flight tickets and 46% of the respondents were also booking hotel rooms from the OTA's.

From the fig. 6, it is clear that 100% OTA's in India are providing the services of hotel bookings on web, 86% of the OTA's are providing the services of flight bookings online to the customers. 73% of the OTA's are providing holiday/tour packages online, 46% of OTA's are providing car rentals online.

Major issues associated in e-tourism

- Fraud
- Transaction security
- Hacking
- Link failure
- Password security in case of B2B transactions
- Virus
- Bounced reservations
- failure in service delivery
- discrepancy in service

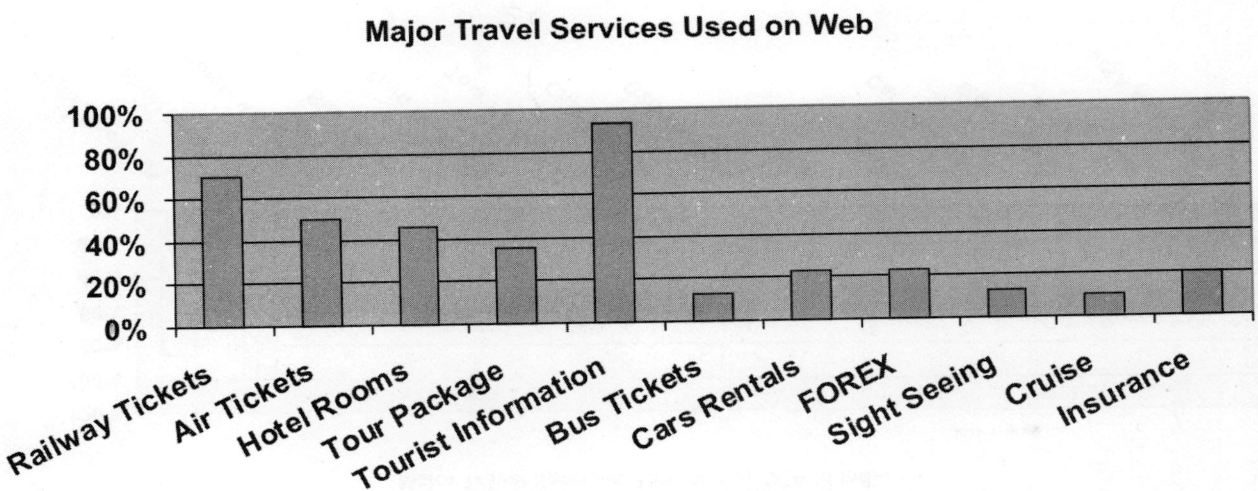

Fig. 5. Major travel services used on web
Source: Primary Data

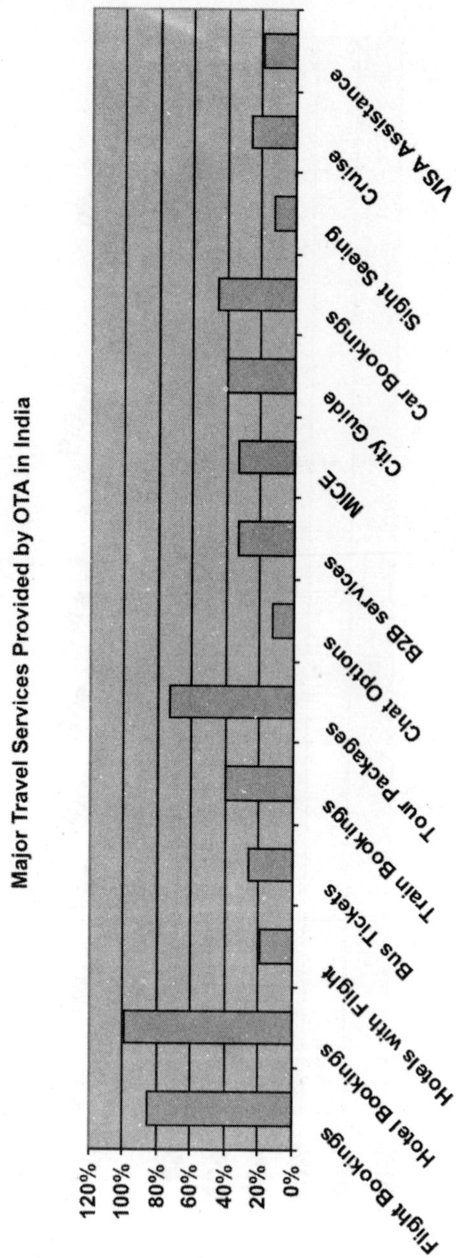

Fig. 6. Major travel services by OTA in India
Source: Primary Data

Suggestions:

- The information provided on the web site should be genuine and websites need to be updated regularly.
- All the terms and conditions should be clearly mentioned in the website
- Any hidden charges, taxes, must be mentioned.
- The website should publish detail information about destinations from customs, traditions, food habits, do's and don't.
- All the payment details and security concerns should also be highlighted.
- Plenty of websites shows link failure, it should be corrected immediately.
- Toll free help line numbers/customer care services should be provided.
- A trust should be built between customers and service providers which is essential for overall development of e-tourism.
- A more customer centric approach should be used by the service providers.
- A website should be more users friendly so that even naïve users can use it without any hassle.

2. CONCLUSION

The e-tourism has become a buzz word around the globe and all the major associated players have now started to realize its importance. The present study illustrates that e – tourism is all set to have prominent growth in future. With the increased projection in the number of internet users, we can presume that web based travel services will play a significant role in the tourism business. The e-tourism will be more fruitful, if the service providers will ensure authenticity and follow the business ethics associated with the web based services, at the same time, it is the duty of the government to make tough cyber laws to ensure that, all the clients gets accurate, timely and reliable information.

REFERENCES

1. C.R. Kothari, (2006), "Research Methodology: Methods and Techniques", New age international publishers, New Delhi, 7-8.
2. Information & Communication Technology in public life, University centre for distance learning, Chaudhary devil lal, university, Sirsa, Haryana
3. *http://www.internetworldstats.com/asia/in.htm.*
4. http://www.prlog.org/10269120-online-travel-market-in-india-is-booming-and-attracting-pevc-investments-finds-netscribes-report.html
5. http://www.phocuswright.com/the_phocuswright_india_travel_summit_2009_india_travel_market
6. http://www.traveldailynews.com/pages/show_page/38651-Online-travel-market-in-India-is-evolving-and-attracting-new-players-and-investors
7. http://etc-etcetera.com/what.htm
8. *http://www.vccircle.com/500/news/there-are-many-makemytrip-like-internet-biz-stories-in-india.*

❑❑❑

20

Media Changing the Youth Culture

An Indian Perspective

Dr. Ritu Soni, Mrs. Bharati Kamboj***

Abstract – *A study of the effect of electronic media on the Indian youth has been carried out. The internet has revolutionized the entire world. The Indian youth is being exposed to all that is being offered by it. As a result, the Indian traditions are getting diffused to western culture. The way youth is doing purchases or helping others or raising their voices against corruption or any political matters, information access rights are changing with times. Along with the benefits of internet, the youth is also being influenced by its negative aspects. With the technology embedded society emerging, India is undergoing contradicting cultural changes.*

*Head, Department of Computer Science, Guru Nanak Girls' College, Yamuna Nagar, Haryana, India-135003. E-mail- ritusoniynr@yahoo.com

**Department of Physics, Guru Nanak Girls' College, Yamuna Nagar, Haryana, India-135003. E-mail- bharatikamboj@gmail.com

1. INTRODUCTION

The term "**culture**" originates from Latin term for "cultivation", the preparation of land for producing crop[1]. It is defined as all of the beliefs, behaviors, and products common to a particular group. These include the values and customs that we hold in common with others; the language that we speak; the rules we follows; the tools and technologies we use to make things; the goods we consume; the organizations we belong to; and the larger institutions of society[2].

2. TRADITIONAL INDIAN CULTURE

If we talk about **Indian Culture**, we have certain diverse traditions according to different societies. For example : It is tradition in India that youngsters follows their elders in house hold work & in business, maintain localized traditions for worshipping god, beliefs, cooking traditions, dressing traditions, folk etc. this is possible due to joint family structure available in India. Work is divided between family members, children and older generation get cared, money is pooled, resources are shared. Such a system leads to emotional balance, proper care of every body, high tolerance among family members, helping attitude etc

But due to globalization, the Indian traditions are getting diffused to western culture or within other communities or other social cultures. Media plays a very important role in this kind of diffusion.

How media is changing culture: old media

Different media emerging from time to time- may it be newspaper or radio or films or TV and now internet- has a huge impact on Indian culture as well as society. News paper creates mass awareness, gives right to pen where as radio and films and TV provide entertainment along with mass awareness and right to voice.

With the advent of TV, people are more exposed to different cultures and their traditions. Advertisers use TV as media to promote their products. Social life is taken up by TV rooms. All kinds of programs are viewed by all generations, thereby giving adulthood exposure to children. Thus the cultural impact of all this exposure on society is huge. Ministry of Broadcasting of India has made some polices for certifying the films but there is no such certification in TV programs.

Amazing internet

And then comes the internet!!!! It has revolutionalized the entire world, making it a small global village. Every kind of information is available at the click of mouse. Traditionally, the Internet was used by scientists, academics and engineers to send emails and share information. Today, the internet is also used for the downloading of music, the forming of virtual communities, and the establishment of news groups. **Internet Access Reports** [3] verify that internet is accessed mostly for information retrieval, checking mails and getting sports updates.

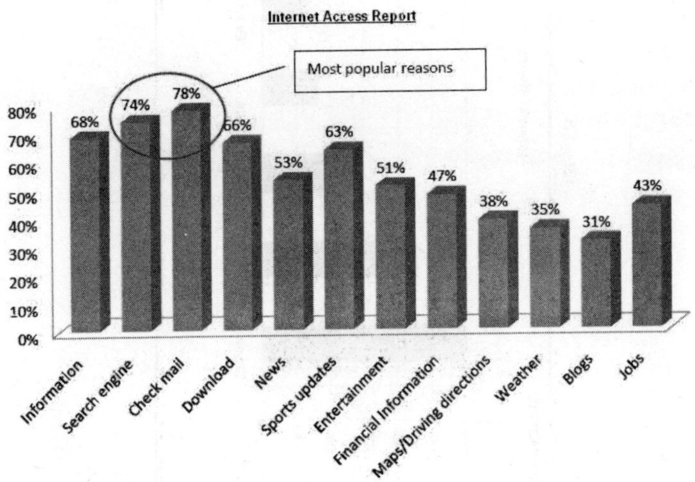

Fig. 1

In the age of digital literacy, children could well overtake their parents when it comes to using the internet for social

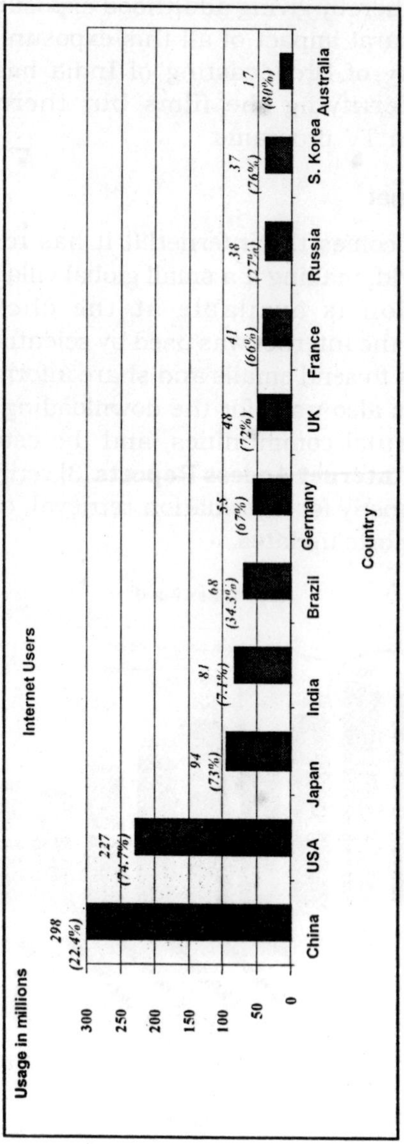
Internet Users
Usage in millions
300
250
200
150
100
50
0
298 (22.4%)
227 (74.7%)
94 (73%)
81 (7.1%)
68 (34.3%)
55 (67%)
48 (72%)
41 (66%)
38 (27%)
37 (76%)
17 (80%)
China
USA
Japan
India
Brazil
Germany
UK
France
Russia
S. Korea
Australia
Country

Fig. 2

networking, social gathering, tweeting, chatting, sending emails and downloading movies and songs. According to a recent survey by IMRB and IMAI (internet and mobile association of India), nearly 22 million school going children between the ages 8-14 are internet savvy. E-mailing continues to be a popular draw with 91% of those surveyed; general information gathering comes second with 76%.

Nearly 41% of Indians enjoy chatting and online gamming account for 41%. A 2008 study conducted by IMAI showed that 25% of respondent use the internet to hunt for a life partner. (TOI Dec 4th 2009)[4]. Some of the news from Times of India shows that "India has recently become the third largest market for twitter in just a few months, with 5 million subscribers of total of over 11.5 millions".

3. YOUTH POPULATION

TCS [5] has identified the youth in four categories -

The Globetrotter: The Globetrotter has global ambitions and wants to study and work abroad. However, a growing confidence in the economic future in India is also reflected in the survey as many students are also keen to bring skills back to India and put them to use here.

The Gadgetphile: Students from both metros and mini-metros who love gadgets and with access to a web enabled mobile, the latest gaming console, i-Pods and if he/she doesn't have one, then aspires to own an i-Phone.

The Nation-Builder: The Indian student is focused on his/her career but is as much interested in the additional benefits that careers brings such as travel, learning new skills, experience to be gained, interesting workplace and salary.

The Social networker: A true digital native, the Social Networker is likely to have as many online friends as real ones and these friendships go beyond the traditional boundaries of gender, caste, and geographies.

History of Youth Culture and New Technologies:

The concept of youth culture and new technologies is a relatively new term. However the rate at which technology has moved into the lives of the young as stated by Seel [7] is unprecedented. Growth within this area began in August 1981 when IBM released the IBM PC [6]. The next major development was the internet established in the 1990's, which "created an entirely new means of social interaction? [7].

More recently, there has been the convergence of individual technologies. An example of this is the convergence of mobile phone technologies with that of the internet.

4. YOUTH CONTRIBUTION IN CULTURE BUILDING:

Any culture is reorganized by its unique identity. For youths there are three processes in the formation and construction of their identity; **reflexivity, makeability and individualization** (Aakhus & Katz 2002, p.255). **Reflexivity**: is a cultural way of mirroring (individual, subjective, social, cultural) selves or identities through symbolic images in media, verbal language or face-to-face interaction. **Makeability**: is the perspective that sees personality and lifestyle factors as being open to influence; individuals are able to make choices about their content. **Individualization**: means that as industrial society develops, the significance of social background decreases while the subjective importance of the inner world increases. (Aakhus & Katz, 2002, p.255). The following are some of the areas where the influence of youth culture is recognized:

Youth trends for purchasing:

The effort to commercialize and commodity anything and everything not only leads to the degradation of Indian culture, it is harmful to us as citizens. According to the survey, 57 per cent of the respondents browsed the Internet on their mobile phones, and close to one-third of those were engaged with brands that advertise. If India could use youth as a hook to lure top brands, it would be the world's most brand-rich country. This is the reason why international brands are making a beeline to tap the Indian youth..

Youth mindset for social networking:

One of the biggest innovations of technology is social networking. A web based social network service focuses on building online communities of people who share interests or activities, attracting people based on common language, sex, religion, or nationality-based identities. These sites also integrate new information and communication tools, such as mobile connectivity, blogging, and photo/video-sharing. Variety of services like **c**reating your own FREE profile webpage, chatting, Instant messaging, playing online games, sharing ideas- sending a friend request or a secret crush etc., are provided by them. It is surveyed that 63% of urban students spend over an hour online daily; 93% are aware of social networking; Orkut and Facebook are most popular online destinations. Other popular social networking sites are MySpace, Friendster, Cyworld, Orkut, Zorpia, Hi5 and Bebo.

Youth mindset for crime:

Every technology has its own negative aspects. **Cyber bullying** is a disturbing new trend among young people abusing the technology The study shows that 15% of children experience C**yber sexual harassment** on social sites & chat rooms.

Networking sites also helps burglars home in as they get information via scraps, tweets sent by user to inform their friends that users are away on holiday.

Terrorists also use internet to pass their information or scaring the innocent people by sending emails, sms or tweets or by writing blogs. Since media is a one sided communication from "media to masses"; sometime wrong information or view point is also transmitted to masses.

Youth mindset for helping others:

Indians are very helpful by nature. One can find lots of emails asking help for people financially, blood requirements or helping people **in natural disasters** in India. Colleges are embracing student blogs on their websites, seeing them as powerful tool for admissions. **On-line helps** during admission days are very common in India.

Online car sharing portals are already a popular way of commuting longer distances between towns and cities. Rising fuel and train ticket prices coupled with an increasing environmental awareness are all helping to boost its popularity.

Youth mindset for open sex:

Traditional Indian values about male female relationships, marriages have had a severe blow from the pornography available on internet. Online friendships sometimes turn into violent rapes on actual meeting. Youth is totally confused who want to be westernized but their deep rooted Indian values stops them to be free. Flirting and sexting – sharing sexually explicit photos, videos, and chat by cell phone or internet – is fairly commonplace among young people. In general, 28% Indians flirted with someone other than partner.

Youth mindset for marriage:

Survey reveals that most of the Indians (80%) have used a mobile phone or internet for weddings; Along with that romances occur on the internet without physical or visual contact (Wiseman, 1998), which may end to marriage.

Media using youth as audience for advertising:

Mobile and internet are clearly becoming a mass medium in India. The advanced technology enables advertisers to discover their target audience on mobile Internet sites in a measurable manner. It is a well known fact that the Youth segment in India is one of the most lucrative consumer groups for marketers around the world.

Youth for politics:

As Dante Motes, a Bronx high school student who works at Youth Force, points out, "Instead of young people wanting to fight or just hanging out, they should be down and make a voice for themselves. If they don't, then who's going to be talking for us?" Such type of activity is gaining in India also.

Youth for voice rise:

Many youth argue that they don't need to be protected. Many believe that they should have access to all information, without it being censored by the obscenity and indecency laws theoretically meant to protect them. While allowing youth to access censored material like hard core pornography is highly debatable; it does suggest that perhaps we should start listening to youth, and their thoughts about the media.

5. YOUTH AND HEALTH

The ability to interact with various people without having to leave the comforts of their house leads to lack of social competencies and interpersonal skills to deal with the real world [8]. Internet addiction makes a person more aggressive, frustrated and isolated and leads to certain physical symptoms, such as back aches, dry eyes, migraine and other physical symptoms. Excessive use of mobiles can cause **Tumors and Acoustic Neuroma** - a study by a team from the Karolinska Institute found.

It also decreases the user's physical identity amongst their families, peers and co-workers. People tend to become isolated from the rest of the world as they continue to live in a fantasy of unreal identities. This is causing concern within society as people are thought to lose their sense of reality, interaction, and their personal identity. Online sharing has one of the most disadvantages of keeping all you have shared, in memory for ever. In reality, with passage of time, life changes and man gets matured and then all past memories simply disturb present life.

Virtual and multiple identities have further multiplied the human psychological problems as users lose touch with the sense of reality. This in turn can lead to depression about themselves, as once reality sets in that they are not who they created online, people can feel despondent about their lives and those in it.

On the positive side, young people may self-examine themselves by changing their character as more appealing. People can enhance their self esteem by forming on-line friendships and relationships.

6. CONCLUSION

We live today in an ever-increasingly hyper-interconnected world, a global society of communicative interactions and exchanges that stimulates profound cultural transformations and realignments. Indian youth is the most influenced segment that uses the innovative methods of communication and interaction. Young generation of India is very eager to set their career and make money sideways.With high traditional values in Indian society, cultural diffusion is occurring. India is also going through contradicting cultural changes. Our older generation is not comfortable with the way people work, interact, relate, learn, process information and view their community and their standing in the world. Within business, the changes are getting more and more adaptable but with the Indian tradition living styles, the education system still needs time for adaptation.

References

[1] Richard Process Appelbaum, William J. Chambliss "Sociology"

[2] Greetz, Clifford "The impact of culture on the Concept of man", 1968, The interpretation of culture, New York Basic books.

[3] http://vitalanalytics.in

[4] Indian leading newspaper "Times of India"

[5] TCS Generation Web 2.0 Trends 2008-09 Posted on August 04th, 2009

[6] Bellis, M. (2005) "Inventors of the Modern Computer?? retrieved September 3, 2005, from http://inventors.about.com/library/weekly/aa031599.htm/

[7] Seel, J. (1997) "Plugged in, spaced out, and turned on: electronic entertainment and moral mindfields,?? Academic Search Elite

vol.179, no.3, pp. 1-11 retrieved August 30, 2005, from Academic Search Elite database

[8] http://www.futureofchildren.org

[9] M/Cyclopedia of New Media (2004) "Virtual Identities?? retrieved August 28, 2005, from http://newmediawiki.ci.qut.edu.au/index.php/Virtual_Identities/

❒❒❒

21

E-Government and Knowledge Management

Subhash Chander, Ashwani Kush***

Abstract – *India is democratic developing nation. New technologies are taking birth day by day. In the modern world we make use of Internet for our daily routine work. In a democratic country like India Government is for the people, of the people and by the people. Hence needs of people must be taken into account. More stress is to be given to the needs of a common man who is residing at his native place and visited by the politicians only at the time of election to know about their problems-Government can help in sorting out some of the issues related to the rural public. The primary objectives of government is to provide the services citizens want, and with minimum cost and bureaucracy. E-government is not a panacea rather a tool*

*Assitant Professor (Computer Sc.), Govt. College, Sec-14, Karnal (Haryana)

**Associate Professor, University College, Kurukshetra University, Kurukshetra

to reduce certain problems. Now it has become necessity not a need. It can change the whole Scenario of functioning of a govt.? It would make the process easy that will be beneficial for the general public. In this paper it has been shown that by utilization of knowledge management and data mining techniques better e-government services can be provided to rural people at their native place in the modern information society.

Keywords – *E-Government, Knowledge Management, ICT, Data Mining.*

1. INTRODUCTION

Throughout the world the Internet is impacting all areas of life – business and politics as well as the cultural and private spheres. For some time the dynamism of these seismic changes has also been felt in the public sector – in the activity of local authorities, the State and administration [3]. In the today's world of IT there is a need of direct involvement of citizens and businesses in the process of e-government development. Many online delivery channels can be used by government officials to know needs of their citizen. Citizens wanted, but found out later they were only satisfying the needs of government departments and users weren't interested in using the services. E-Government should be about putting citizens and businesses at the heart of the process [1].There is no scarcity of information & knowledge and major part of this information is available with the government in Government records. Due to advent of Internet the Information has become manifold in this decade as compared to last forty years. The focus is also on the integrity of information created through electronic means and applications. As government services move online e-records will be used to confirm pensions and other entitlements, register births and deaths, verify citizenship, certify voting rights, enable the collection of taxes and censuses, support financial management and audits help resolve land claims, support litigation, document intergovernmental agreements, enable economic planning, document development, and support countless other information-intensive activities[2] . Hence there is need of adequate infrastructure for managing e-records; otherwise benefits of e-government can not be tapped [2]. In E-Government the primary interest of decision-makers is to make available the traditional spectrum of services in electronic form. Also much stress has also been given on this side. Just recently, however, more attention has also been paid to the inclusion of forms of direct democracy and immediate citizen participation.[3]. These two factors (providing services online and to take views of general public through direct democracy and immediate citizen participation) are the two sides of same coin. Hence there is also need to concentrate on both the factors.

2. E-GOVERNMENT

Generally, there is broad agreement on the definition of e-government and what it encompasses. There are, however, differences in scope, depending on government structure, budget allocations, resources, availability of skills and technology, and central government vision. For development teams just getting started, a good first step is to agree on your working definition of E-Government [1]. E-Government refers to the use by government agencies of information technologies (such as Wide Area Networks, the Internet, and mobile computing) that have the ability to transform relations with citizens, businesses, and other arms of government. These technologies can serve a variety of different ends in much better way by delivering of government services to citizens, improved interactions with business and industry, citizen empowerment through access to information, or more efficient government management. The resulting benefits can be less corruption, more transparency, greater convenience, revenue growth, and/or cost reductions. E-Government matures along E-Commerce development path that witnesses broadcasting, interaction, transaction, and finally integration. In broadcasting Government's presence is simply a presence having static web pages and one way communication. In Interaction mode websites are able to exchange information or services with citizens, where citizens can inquire, and obtain some resources from database backed websites located behind a portal. At the transaction stage general public can carry out (financial) transactions with the government. It requires higher levels of processing capability, as well as payment Gateways and security implementation and Finally in Integration stage when departments collaborate in significant ways to avoid duplication of efforts, and when a one-stop contact point, which is knowledgeable about the procedures of all involved departments, is created. Traditionally, we go in offices to accomplish our normal routine work and interaction between citizens or business and a government agency take place in a government office. Since the advent of World Wide Web (WWW) the global business environment has gone through a lot of changes particularly in the B2B and B2C sectors. That is the reason that Governments have started to adapt Internet and related technologies in various departments and it provides various benefits to general public. With emerging information and communication technologies (ICTs) it is possible to locate service centers closer to the clients. Such centers may be named Common Service Centers (CSCs) or Soochnalyas or Bharat Nirman Centres (BNCs). Puprpose will be to provide services, benefits to masses at their doorsteps. For a successful e-Government implementation, any country should adopt its own implementation approach, which is molded according to the unique characteristics of the country [4]. Even the developed countries have not been able to tap this resource fully. But it does not mean E-government is a tool limited to the richer countries. In Fact , some of the most innovative uses of the Internet & ICT in governance are appearing in the developing countries, like 'Web-based Blood Bank Management System' by Department of Health and Family Welfare, Government of Delhi[7] , 'Computerized Bus Pass System' by Delhi Transport Corporation[8], 'Community-owned Rural Intranet Kiosk ',by Government of Dhar District[9] and 'Management Information System for Education' by Education Department, Government of

Delhi[10] In India [6]. E-Government is also defined as utilizing the Internet and the world-wide-web for delivering government information and services to citizens as United Nations [11]. According to World Bank (2005) definition- Government refers to the use of IT by Government organizations, which have the ability to transform relations with the citizens, business and other arms of the Government. [4] E-government means different things to different people. Some observers define e-government in terms of specific actions: using a government kiosk to receive job information, applying for Social Security benefits through a web site, or creating shared databases for multiple agencies, as examples. Other observers define e-government more generally as automating the delivery of government services. While perceptions of e-government vary widely, some common themes can be identified that capture its evolutionary nature. E-government involves using information technology, and especially the Internet, to improve the delivery of government services to citizens, businesses, and other government agencies [12].

3. KNOWLEDGE MANAGEMENT & E-GOVERNMENT

Managing Knowledge is more challenging than managing information. Knowledge in peoples' mind obtained through a long process of their experience transformed their organization to knowledge based organization. Knowledge workers are the greatest organizational assets [14]. The objective of KM is to focus on organizational objectives, such as improved performance, competitive advantage, innovation, sharing of lessons learned, integration and continuous improvement of the organization. KM efforts can help individuals and groups to share valuable, organizational insights, to reduce redundant work, to avoid reinventing the wheel per se, to reduce training time to new employees, to retain intellectual capital as employees turnover in an organization and to adapt to changing environment and markets [5]. At this time the work of e-government is increasing and most of the Government Departments have created their own portal. How to manage all Government information resources effectively in the e-government, how to make users to facilitate the retrieval of information through e-government system, analysis and sharing better government services, how to enhance the image of the government, it is urgent need for the e-government construction and development of knowledge management. An organization's knowledge management framework consists of the creation, storage, transfer, and application processes. Knowledge is a competitive tool for e-government and effective knowledge management can produce knowledgeable informed leadership, sound strategic planning, and a better understanding of customers' needs. E-government that succeeds in the digital environment is likely to value knowledge and knowledge management and, as a result, to treat knowledge as an asset. Accordingly, developing organizational norms and values can support the creation and sharing of knowledge [20]. Knowledge management can build an effective knowledge precipitation, clear up various channels of information flow, realize knowledge sharing, and promote e-government's development. Knowledge Management has basically three subsystems namely knowledge collection, knowledge organization and knowledge application [13]. Knowledge management is needed to facilitate information exchange and transaction processing with citizens, as well as to enable inter-government knowledge sharing and integration. current e-government practice in developing economies is project-specific and not government-wide with the consequence that e-government impact often fizzles out at the level of a project and is not felt at the government level where decision-makers usually operate [19].

4. NEED OF KNOWLEDGE MANAGEMENT

Knowledge management has been described as a cultural shift from the old maxim that"knowledge is power" into a new state of mind which considers that "sharing knowledge is power." In developing countries, where governments usually suffer from low levels of trust coupled with low levels of citizens' technology acceptance, e-voting should be introduced cautiously. In such countries, knowledge management approaches can be utilized when introducing an e-voting process to accelerate citizens' acceptance of the process through increasing transparency. However, overall trust in the political system would clearly require a more comprehensive government overhaul of the economic, Societal and democratic approaches [18].Knowledge management can be defined as a process, applied by organizations, for acquiring, organizing, and communicating both tacit and explicit knowledge so that others may use the knowledge to be more effective and productive. Genearlly There is need of KM in three areas in public relationship, in various Govt. departments, and for coordination between Government departments. In public relationship there is need to answer citizen's e inquiries. The demand of these queries arises more prominently in the interaction and transaction phases of E-Government. In these stages people expect solution of their problems online which is neither possible nor feasible in the absence of proper knowledge management. Proper Knowledge Management also helps in reduction of duplication of same work in various departments.

5. KNOWLWDGE PORTALS IN E-GOVERNMENT

Information and knowledge is not created by Portals rather, but they can collect, organize, and distribute it and hence they are focus for information and knowledge exchange. Apart from providing functions specifically contributing to knowledge management, portals can provide their users many features, such as, email, chat rooms, personalized news, and a search engine, many of which benefit information and knowledge exchange [15]. Many state as well centre Governments have created their Portals but the these are not very much used. The reasons may include the development costs and effort, on-going maintenance and periodic pupation. If there is no updating on portals then it reduces the number of visitors and that becomes a total loss if the service is being provided to you at the cost of time and money. Among other causes of dissatisfaction may be out-of-date information, difficult-to-locate web sites, difficult-to-find information, lack of needs orientation, and dead links. Knowledge management portals are an extension of the portal concept, with the purpose of adding superior knowledge representation, search capabilities, and supporting knowledge workers in their activities. Knowledge management portals provide tools to extract, analyze and categorize both structured and unstructured information, and reveal the relationship between content, people, topics and user activities in the organization [15]. To build portals cost-effectively, governments use their portals as e-Commerce sites. Knowledge management portals are still at an early development stage, with no single leading technology.

6. DATA MINING AND TEXT IN E-GOVERNMENT

Data Mining is a technique in which various technologies for gathering, analyzing and storing and providing access to data a, are employed to help the decision maker in making decisions. It is a technique to draw out useful information from a large database. It is also known as analytical tool as it helps the user to analyze the data. From different fields, integrate them and identify the relationship between them [16]. Now a days data mining has become very popular for extracting appropriate information from raw data which has more value than when it was not mined. The data . which is presently in two forms structured and unstructured in the raw form does not usually help in adding to the knowledge and so data mining techniques are used to work over this data and torture it till it yields the knowledge which was required in the first phase and tools of torture are algorithms techniques of data mining usually comprising of pattern matching algorithms and artificial Intelligence methods [17]. Data mining can be utilized for deducing useful information for the general users from the database which is already available with the Government. Many types of services like checking the status of loan by a particular general man can be sent to him electronically. As this information is already available with the Government and a person who is in need of a loan would like to know how much time it would take. Such type of Information can be availed to users if we make proper use cf Data Mining and knowledge Management.The objective of data mining is to identify hidden useful relationships and patterns in existing large datasets, which makes it an important knowledge management technology. The result is typically the extraction of a relationship, formula, or rule that can be applied as a heuristic to complete future activities. Within e-government, the focus of data mining is predominantly on the management of interactions between the government and citizens or business. In these applications, data mining can extract knowledge from transaction data, can lower the burden of dealing with large volumes of transactions, and can improve decision making ability. Text mining applies data mining techniques to look for patterns in natural language text. Examples of text mining applications include screening email messages from customers in an organization, short listing resumes of job applicants. Text mining can be one of the important technologies in the future when large organizations, including government need to reply to their "customer" e-mail in fast, efficient, and meaningful manner. Already today, some organizations are using this technology as part of their e-mail response systems, but there is still great potential for the breadth of use and the quality of the technology's responses.

7. CONCLUSION

E-Government is the new challenge for public administration in the 21st century. Every society has always been a knowledge society in the sense that it has been using knowledge - formally and informally - in economic growth and in social development. However, the ICT revolution at the end of 20th century revamped the ways in which all knowledge can be created, harvested, assembled, combined, manipulated, enhanced and channeled. This increases the efficiency and effectiveness of using knowledge in economic growth and development to the extent that it is becoming the leading factor for adding value and for wealth creation in the market economy. In this Knowledge Age, intellect and creative, innovative and inventive ideas become a primary source of advantage and wealth. Therefore, a nation's capacity to develop systems that support the creation and application of knowledge within government, as well as throughout society, increases in importance and warrants greater consideration. E-Government indeed work with immense amount of information that is being used or created every day, there is also immense amount of knowledge (tacit and explicit) embedded in the bureaucracy and civil servants, so the need to manage the knowledge in an effective way is important. Kknowledge Management in the public sector can be a challenging task, especially when the state services evolve towards higher levels of electronic government. Public documents, legal elements, service descriptions and all forms of information stored in back-office and front-office systems Knowledge Management and Data mining techniques can help a lot in E-Government and provide solution of many problems faced by general public.

REFERENCES

[1] E-Government from a User's Perspective, a Report published in 2004 & available at http://egov.sonasi.com/

[2] Anni Thurston, "Fostering trust and transparency through information systems" Feb, 2005, Number 97 also available at http://egov.sonasi.com/

[3] Bertelsmann Foundation + Booz Allen Hamilton "Balanced E-Government" A report published in March 2002 & also available at www.begix.de

[4] W.G. Crishantha D. Nanayakkara, and Shahani Markus weerawarana "E-governance programme Implementation in Sri lanka" Volume 5 , Issue 12 , December 2009 , E-Gov, asia's monthly magazine on e-governance , also available at www.egovonline.net

[5] Rupinder Kaur, Munish Sethi "E-learning and Knowledge Management an evolving initiative for an evolving world", proceedings of the International Conference on Education Informatics (Edumatics-2010), May 22-23,2010 organised at CIET in association with INDO-US collaboration for Engineering Education.

[6] United Nations Department of Economic and Social Affairs (UN/DESA) "Compendium of Innovative e-Government practices: Volume 1", A report published in 2005 & available at http://egov.sonasi.com/

[7] Available at http://www.bloodbanksdelhi.com/

[8] Available at http://dtc.nic.in/

[9] Available at http://www.bloodbanksdelhi.com/

[10] Available at http://www.edudel.nic.in/

[11] Avaialable at www.unpan.org

[12] Available at www.fas.org/sgp/crs/RL31057.pdf

[13] Zhitian Zhou, Feipeng Gao, "E-Government and Knowledge Management "IJCSNS International Journal of Computer Science and Network Security, pp 285-289, Vol. 7 No. 6, June 2007

[14] Lai Prabhakar, S.Somokanta Singh & S. Keshorjit Singh "Gaining Competitive Advantage Through Knowledge Management" International Journal of Information Technology and Knowledge Management, January-June 2009, pp 61-64, Volume 2, No 1.

[15] Christian Wagner, Karen Cheung, Fion Lee and others "Enhancing E-government in Developing Countries: Managing Knowledge through Virtual Communities" EJISDC, (2003), pp 1-20, 14,4 and also Avaialble at http\\:www.ejisdc.org

[16] Sushil Kumar,Himanshu Aggarwal,Upinder Kaur & Sumati," E-governance and Data Mining: A methodology for e-voting", International Journal of Information Technology and Knowledge Management, January-June 2009, pp 139-144, Volume 2, No 1.

[17] Ajendra Issacs,Rajeev Paulus, Navendu Nitin and Narender Gupta," Data Mining for digital libraries- A New paradigm", Proceedings for 4th National Conference; IndiaCom-2010, Computing For Nation Development, February, 25-26, 2010, BVICAM, New Delhi

[18] Available at http://ssrn.com/abstract=1498505

[19] D.C. Misra, "Ten Guiding Principles for Knowledge Management in E-Government in Developing Countries" First International Conference on Knowledge Management for Productivity and Competitiveness, January 11-12, 2007, New Delhi organized by National Productivity Council, also available at http://www.npcindia.org/

[20] Xiaoni Zhang, Victor R. Prybutok, Jason H. Sharp," A Leadership Knowledge Management Model for E-Government: A Preliminary Empirical Test" Proceedings of the Fourteenth Americas Conference on Information Systems, Toronto, ON, Canada August 14th-17th 2008.

□□□

22

Security Concerns of Saodv, Aran, Ariadne and Sar Routing Protocols in Mobile Ad Hoc Networks

Sudesh K. Sharma, Bharat Bhushan***

Abstract – *Mobile Ad Hoc Network (MANET) consists of a collection of wireless mobile hosts which does not require any existing infrastructure or centralized access point such as base station. The dynamic topology of MANET works by allowing the nodes to join and leave the network at any point of time. So in the absence of any fixed infrastructure in mobile ad-hoc networks, it is difficult to utilize the existing techniques for network services, and faces number of various challenges in this area. The top most and the main challenge in MANET is to discover and maintain the security of the route and also in*

*Dept. of Statistics, Guru Nanak Khalsa College, Yamunanagar, Haryana, India. Email: atrisk@gmx.net

**Dept. of Computer Sc. & Applications, Guru Nanak Khalsa College, Yamunanagar, Haryana, India. Email: bharat_dhiman@sify.com

ensuring the security of the communication. Many of the ad hoc routing protocols that deal in security issues are dependent on implicit trust relationships to route packets among participating nodes. This paper provides a comparison of various on demand routing protocols for their security concerns. The objective is to standardize the parameters of the security concerns and making protocol robust.

1. INTRODUCTION

An ad hoc network is a group of wireless mobile computers (or nodes) in which nodes cooperate by forwarding packets for each other to allow them to communicate beyond direct wireless transmission range. Due to the absence of centralized administration or fixed network infrastructure, ad hoc networks can be quickly and inexpensively set up as and when needed like in military exercises and disaster relief. However, secure and reliable communication is a necessary prerequisite for such applications. In early time, the main emphasis of the researchers in ad hoc networking was to study the routing problems in a non adversarial network setting by making an assumption that they are working in trusted environment. So very little research has been done in a more realistic way to face the adverse situation where attempts are made to disrupt the communication. As a result current mobile ad hoc networks have no security mechanism. This openly invites the attackers to easily manipulate, exploit or disable the mobile ad hoc network. So far, secure routing protocols emerged but mainly depends on the key management, authentication and encryption algorithms used. These traditional routing protocols such as SAODV, SRP and SAR do not maintain a highly secured level route because it is not the part of their normal operation to maintain security. Therefore, special secure routing protocols are very much needed in mobile ad hoc networks to address security concerns.

2. SECURITY PROBLEMS

In the wired environment, the routing protocols are based on trust relationship of two participating nodes when exchanging routing information since a lot of routers in the internet usually have been operated by trustworthy companies. So security in wired environment is not a big problem. Current ad hoc routing protocols also trust all participants like wired environment because most of them uses the routing protocols of wired networks. Thus, the most ad hoc routing protocols cooperate and depend on their neighboring nodes to route packets. However, this native trust model allows a malicious attacker to manipulate and disrupt an entire ad hoc network in very easy way, such as inserting routing information which is wrong, incorrect and contains errors and mistakes. To achieve availability of ad hoc networks, routing protocols should be robust against this kind of malicious attacks [4, 9]. The common security threats in ad hoc routing protocols faces two kinds of attacks [4]. The first one is done by external attackers by inserting or injecting error generating routing information, replaying old routing information, or distorting routing information. In this an attacker could successfully partition a network or introduce excessive traffic load into the network by causing re-transmission and making the routing inefficient. The second one, which is more dangerous, is done by compromised nodes, which might deliver incorrect routing information to other nodes. In this attack, detection of such incorrect information and compromised node is very tough and difficult.

Attacks can either be passive or active ones [6]:

2.1 Passive attack

It means that the attacker does not obstruct the operation of a routing protocol but only attempts to recognize important information by listening to the routing traffic. The major advantage for the attacker in passive attacks is that in a wireless environment it is usually impossible to detect the attack. Moreover, routing information can reveal the relationships between the nodes; disclose their IP addresses, or even the network topology. If a route to a particular node is being used frequently than to other nodes, the attacker might understand that the node is important for the functioning of the network, and can make that particular node as a victim of his attack, which might bring the entire network down.

2.2 Active attack

Besides the passive attack, this active attack is performed by the attacker who can inject irresponsible and inconsistent packets into the network. The goal may be to attract packets inevitable to other nodes to the attacker for analysis or just to disable the network. A major difference is that an active attack can sometimes be detected. Here are some types of active attacks that can be easily performed in an ad hoc network.

(a) Black hole: The black hole attack is that a mischievous node uses the routing protocol to proclaim itself as having the shortest path to the node whose packets it wants to obstruct and make the route redirected to it. This redirection attack is possible in certain protocols, such as AODV [1]. The attacker listens to requests for routes. When the attacker receives a request for a route to the target node, the attacker creates a reply where an extremely short route is proclaimed. If the malicious reply reaches the requesting node before the reply from the actual node, a spurious or forged route has been created. Once the malicious device has been able to insert itself between the communicating nodes, it is able to do anything with the packets passing between them. It can choose to drop the packets to perform a denial-of-service (DOS) attack, or alternatively, use its place on the route as the first step in a man-in-the-middle attack.

(b) Routing table overflow: The attacker attempts to create route to non existent nodes. The goal of the attack is to make some node to create enough false routers to prevent new routes from being created or overwhelm the protocol. In recent routing protocols, proactive routing algorithms attempt to discover routing information even before they are needed, while reactive algorithms create only when they are needed. This nature makes proactive algorithms more exposed to this kind of attack [9].

(c) Sleep deprivation: Usually, this persecution is practical only in ad hoc networks, where battery life is a critical parameter. Battery powered devices try to conserve energy by transmitting only when absolutely necessary. An attacker can attempt to consume batteries by requesting routes, or by forwarding unnecessary packets to the node. This attack is especially suitable against devices that do not offer any services to the network or offer services only to those who have some special recommendations. Regardless of the properties of the services, a node must participate in the routing process unless and until it is willing to become unreachable to the network.

(d) Impersonation: Current ad hoc routing protocols do not authenticate source IP address. IP address information of a packet can be simply modified by the compromised node or malicious attacker and even MAC address can be changed since most open source device drivers now allow the user to change the MAC address [11]. A malicious node can launch many attacks by altering its MAC or IP address. Both AODV and DSR [1, 9] are influenced to this attack.

3. SECURED PROTOCOLS

Many existing schemes have been studied for secured routing. Some of the studied protocols discussed here are ARAN, ARIDANE, SAODV and SAR.

(A) ARAN [5]: Dahill et al. proposed ARAN [5], which assumes managed-open environment, where there is a possibility for pre-deployment of infrastructure. It consists of two distinct stages. The first stage is the certification and end-to-end authentication stage. Here the source gets a certificate from the trusted certification server and then, using this certificate, signs the request packet. Each intermediate node in turn signs the request with its certificate. The destination then verifies each of the certificates, thus the source gets authenticated and so do the intermediate nodes. The destination node then sends the reply along the route reverse to the one in the request, using the certificate of the destination. The second stage is a non-mandatory stage used to discover the shortest path to the destination, but this stage is computationally expensive. It is prone to reply attacks using error messages unless the nodes have time synchronization. Authenticated Routing for Ad-hoc Networks (ARAN) detects and protects against malicious actions by third parties and peers in Ad-hoc environment. ARAN introduces authentication, message integrity and non-repudiation to an Ad-hoc environment [7].

Characteristics:

(i) ARAN is able to take care of Replay attacks

(ii) It is able to eliminate Rushing attacks

(iii) It does not effectively deals with location disclosure

(iv) It has no provision for Black Hole and Worm Hole

(v) It does not secure for the Denial Of service (DOS) attack

(vi) ARAN is loop free

(vii) It is based on online trusted certification authority

(B) Secure AODV (SAODV): Secure AODV (SAODV) [2, 3] is a security extension of the AODV protocol, based on public key cryptography. SAODV routing messages (RREQs, RREPs, and RERRs) are digitally signed to guarantee their integrity and authenticity. Therefore, a node that generates a routing message assigns it with its private key and the nodes that receive this message verify the signature using the sender's public key. The hop count cannot be signed by the sender, because it must be incremented at every hop. Therefore, to protect it (i.e., not allow malicious intermediate nodes to decrement it), a mechanism based on hash chains is used. In its basic form, this makes it impossible for intermediate nodes to reply to RREQs if they have a route towards the destination, because the RREP message must be signed by the destination node. To preserve the combination mechanism of AODV, SAODV includes a kind of delegation feature that allows intermediate nodes to reply to RREQ messages. This is called the double signature. When a node A generates a RREQ message, in addition to the regular signature, it can include a second signature, which is computed on a fictitious RREP message towards A itself. Intermediate nodes can store this second signature in their routing table, along with other routing information related to node A. If one of these nodes then receives a RREQ towards node A, it can reply on behalf of A with a RREP message, similarly to what happens with regular AODV. To do so, the intermediate node generates the RREP message, includes the signature of node A that it previously cached, and signs the message with its own private key.

SAODV does not require additional messages with respect to AODV. Nevertheless, SAODV messages are convincingly bigger, mostly because of digital signatures. Moreover, SAODV requires heavy weight asymmetric cryptographic operations. Every time a node generates a routing message, it must generate a signature, and every time it receives a routing message (also as an intermediate node), it must verify a signature. This gets worse when the double signature mechanism is used, because this may require the generation or verification of two signatures for a single message. In the SAODV operations, SAODV allows to authenticate the AODV routing data. Two mechanisms are used to achieve these signatures and hash chains as SAODV digital signatures and signature extension.

Characteristics:

(a) SAODV is able to take care of Replay attacks

(b) It is not able to eliminate Rushing attacks

(c) It does not effectively deal with location disclosure

(d) It has no provision for Black Hole and Worm Hole

(e) It does not secure for the Denial Of service (DOS) attack

(f) SAODV uses online key management scheme for acquisition and verification of keys

(g) It is loop free and uses Distance as routing metric

(C) Security Aware ad hoc Routing (SAR): There is another approach to secure the ad hoc routing protocol motivated from traditional wired routing matrices where same security levels of nodes incorporate each other [10]. Instead of discovering the shortest path between two nodes,

Security Aware Ad Hoc Routing (SAR) protocol can discover a path with desired security attributes, such as a path through nodes with a particular shared key. For this purpose to determining a secure route, the information in the routing messages must be protected against alteration that can change routing behavior. A node initiating route discovery determines the required minimal trust level for nodes participating in the query and reply propagation. Since only nodes at each trust level share equal encryption keys, intermediate nodes of different levels cannot decrypt in-transit

routing packets or determine whether the required security attributes can be satisfied and then drop them. Only the nodes with the correct key can read the header and forward the packet. So, if a packet has reached the destination, it must have been propagated by nodes at the same level. Therefore, Routes discovered by SAR come with "quality of protection" guarantees. One of the merits SAR has is that it can be implemented based on any on-demand ad hoc routing protocol with suitable modification. The security metric can be embedded into RREQ packet. It also showed the practical implementation and experimental data by mixing with AODV [10].

Characteristics:

(a) It uses Security requirement as Routing metric

(b) SAR is loop free

(c) SAR uses Key distribution or secret sharing mechanism

(d) SAR is not loop free, it depends upon selected security requirement

(e) It is able to take care of Replay attacks

(f) It is not able to eliminate Rushing attacks

(g) It does not effectively deals with location disclosure

(h) It does secure for Denial Of service (DOS) attack

(D) ARIADNE: It is a Secure On Demand Routing Protocol for Ad Hoc Networks (ARIADNE) using the TESLA [10] broadcast authentication protocol for authenticating routing messages, since TESLA is efficient and adds only a single message [8] authentication code (MAC) to a message for broadcast authentication. Adding a MAC (computed with a shared key) to a message can provide secure authentication in point-to-point communication; for broadcast communication, however, multiple receivers need to know the MAC key for verification, which would also allow any receiver to forge packets and impersonate the sender. Secure broadcast authentication thus requires an asymmetric primitive, such that the sender can generate valid authentication information, but the receivers can only verify the authentication information. It is used with DSR. It is prone to selfish node attack. It prevents attackers from tampering uncompromised routes.

Characteristics:

(a) ARIADNE is able to take care of Replay attacks and immune to wormhole attack
(b) It is able to eliminate Rushing attacks
(c) It does not effectively deal with location disclosure
(d) It has no provision for Black Hole.
(e) It does secure for Denial Of service
(f) It uses TESLA keys distributed to participating nodes
(g) It is loop free and uses Distance as Routing metric.

4. CONCLUSION

An analysis has been made on various routing schemes with regards to their security issues. A detailed study has been carried out for a few ad hoc networks and security problems. Their characteristics, merits and demerits have been elaborated. Ad hoc networking is still in its infancy as can be seen with the problems that exist in these networks and the emerging solutions. There is a need to make them more secure and robust to adapt to the demanding requirements of their users. It remains a challenging task to design routing protocols resistant to multiple attacks.

REFERENCES

[1] A. Kush, P. Gupta, R. Kumar; "Performance Comparison of Wireless Routing Protocols", Journal of CSI, Vol. 35 No.2, April-June 2005.

[2] Ashwani Kush, "Performance Evaluation of Protocols for Secure Routing over MANET", Proceedings of the 4th National Conference; INDIACom-2010 Computing For Nation Development, February 25 – 26, 2010 Bharati Vidyapeeth's Institute of Computer Applications and Management, New Delhi.

[3] A. Kush, V. Rishiwal, "A SECURE ROUTING PROTOCOL FOR WIRELESS AD HOC NETWORKS", Proceedings of International Cryptology Workshop and Conference, Malaysia, ICIIS 2008.

[4] L. Zhou and Z. J. Haas. "Securing Ad Hoc Networks", IEEE Network Magazine, 13(6), 1999.

[5] B. Dahill, B. N. Levine, E. Royer and C. Shields, "A secure routing protocol for ad hoc networks", Technical Report UM-CS-2001-037, University of Massachusetts, Department of Computer Science, Aug. 2001.

[6] Janne Lundberg, "Routing Security in Ad Hoc Networks", Telecommunication Software and Multimedia Laboratory, Helsinki University of Technology.

[7] Hongmei Deng, Wei Li, and Dharma P. Agrawal, "Routing Security in Wireless Ad Hoc Networks", IEEE Communications Magazine October 2002.

[8] Y.C. Hu, A. Perrig and D. Johnson, "Ariadne: A secure on-demand routing protocol for ad hoc networks", Technical Report TR01-383, Rice University, Dec. 2001.

[9] Arun Kumar Bayya et al. "Security in ad hoc network", University of Kentucky.

[10] A. Perrig, R. Canetti, D. Tygar, and D. Song, "TESLA Broadcast Authentication Protocol, RSA Cryptobytes (RSA Laboratories)", Vol. 5, No. 2, Summer/Fall 2002, pp. 2-13.

[11] Russ Housley and William Arbaugh, "Security problems in 802.11-based networks", Communication of the ACM, Vol. 46. No. 5, pages 31-34, May 2003.

23

Modelling of Web Search Engine

*Shikha Singh**

Abstract – *A Web search engine is a search engine designed to search for information on the World Wide Web. Information may consist of web pages, images, information and other types of files. Some search engines also mine data available in newsbooks, databases, or open directories. Unlike Web directories, which are maintained by human editors, search engines operate algorithmically or are a mixture of algorithmic and human input. In this paper I have discussed the web search engine and how they can model and implement to retrieve the information.*

1. INTRODUCTION

Web search engines work by storing information about many web pages, which they retrieve from the WWW itself.[1] These pages are retrieved by a Web crawler (sometimes also

*(Lecturer, Department of Computer Science & Engineering), Ideal Institute of Technology, *Sadarpur-Sikroad, Behind Govind Puram, Ghaziabad* (U.P.) Tel.: 0120-2768481,2767351,2767818

known as a spider) an automated Web browser which follows every link it sees. Exclusions can be made by the use of robots.txt. The contents of each page are then analyzed to determine how it should be indexed (for example, words are extracted from the titles, headings, or special fields called meta tags). Data about web pages are stored in an index database for use in later queries. Some search engines, such as Google, store all or part of the source page (referred to as a cache) as well as information about the web pages, whereas others, such as AltaVista, store every word of every page they find.[2] This cached page always holds the actual search text since it is the one that was actually indexed, so it can be very useful when the content of the current page has been updated and the search terms are no longer in it. This problem might be considered to be a mild form of linkrot, and Google's handling of it increases usability by satisfying user expectations that the search terms will be on the returned webpage. This satisfies the principle of least astonishment since the user normally expects the search terms to be on the returned pages. Increased search relevance makes these cached pages very useful, even beyond the fact that they may contain data that may no longer be available elsewhere.

When a user enters a query into a search engine (typically by using key words), the engine examines its index and provides a listing of best-matching web pages according to its criteria, usually with a short summary containing the document's title and sometimes parts of the text. Most search engines support the use of the boolean operators AND, OR and NOT to further specify the search query. Some search engines provide an advanced feature called proximity search which allows users to define the distance between keywords.

2. USAGE OF SEARCH ENGINES

The usefulness of a search engine depends on the relevance of the result set it gives back. While there may be millions of webpages that include a particular word or phrase, some pages may be more relevant, popular, or authoritative than others. Most search engines employ methods to rank the results to provide the "best" results first. How a search engine decides which pages are the best matches, and what order the results should be shown in, varies widely from one engine to another.[3] The methods also change over time as Internet usage changes and new techniques evolve.

A web crawler (also known as a web spider, web robot, or especially in the FOAF community web scutter) is a program or automated script that browses the World Wide Web in a methodical, automated manner. Other less frequently used names for web crawlers are ants, automatic indexers, bots, and worms.

This process is called web crawling or spidering. Many sites, in particular search engines, use spidering as a means of providing up-to-date data. Web crawlers are mainly used to create a copy of all the visited pages for later processing by a search engine that will index the downloaded pages to provide fast searches. Crawlers can also be used for automating maintenance tasks on a website, such as checking links or validating HTML code. Also, crawlers can be used to gather specific types of information from Web pages, such as harvesting e-mail addresses (usually for spam).

A web crawler is one type of bot, or software agent. In general, it starts with a list of URLs to visit, called the seeds. As the crawler visits these URLs, it identifies all the hyperlinks in the page and adds them to the list of URLs to visit, called the crawl frontier.[4] URLs from the frontier are recursively visited according to a set of policies.

3. STANDARD CRAWLER

Crawler with one thread that uses 'depth first' searching when searching a repository. This crawler type is aimed at searching repositories with moderate CPU usage.

Web crawler – Crawler with one thread that uses 'breadth first' searching when searching a repository. This crawler type is aimed at searching Web repositories with moderate CPU usage.

Crawler with several threads – Crawler with more than one thread that uses 'breadth first' searching when searching a repository. This crawler type is aimed at searching repositories with high CPU usage.

4. ARCHITECTURE OF A SCALABLE WEB CRAWLER

The basic algorithm executed by any web crawler takes a list of *seed URLs* as its input and repeatedly executes the following steps. Remove a URL from the URL list, determine the IP address of its host name, download the corresponding document, and extract any links contained in it. For each of the extracted links, ensure that it is an absolute URL (derelativizing it if necessary), and add it to the list of URLs to download, provided it has not been encountered before. If desired, process the downloaded document in other ways (e.g., index its content).[5] This basic algorithm requires a number of functional components:

- a component (called the *URL frontier*) for storing the list of URLs to download;
- a component for resolving host names into IP addresses;
- a component for downloading documents using the HTTP protocol;
- a component for extracting links from HTML documents; and
- a component for determining whether a URL has been encountered before.

This paper describes how Mercator refines this basic algorithm, and the particular implementations we chose for the various components.[6] Where appropriate, we comment on design alternatives and the tradeoffs between them.

Scalable web crawlers are an important component of many web services, but they have not been very well documented in the literature. Building a scalable crawler is a non-trivial endeavor because the data manipulated by the crawler is too big to fit entirely in memory, so there are performance issues relating to how to balance the use of disk and memory. This paper has enumerated the main components required in any scalable crawler, and it has discussed design alternatives for those components.

In particular, the paper described Mercator, an extensible, scalable crawler written entirely in Java.

Mercator's design features a crawler core for handling the main crawling tasks, and extensibility through protocol and processing modules. Users may supply new modules for performing customized crawling tasks. We have used Mercator for a variety of purposes, including performing random walks on the web, crawling our corporate intranet, and collecting statistics about the web at large.[7]

Although our use of Java as an implementation language was somewhat controversial when we began the project, we have not regretted the choice. Java's combination of features including threads, garbage collection, objects, and exceptions made our implementation easier and more elegant. Moreover, when run under a high-quality Java runtime, Mercator's performance compares well to other web crawlers for which performance numbers have been published.

Mercator's scalability design has worked well. It is easy to configure the crawler for varying memory footprints. For example, we have run it on machines with memory sizes ranging from 128 MB to 2 GB.

The ability to configure Mercator for a wide variety of hardware platforms makes it possible to select the most cost-effective platform for any given crawling task. Mercator's extensibility features have also been successful. As mentioned above, we have been able to adapt Mercator to a variety of crawling tasks, and as stated earlier, the new code was typically quite small (tens to hundreds of lines). Java's dynamic class loading support meshes well with Mercator's extensibility requirements, and its object-oriented nature makes it easy to write variations of existing modules using sub classing. Writing new modules is also simplified by providing a range of general purpose reusable classes, such as classes for recording histograms and other statistics.

Mercator is scheduled to be included in the next version of the *AltaVista Search Intranet* product, a version of the AltaVista software sold mostly to corporate clients who use it to crawl and index their intranets.

A focused crawler or topical crawler is a web crawler that attempts to download only web pages that are relevant to a pre-defined topic or set of topics. Topical crawling generally assumes that only the topic is given, while focused crawling also assumes that some labeled examples of relevant and not relevant pages are available. Topical crawling was first introduced by Menczer.

Internet bookmarks are stored Web page locations (URLs) that can be retrieved. As a feature of all modern Internet web browsers, their primary purpose is to easily catalog and access web pages that a user has visited and chosen to save. Saved links are called "favorites" in Internet Explorer, and by virtue of the browser's large market share, the term favorite has been synonymous with bookmark since the early days of widely-distributed browsers. Bookmarks are normally visible in a browser menu and stored on the user's computer, and commonly a folder metaphor is be used for organization. In addition to bookmarking methods within most browsers, many external applications exist for bookmark management.[8]

Bookmarks have been incorporated in browsers since the Mosaic browser in 1993. Bookmark lists were called Hotlists in Mosaic and in previous versions of Opera; this term has faded from common use. Other early web browsers such as Viola WWW and Cello also had bookmarking features.

Bookmarks are a fundamental feature of web browsers, but some users have expressed frustration with bookmark collections that become disorganized and have looked for other tools to help manage their links. These tools include browser synchronizers and desktop applications.

HTTP cookies, more commonly referred to as Web cookies, tracking cookies or just cookies, are parcels of text sent by a server to a Web client (usually a browser) and then sent back unchanged by the client each time it accesses that server. HTTP cookies are used for authenticating, session tracking (state maintenance), and maintaining specific information about users, such as site preferences or the contents of their electronic shopping carts. The term "cookie" is derived from "magic cookie," a well-known concept in UNIX computing which inspired both the idea and the name of HTTP cookies.

Because they can be used for tracking browsing behavior, cookies have been of concern for Internet privacy. As a result, they have been subject to legislation in various countries such as the United States, as well as the European Union. Cookies have also been criticized because the identification of users they provide is not always accurate and because they could potentially be a target of network attackers. Some alternatives to cookies exist, but each has its own uses, advantages, and drawbacks.

Cookies are also subject to a number of misconceptions, mostly based on the erroneous notion that they are computer programs. In fact, cookies are simple pieces of data unable to perform any operation by themselves. In particular, they are neither spyware nor viruses, although cookies from certain sites are described as spyware by many anti-spyware products because they allow users to be tracked when they visit various sites.

Most modern browsers allow users to decide whether to accept cookies, but rejection makes some websites unusable.[9] For example, shopping carts implemented using cookies do not work if cookies are rejected

A progress indicator is an element of a command line interface, a textual user interface, or a graphical user interface that is intended to inform the user that an operation is in progress, to reassure that the system is not hung or waiting for user input, and often to provide the user with an estimate of how far through a task the system has progressed.

5. EXAMPLES OF PROGRESS INDICATORS

A progress bar is a component in a graphical user interface used to convey the progress of a task, such as a download or file transfer. Often, the graphic is accompanied by a textual representation of the progress in a percent format. A more recent development is the indeterminate progress bar, which is used in situations where the extent of the task is unknown or the progress of the task can not be determined in a way that could be expressed as a percentage.[10] This bar uses motion or some other indicator to show that progress is taking place, rather than using the size of the filled portion to show the total amount of progress, making it more like a throbber than a progress bar.

6. CONCLUSION

A web search engine is designed to search for information on the World Wide Web and FTP servers. The search results are generally presented in a list of results and are often called hits. The information may consist of web pages, images, information and other types of files. Some search engines also mine data available in databases or open directories. Unlike Web directories, which are maintained by human editors, search engines operate algorithmically or are a mixture of algorithmic and human input. Most Web search engines are commercial ventures supported by advertising revenue and, as a result, some employ the practice of allowing advertisers to pay money to have their listings ranked higher in search results. Those search engines which do not accept money for their search engine results make money by running search related ads alongside the regular search engine results. The search engines make money every time someone clicks on one of these ads.

REFERENCES

[1] Y. Hafri and C. Djeraba. High performance crawling system. In Proceedings of the 6th ACM SIGMM international workshop on Multimedia information retrieval, pages 299–306. ACM Press, 2004.

[2] M. Henzinger, A. Heydon, M. Mitzenmacher, and M. Najork. On near–uniform url sampling. In Proceedings of the Ninth Conference on World Wide Web, pages 295–308, Amsterdam, Netherlands, May 2000. Elsevier Science.

[3] M. Hersovici, M. Jacovi, Y. S. Maarek, D. Pelleg, M. Shtalhaim, and S. Ur. The shark-search algorithm. An application: tailored Web site mapping. In Proceedings of the seventh conference on World Wide Web, pages 317–326. Elsevier Science, April 1998.

[4] T. E. Anderson, M. D. Dahlin, J. M. Neefe, D. A. Patterson, D. S. Roselli, and R. Y. Wang. Serverless network .le systems. In Proc. of SOSP, 1995.

[5] A. Barabasi and R. Albert. Emergence of scaling in random networks. Science, 286(509), 1999.

[6] A. Z. Broder, S. R. Kumar, F. Maghoul, P. Raghavan, S. Rajagopalan, R. Stata, A. Tomkins, and J. L. Wiener. Graph structure in the web. In Proc. of WWW Conf., 2000.

[7] A. Heydon and M. Najork. High-performance web crawling. Technical report, SRC Research Report, 173, Compaq Systems Research Center, September 2001.

[8] D. Hirschberg. Parallel algorithms for the transitive closure and the connected component problem. In Proc. of STOC Conf., 1976.

[9] D. Nassimi and S. Sahni. Parallel permutation and sorting algorithms and a new generalized connection network. Journal of ACM, 29:642–667, July 1982.

[10] M. T. Ozsu and P. Valduriez. Principles of Distributed Database Systems. Prentice Hall, 1999.

24

Methodology and Implementation of Databases in Multimedia

Dr. Sudhir Dawra, Manisha***

Abstract – *Multimedia may include text, spoken audio, music, images, animation, and video. The large amounts of data required for computer multimedia files makes CD-ROMs a good option for storage; but there are other ways of receiving multimedia communications, such as the Web. Our houses will be wired for Bandwidth to handle interactive multimedia applications. Our high definitions TV/ Computers/ 'workstations will have access to a large number of databases including digital libraries that will distribute vast amount of multi-source multimedia content. This paper deals with various aspects of multimedia database.*

*(HOD & Associate Professor, Department of Computer Science & Engineering), Ideal Institute of Technology, *Sadarpur-Sikroad, Behind Govind Puram, Ghaziabad* (U.P.) Tel.: 0120-2768481,2767351,2767818 Email: {dawra1211@yahoo.com}

**(Lecturer, Department of Computer Science & Engineering) Al- Falah School of Engineering and Technology, Dhuaj, Faridabad, Haryana-12004 (India) Tel.: 0129-2206223, 2206593

Some of them are as follows: Types of multimedia data available, Data-management issues, Retrieval and storage methods, Research issues and Search Engines used for multimedia.

1. MULTIMEDIA DATABASES

The dramatic development of computer technology in the last decades, we have seen a growing interest in supporting multimedia data, Compared with traditional data, the most noticeable features of multimedia data are their spatiality (the spatial layout of objects and their relationships), temporality (time-dependence in media such as video and audio) and presentation requirements (imposed in response to years queries, such as synchronization of different media)[1]. The intensive use of multimedia documents in a variety of formats and at different level of quality demand on optimized storage of multimedia documents together with the integration of knowledge on multimedia formats into web servers and clients For example, Video Database System. The availability of video as an accessible media leads to a new set of applications including video conferencing, video telephony, movie-on-demand, and distance learning, most of these applications however assume the viability of constructing substantial databases of video content.

2. NATURE OF MULTIMEDIA APPLICATIONS

Multimedia data may be stored, delivered, and utilized in many different ways. Applications may be categorized based on their data management characteristic as follows:

Repository Application: A large amounts of multimedia data as well as metadata is stored for retrieval purposes. A central repository containing multimedia data may be maintained by DBMS and may be organized into a hierarchy of storage levels-local disks, tertiary disks and tapes, optical disks, so on. Examples include repositories of satellite images, engineering drawings and designs, space photographs and radiology-scanned pictures.

Presentation Application: A large number of applications involve deliver multimedia data subject to temporal constraints. Audio and video data are delivered his way in these application optimal viewing and listening condition require the DBMS to deliver data at certain rate offering "quality of service".[2] Data is consumed as it is delivered, unlike in repository applications, sphere it may be processed later simple multimedia viewing of video data requires a system VCR like functionality. Complex and interactive multimedia presentations involve orchestration directions to control the retrieval order of component in a series or in parallel. Interactive environment must support capabilities such as real editing analysis or annotating of video audio data.

Collaborative work using multimedia information: There is a new category of application in which engineers may execute a complex design task by merging drawing, fitting subjects to design constraints, and generating new documentation, change notification, and so forth, intelligent healthcare networks as well as telemedicine will involve doctors collaborating among themselves, analyzing multimedia patient data information in real time as it is generated.

3. DATA MANAGEMENT ISSUES

Multimedia applications dealing with thousands of images, documents, audio and video segments, and free text data depend critically on appropriate modeling of the structure and content of data and then designing appropriate database schemas for storing and retrieving multimedia information.[3] Multimedia information systems are very complex and embrace a large set of issues, including the following:

Modeling: This area has the potential for applying database versus information retrieval techniques to the problem. There are problems for dealing with complex object made up of a wide range of types of data: numeric, text, graphics, animated graphic image, audio stream, and video sequence.

Design: The conceptual, logic, and physical design of multimedia databases has not been addressed fully, and it remains an area of active research. The design process can be based on the general methodology, but performance and tuning issues at each level are far more complex.

Storage: Storage of multimedia data on standard dislike devices present's problems of representation, compression, mapping to device hierarchies, archiving, and buffering during the input/output operation. Adhering to standards such as JPEG or MPEG is one way most vendors of multimedia product are likely to deal with this issue. In DBMS, a" BLOB"(binary large object) facility allows untyped bitmaps to be store and retrieved. Standardized software will be required to deal with synchronization and compression/decompression will be coupled with indexing problems.

Queries and Retrieval: The "database" way of retrieving information is based on query language and internal index structures. The "information retrieval" way relies strictly on keywords or predefined Index terms. For Images, video data, and audio data, this opens up many issues, among them efficient query formulation, query execution, and optimization. It is believed that true multimedia database systems provide content-based retrieval facilities. Multimedia objects in such a database are first-class citizens. It should be possible to formulate queries referring to several types of data simultaneously.[4] The querying strategy used in Multimedia database is known *as* Query-by-example. A somewhat related strategy to find interesting documents in a multimedia database is the navigational querying paradigm. Similar document are grouped arte together and by wandering through the search you can and answers to the queries.

Performance: For multimedia applications involving only documents and text, the user subjectively determines performance constraints. For application involving video playback or audio-video synchronization, physical limitations dominate. For instance, video must be delivered at a steady rate of 60 frames per second Techniques for query optimization may compute expected response time before evaluating the query. The use of parallel processing of data may alleviate some problems, but such efforts are currently subject to further experimentation.

4. OPEN RESEARCH PROBLEMS

Databases versus Information Retrieval Perspectives: Modeling data constrain has not been an issue in database model and systems because the data has structure and the meaning of a data instance can be informed from the sachems contrast information retrieval (IR) is mainly concerned with modeling the contain text document (through the use of keyword, Phrasal indexes, semantic is networking word frequencies sounder encoding and so on) for which structure is generating neglected. By modeling content, the system can determine whether a document relevant to a query by examining the content descriptors of the document. for example, an insurance company's accident claim report as a multimedia object includes images of accident, structured insurance forms.[5] Audio recording of parties involved in the accident, the text report of insurance company representative multimedia information such as this? How should queries of formulated against this data? Efficient execution thus becomes a complex issues and the semantic heterogeneity and representational complexity of multimedia information gives rise to many new problems.

Requirements of Multimedia/ Hypermedia data Modeling and Retrieval: Capture the full expressive power of multimedia data modeling, the system show have a general construct that lets the user specify links between any two arbitrate nodes. Hypermedia links or hyperlinks have a number of different characteristic Links can be specified with or without associated information, and they may have large descriptions associated with them. Links can start from a specific point with a node or form the whole node. Links can be directional or non-directional when they into account all of these variations. When content-based retrieval of multimedia data is needed the query mechanism should have access to the links and the link-associated information the system should provide facilities for defining views over all links-private and public. Valuable contextual information can be obtained from the structure information. Automatically generated hypermedia links do not reveal any thing about the two nodes, and in contrast to manually generated hypermedia links would have different significance. Facilities for creating and utilizing such link as well as developing and using navigational query languages to utilize the links are important features of any system permitting effective use of multimedia information.

Indexing of Images: There are approaches to indexing images: (1) identify object automatically through image processing techniques, and (2) assign index terms and phrases through manual indexing. An important problem in using image-processing techniques to index pictures relates to scalability. The current state of the art allows the indexing of only simple patterns in images Complete increases with the number of the art allows the indexing of only simple patterns images. Complexity increases with the number recognizable features. Another important problem relates to the complexity of the query. Rules and inference mechanisms can be used to derive higher-level facts from simpler features images. This allows high-level queries like" find hotel buildings that have Open foyers and allow maximum sunshine in the front desk area" in an architecture application.

The information retrieval approach to image indexing is based on one of this indexing schemes:

Classificatory systems: Classifies images hierarchically into predetermined categories. In this approach, the indexer and the user should have a good knowledge of the available categories. Finer details of a complex image and relationships among objects in an image cannot be captured.

Keyword-based systems: Users an indexing vocabulary similarity to that used in the indexing of textual documents, Simple facts represented in the images (like "ice capped region") and facts derived as a result of high-level interpretation by humans like permanent ice, recent snowfall and polar ice) can be captured

Entity attribute relationship system: all object in the picture and the relation ship between object and the attributes of the object are identified

Problems in Text Retrieval: Text retrieval has always been the key feature in business application and library systems, and although much work has gone into some of the following problems, there remains an ongoing need for improvement, especially regarding the following issues

Phrase indexing: Substantial improvements can be realized if phrase descriptions (as opposed to single-word terms) are assigned to documents and used in queries, provided that these descriptors are good indicators of document content and information need.

Use of thesaurus: One reason for the poor recall of current systems is that the vocabulary of the user differs from the vocabulary used to index the documents. One solution is to use a thesaurus to expand the user's query with related terms.[6] The problem then becomes one of finding a thesaurus for the domain of interest.

Resolving ambiguity: One of the reasons for low precision in text information retrieval systems is that words have multiple meanings. One way to resolve ambiguity is to use an on-line dictionary another is to compare the contexts in which the two words occur.

5. MULTIMEDIA DATABASE APPLICATIONS

Large-scale applications of multimedia databases can be expected to encompass a large number of disciplines and enhance existing capabilities. Some important applications will be involved:

Documents and records management: A large number of industries and businesses keep very detailed records and a variety of documents the data may include engineering design and manufacturing data medical record of patients publishing materials encyclopedia and repositories of in formation on many topic.

Knowledge dissemination: the multimedia mode, a very effective means of knowledge dissemination, will encompass a phenomenal growth in electronic books, catalogs, manuals, encyclopedia and repositories of information on many topics.

Education and training: Teaching materials for different audiences from kindergarten students to equipment operators to professional can be designed from multimedia sources. Digital libraries are expected to have a major influence on the way future students and researchers as well as other users will access vast repositories of educational material.

Marketing advertising, retailing, entertaining, and travel: There are virtually no limits to using multimedia information in these applications-from effective sales presentations to virtual tours of cities and art galleries. The film industry has already shown the power of special effects in creating animations and synthetically designed animals, aliens, and special effects.[8] The use of pre-designed stored objects in multimedia databases will expand the range of these applications.

Real-time control and monitoring: Coupled with active database technology. Multimedia presentation of information can be very effective means for monitoring and controlling complex tasks such as manufacturing operations, nuclear power plants, patients in intensive care unit and transportation systems,

6. MULTIMEDIA STORAGE AND RETRIEVAL

There are 3 requirements for the support of multimedia databases that differ from the support of relational databases:

1. Volume of data. For example one compressed video frame typically exceeds 10 KB consequently, 30 frames per second requires a volume of over 300 KB/s- far more than that required by typical relational queries.

2. Continuity within each video or audio stream (i.e., inter-frame and inter-segment time constraints)

3. Synchronization of multiple streams of data (e.g., video, closed caption, left speaker's audio). We note that individual streams of data should not be viewed as separate clients.

Furthermore, interleaving is impractical if the only difference is say closed captioning or foreign language subtitles for a video.

Resources of Consider

Network

Bandwidth.

Communications protocols

Buffering

Disk Bandwidth

Amount of data that can be read per unit of time

CPU

May be needed for decompression; however, JPEG and MPEG hardware decoders

Exist

Disk buffers to facilitate I/O

Admission Control and Buffer Allocation

These policies are influenced by a number of factors:

The reference patterns of query (e.g.. pause, fast forward. Rewind) we call this the "demand" side. From an operating systems perspective, the reference patterns in programs are typically too complicated to analyze and predict. In relational DBMS's however, reference patterns are defined by the relational algebra (6 basic operations). Good RDBMS's can exploit reference 'patterns for performance gains with multimedia databases. The reference patterns are simpler than those for Relational database since the types of queries tend to be quite limited (and hence it is easier to determine and calculate the demand side) the number of buffers available at the time the query is serviced. We call this the supply side. Quires in multimedia database are not unless an adequate number of buffers exist. The characteristics of all active queries in the system

Continuous Media Streams

Each video or audio stream typically has a fixed display rate. The display rate is what the user sees and is concerned with. The consumption rate, on the other hand is determined from the perspective of the disk(s). In an uncompressed stream, the display rate equal the consumption rate in a compressed stream there are 2 scenarios:

With constant compression "r" (e.g. JPEG),

display_rate = r*consumption_rate

with variable compression (e.g., MPEG)

display_rate > min_constant.

consumption_rate to satisfy the continuity requirements of a multimedia database system; the reading curve must not be below the consumption curve. Obviously, the scheduling of multimedia streams requires more planning since reading rates, consumption rates, switching times (e.g., disk seek time), and disk utilization rates need to be considered.

Buffer sharing can yield significant efficiencies in multimedia systems. Buffer sharing can be facilitated by careful interleaving. For example, each stream requires its maximum number to buffers only right after completing its reading period. The total number of buffers required is not necessarily constant throughout a given time period for a number of reasons: consumption rates often differ, data streams are not contiguously placed on disk, and idle periods exist.

Non-contiguous streams can be handled better if the data is put into clusters (subsets of the data) are stored contiguously. Clustering avoids time-consuming seek operations within a stream's reading period, This kind of buffer analysis needs to be carried out at design time rater than at execution time (unlike admission control, which is dynamic).

Although continuity requirements must be met we are not forced to follow a fixed reading order in fact intelligent disk scheduling can be used to reduce the total seek time For example, a strategy can be used to restrict the maximum inter-piece (or Cluster) distance on disk. This distance is referred to as a scattering parameter. Of course, some disk strategies are impractical to implement, especially if updates are, involved, since a complete disk reorganization may be required.

On-going or Future Work

Buffer allocation strategies for variable compression rates statistical models of variable compressed streams analyzing display orders (e.g., news-on-demand systems in which users may not care about the order of most, or all, of the short video clips requested) content-based retrieval of videos (e.g., search for the goals scored in a hockey game).

7. DIGITAL VIDEO INDEXING

Typically the indexing of a digital video program consists of the following steps:

1. Segment the video hierarchically into sequences, scenes, and shot. (A shot is a continuous sequence of frames captured from one camera, A Scene is composed of the of more shots, which present different views of the same even, related in time or space. A segment is composed of one or more related scenes.)
2. Describe the complete video using bibliographic information (title, creator, dates, subjects, item numbers, publisher details; names synopsis etc.) plus format, frame rate, duration etc.
3. Described each sequence id, start time/frame end time /frame brief textual summary.
4. Described each scene id, start time/frame end time / frame brief textual transcript (ideally derived from a closed caption decoder).

5. Described each shot id, start time/frame end time / frame key frame (first frame of the shot ideally derived from an automatic shot detection algorithm).

If captions are available then a closed caption decoder may be used to extract the transcript. However the majority of the videos, which are acquired by the audiovisual unit, do not contain closed captions, and when they do, the method by which the closed captions are encoded varies from country to country, often making their extraction highly problematic. Assuming closed captions have been extracted then there is still a need for the time-consuming step of generating scene summaries from the transcript. Software is available, which is capable of detecting scene changes (the first frame each new scene) and saving them as image files e.g. GIF or JPEG images.[7] However there are a number of problems with this automated approach Scene change detection methods are improving but they can experience difficulties when there are fades, pans between scans and fast motion within scenes. But more importantly, scene changes are often not the most visually impressive aesthetic. Evocative or even representative images for a particular scene. Image processors which are capable measuring aesthetics or visual impact; An international closed caption encoding standard or decoders capable of handling the different video formats (PAL, NTSC and closed-caption encoding methods Software. which can automatics generate summaries from transcripts.

REFERENCES

[1] Lockemann, PC "Multimedia Databases Paradigm Architecture survey and issues" report no. NP S52-88-047. Naval Postgraduate School. Monterey, CA sept 1988

[2] Masunga, Y, "Multimedia Databases: A formal Framework" in Proc. IEEE CS Office

[3] Automation Symp. (Gaithersburg. MD, Apr. 1987), IEEE CS Press, order no.770, Washington, 1987, pp, 36,45

[4] Mindel1, D.A., "Dealing with a Digital World" Byte, vol. 14, no.8, Aug. 1989 pp 246-256

[5] Phi B' Multimedia Systems and Text: in Proc. 4 Int. Conf on data Engineering (Los Angeles, Febt. 1998). IEEE Computer Society Press, order no 827, p.601.

[6] Stonebraker, M., Rowe, L., Lindsey, B., Gray, J., Careyu, M., Brodie M., Brenstein P., and Breech, D., "Third-Generation Database System Manifesto, ACM SIGMOO Record, vol. 19, no.3, Sept. 1990, pp. 31-44.

[7] Woelk, D., and Kim, W., "Multimedia Information Management. in an object Oriented Database System"' in Proc. Int Conf. On VLDB (Brighton, England, sept 1987).

❑❑❑

25

High Performance Model for Focussed and Parallel Web Crawler

*Dr. Sudhir Dawra**

Abstract – *The World Wide Web has grown at a phenomenal pace, from several thousand pages in 1993 to over 3 billion today. This explosion in size has made Web crawlers indispensable for information retrieval on the Web. They download large quantities of data and browse documents by passing from one hypertext link to another. In this paper we are designing a model for focused and Parallel Web Crawler.*

1. INTRODUCTION

Today's search engines are equipped with specialized agents known as Web crawlers dedicated to crawling large Web contents on line. These contents are then analyzed, indexed and made available to users. Crawlers interact with

*(HOD & Associate Professor, Department of Computer Science & Engineering), Ideal Institute of Technology, *Sadarpur-Sikroad, Behind Govind Puram, Ghaziabad* (U.P.) Tel.: 0120-2768481,2767351,2767818 Email: {dawra1211@yahoo.com}

thousands of Web servers over periods extending from a few weeks to several years. This type of crawling process therefore means that certain judicious criteria need to be taken into account, such as the robustness, ?exibility and maintainability of these crawlers. We will describe the technical choices for very high performance crawling.[1]

Crawler?

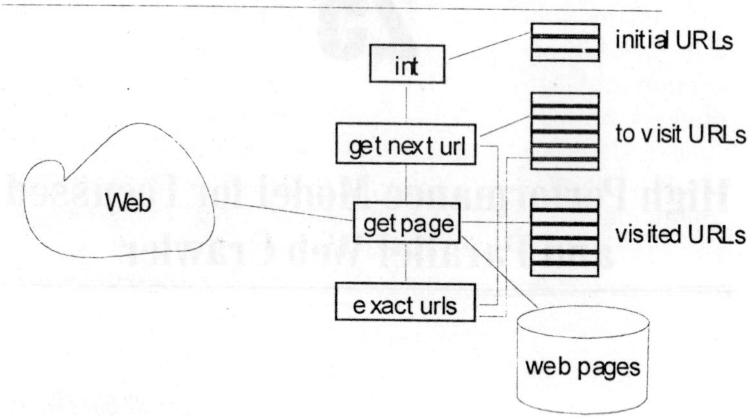

High performance crawling systems first appeared in academic and industrial sectors, allowing hundreds of millions of documents to be downloaded and indexed. Indeed, search engines may be compared on the basis of the number of documents indexed, as well as of the quality of replies obtained.

Any crawling system in this category should other at least the following two features.

1. It needs to be equipped with an intelligent navigation strategy, i.e. enabling it to make decisions regarding the choice of subsequent actions to be taken (pages to be downloaded etc).
2. Its supporting hardware and software architecture should be optimized to crawl large quantities of documents per unit of time (generally per second).

To this we may add fault tolerance (machine crash, network failure etc.) and considerations of Web server resources.

Studies on the first point include crawling strategies for important pages, topic-specific document downloading, page recrawling to optimize overall refresh frequency of a Web archive or scheduling the downloading activity according to time.[2] However, little research has been devoted to the second point.

Most recent studies on crawling strategy fail to deal with these features, contenting themselves with the solution of minor issues such as the calculation of the number of pages to be downloaded in order to maximize/minimize some functional objective. This may be acceptable in the case of small applications, but for real time applications the system must deal with a much larger number of constraints. We should also point out that little academic research is concerned with high performance search engines, as compared with their commercial counterparts

2. LITERATURE REVIEW

Many of the search engines use well-known information retrieval (IR) algorithms and techniques [Salton 1989; Faloutsos 1985].[3] However, IR algorithms were developed for relatively small and coherent collections such as newspaper articles or book catalogs in a (physical) library.

According to Lawrence and Giles 1999; 1998; Bharat and Broder 1999], and while they report slightly different numbers, most agree that over a billion pages are available. Given that the average size of a Web page is around 5 to 10K bytes, just the textual data amounts to at least tens of terabytes. The growth rate of the Web is even more dramatic. According to Lawrence and Giles [1999], the size of the Web has doubled in less than two years, and this growth rate is projected to continue for the next two years.

According to the study ***P.Lyman*** in 2003 the surface web is about 7.5 billion pages and the deep web is more than 5500 billion.Google can indexs about 4 billion of web pages.

According to ***J. Cho, H. Garc'ia-Molina,*** and ***L. Page. E.cient*** crawling through URL ordering. In Proceedings of the seventh conference on World Wide Web. Elsevier Science, April 1998.

Cho et al. made the first study on policies for crawl-ing scheduling. Their data set was a 180,000-pages crawl from the stanford.edu domain, in which a crawling sim-ulation was done with different strategies.[4] The ordering metrics tested were breadth-first, backlink-count and par-tial Pagerank, which are explained later in this article. One of the conclusions was that if the crawler wants to download pages with high Pagerank early during the crawling process, then the partial Pagerank strategy is the better, followed by breadth-first and backlink-count. However, these results are for just a single domain.

According to M. Najork and J. L. Wiener. Breadth-first crawling yields high-quality pages. In Proceedings of the Tenth Conference on World Wide Web, pages 114–118, Hong Kong, May 2001. Elsevier Science.

He performed an actual crawl on 328 million pages, using breadth-first ordering. They found that a breadth-first crawl captures pages with high Pagerank early in the crawl, but they did not attempt to compare it to other strategies.

According to S. Abiteboul, M. Preda, and G. Cobena. Adaptive on-line page importance computation.[5] In Proceedings of the twelfth international conference on World Wide Web, pages 280–290. ACM Press, 2003. He designed a crawling strategy based on an algorithm called OPIC (On-line Page Importance Com-putation). In OPIC, each page is given an initial sum of "cash" which is distributed equally among the pages it points to. It is similar to a Pagerank computation, but it is faster and is done just in one step. An OPIC-driven crawler down-loads first the pages in the crawling frontier with higher amounts of "cash". Experiments were carried in a 100,000-pages synthetic graph with a power-law distribution of in-links. However, there was no comparison with other strate-gies nor experiments in the real Web.[5]

According to P. Boldi, M. Santini, and S. Vigna. Do your worst to make the best: Paradoxical e.ects in pagerank incremental computations. In Proceedings of the third Workshop on Web Graphs (WAW), volume 3243 of Lecture Notes in Computer Science, pages 168–180, Rome, Italy, October 2004. Springer. Boldi et al. used simulation on subsets of the Web of 40 million pages from the .it domain and 100 million pages from the WebBase crawl, testing breadth-first against random ordering and an omniscient strategy. The winning strategy was breadth-first, although a random ordering also performed surprisingly well. One problem is that the Web-Base crawl is biased to the crawler used to gather the data.[6] They also showed that Pagerank calculations carried on par-tial subgraphs of the Web give a bad approximation of the actual Pagerank values.

According to Chakrabarti et al. 1999a, the essential idea in focused crawling is that there is a short range topical locality on the web.

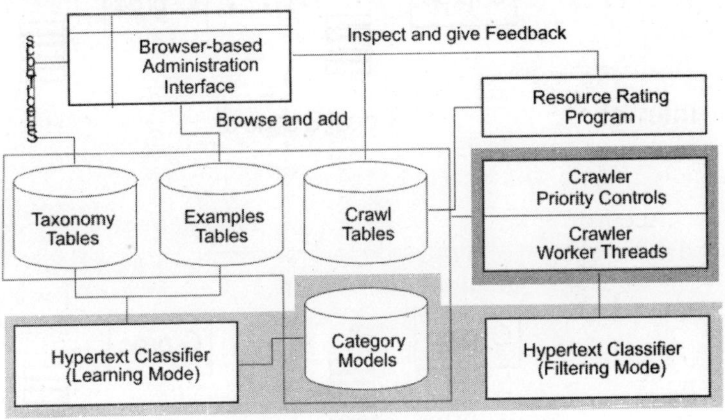

Block- Diagram of Focussed Crawler

This locality may be used in order to design effective techniques for resource discovery by starting at a few well chosen points and maintaining the crawler within the ranges of these known topics focused crawling technique [Chakrabarti et al. 1999a] relies on a restrictive model based on certain pre-ordained notions of how the linkage structure of the World Wide Web behaves. Specifically, the work on focused crawling [Chakrabarti et al. 1999a] assumes two key properties: (1) ***Linkage locality:*** Web pages on a given topic are more likely to link to those on the same topic. (2) ***Sibling locality:*** If a web page points to certain web pages on a given topic, then it is likely to point to other pages on the same topic.

Focussed crawling is a *fixed* model in which it is assumed that the web has specific linkage structure in which pages on a specific topic are likely to link to the same topic. Even though there is evidence [Chakrabarti et al. 1999b; Kleinberg 1998] that the documents on the World Wide Web show topical locality for many broad topical areas, there is no clear understanding of how this translates to arbitrary predicates.

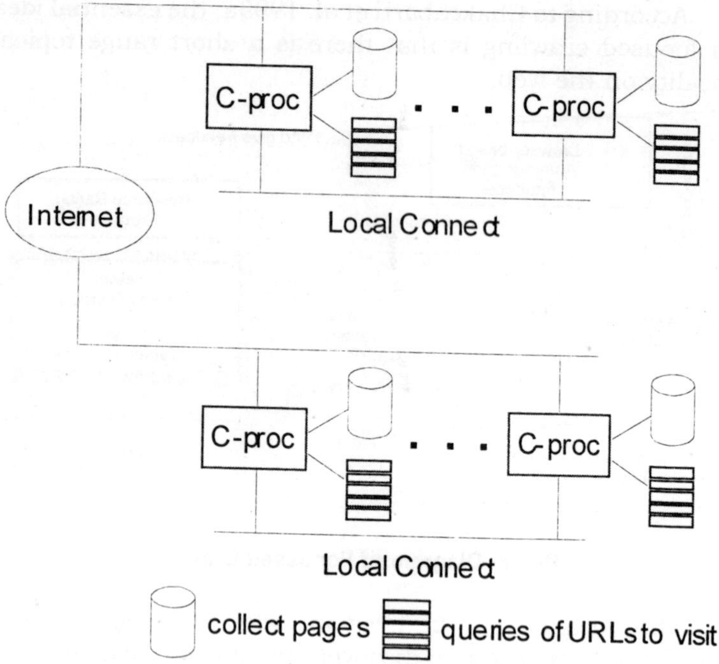

Architecture of Parallel Crawler

According to ***J. Cho*** and H. ***Garcia-Molina***. Parallel crawlers. Technical report, UCLA Computer Science, 2002. As the size of the Web grows, it becomes more difficult to retrieve the whole or a significant portion of the Web using a single process.[7] Therefore, many search engines often run multiple processes in parallel to perform the above task, so that download rate is maximized. We refer to this type of crawler as a parallel crawler.

1. A parallel crawler consists of multiple crawling processes communicating via local network (intra-site parallel crawler) or Internet (distributed crawler)
2. Setting: we have a number of C-proc = crawling process
3. Goal: we wish to crawl the *best* pages with minimum *overhead*

In paral-lel crawler we can maximize its performance (e.g., download rate) while minimizing the overhead from paral-lelization. We believe many existing search engines already use some sort of parallelization, but there has been little scientific research conducted on this topic. Thus, little has been known on the tradeoff among various design choices for a parallel crawler.

The general architecture of a par-allel crawler. A parallel crawler consists of multiple crawling processes, which we refer to as C-proc's. Each C-proc per-forms the basic tasks that a single-process crawler conducts. It downloads pages from the Web, stores the pages locally, extracts URLs from the downloaded pages and follows links.[8] Depending on how the C-proc's split the download task, some of the extracted links may be sent to other C-proc's. The C-proc's performing these tasks may be distributed ei-ther on the same local network or at geographically distant locations.

1. Intra-site parallel crawler: When all C-proc's run on the same local network and communicate through a high speed interconnect (such as LAN), we call it an intra-site parallel crawler. In Figure 1, this scenario corresponds to the case where all C-proc's run only on the local network on the top. In this case, all C-proc's use the same local network when they download pages from remote Web sites. Therefore, the network load from C-proc's is centralized at a single location where they operate.[9]

2. Distributed crawler: When C-proc's run at geograph-ically distant locations connected by the Internet (or a wide area network), we call it a distributed crawler. For example, one C-proc may run in the US, crawling all US pages, and another C-proc may run in France, crawling all European pages. As we discussed in the introduction, a distributed crawler can disperse and even reduce the load on the overall network.

When C-proc's run at distant locations and communicates through the Internet, it becomes important how often and how much C-proc's need to communicate. The bandwidth between C-proc's may be limited and sometimes unavailable, as is often the case with the Internet.

When multiple C-proc's download pages in parallel, differ-ent C-proc's may download the same page multiple times. In order to avoid this overlap, C-proc's need to coordinate with each other on what pages to download. This coordination can be done in one of the following ways:

3. Independent: At one extreme, C-proc's may download pages totally independently without any coordination.[9] That is, each C-proc starts with its own set of seed URLs and follows links without consulting with other C-proc's. In this scenario, downloaded pages may over-lap, but we may hope that this overlap will not be sig-nificant, if all C-proc's start from different seed URLs.

While this scheme has minimal coordination overhead and can be very scalable, we do not directly study this option due to its overlap problem. Later we will consider an improved version of this option, which sig-nificantly reduces overlap.

4. Dynamic assignment: When there exists a central co-ordinator that logically divides the Web into small par-titions (using a certain partitioning function) and dy-namically assigns each partition to a C-proc for down-load, we call it dynamic assignment.

5. Static assignment: When the Web is partitioned and assigned to each C-proc before they start to crawl, we call it static assignment. In this case, every C-proc knows which C-proc is responsible for which page dur-ing a crawl and the crawler does not need a central coordinator. We will shortly discuss in more detail how C-proc's operate under this scheme.

Advantages of Parallel Crawler

1. Scalability: Due to enormous size of the Web, it is often imperative to run a parallel crawler. A single-process crawler simply cannot achieve the required download rate in certain cases.[10]

2. Network-load dispersion: Multiple crawling processes of a parallel crawler may run at geographically distant locations, each downloading "geographically-adjacent" pages. For example, a process in Germany may down-load all European pages, while another one in Japan crawls all Asian pages. In this way, we can disperse the network load to multiple regions. In particular, this dispersion might be necessary when a single net-work cannot handle the heavy load from a large-scale crawl.

3. Network-load reduction: In addition to the dispersing load, a parallel crawler may actually reduce the net-work load. For example, assume that a crawler in North America retrieves a page from Europe. To be downloaded by the crawler, the page first has to go through the network in Europe, then the Europe-to-North America inter-continental network and finally the network in North America.[11] Instead, if a crawl-ing process in Europe collects all European pages, and if another process in North America crawls all North American pages, the overall network load will be re-duced, because pages go through only "local" networks.

Note that the downloaded pages may need to be trans-ferred later to a central location, so that a central index can be built. However, even in that case, we believe that the transfer can be significantly smaller than the original page download traffic, by using some of the following methods:

4. Compression: Once the pages are collected and stored, it is easy to compress the data before send-ing them to a central location.

3. RESEARCH DESIGN

We will combine the both focused crawling technique and Parallel crawling technique on various parameters and will develop a high performance focussed parallel web crawling system.

The main conclusion of our study for the parallel crawling system is: When a small number of crawling processes run in par-allel, the **firewall mode** provides good coverage. Given that firewall mode crawlers can run totally independently and are easy to implement, we believe that it is a good option to consider.

Cross-over mode: In this mode, downloaded pages may clearly overlap (pages g and h are downloaded twice), but the over-all crawler can download more pages than the firewall mode

A crawler based on the **exchange mode consumes** small network bandwidth for URL exchanges (less than 1% of the network bandwidth). It can also minimize other overheads by adopting the batch communication tech-nique. In our experiments, the crawler could maximize the quality of the downloaded pages, even if it ex-changed backlink messages fewer than 100 times dur-ing a crawl.[12]

The main conclusions of our study for focussed crawling system is: a fixed model in which it is assumed that the web has specific linkage structure in which pages on a specific topic are likely to link to the same topic.

It works on the two key properties: (1) ***Linkage locality***: Web pages on a given topic are more likely to link to those on the same topic. (2) ***Sibling locality***: If a web page points to certain web pages on a given topic, then it is likely to point to other pages on the same topic.

4. METHODOLOGY FOR WEB CRAWLER

The crawler module retrieves pages from the Web for later analysis by the indexing module. crawler module typically starts with an initial set of URLs, *S0*. Roughly, it first places *S0* in a queue where all URLs to be retrieved are kept and priorities. From this queue, the crawler gets a URL (in some order), downloads the page, extracts any URLs in the downloaded page, and puts the new URLs in the queue.[13] This process is repeated until the crawler decides to stop. Given the enormous size and the change rate of the Web, many issues arise, including the following:

1. What pages should the crawler download?
2. How should the crawler refresh pages?
3. How should the load on the visited Web sites be minimized?
4. How should the crawling process be parallelized?

The behavior of a Web crawler is the outcome of a combination of policies:

1. A *selection policy* that states which pages to download.
2. A *re-visit policy* that states when to check for changes to the pages.
3. A *politeness policy* that states how to avoid overloading Web sites.
4. A *parallelization policy* that states how to coordinate distributed Web crawlers.

Comparing the Services for Large-Scale Crawling System

1. Flexibility: With some minor adjustments our system should be suitable for various scenarios. However, it is important to remember that crawling is established within a specific framework: namely, Web legal deposit.

2. High Performance: the system needs to be scalable with a minimum of one thousand pages/second and extending up to millions of pages for each run on low cost hardware. Note that here, the quality and efficiency of disk access are crucial to maintaining high performance.

3. Fault Tolerance: this may cover various aspects. As the system interacts with several servers at once, specific problems emerge. First, it should at least be able to process invalid HTML code, deal with unexpected Web server behavior, and select good communication protocols etc. The goal here is to avoid this type of problem and, by force of circumstance, to be able to ignore such problems completely. Second, crawling processes may take days or weeks, and it is imperative that the system can handle failure, stopped processes or interruptions in network services, keeping data loss to a minimum.[14] Finally, the system should be persistent, which means periodically switching large data structures from memory to the disk (e.g. restart after failure).

4. Maintainability and Configurability: an appropriate interface is necessary for monitoring the crawling process, including download speed, statistics on the pages and amounts of data stored. In online mode, the administrator may adjust the speed of a given crawler, add or delete processes, stop the system, add or delete system nodes and supply the black list of domains not to be visited, etc.

We will use java language for implementing and comparing the result of crawling system.

5. CONCLUSION AND SIGNIFICANCE

The out come result of focussed parallel web crawling system will be developed by comparatively study of focussed web crawler and parallel web crawler on the basis of different parameters. The significance of the study we get best high performance focussed parallel web crawler for crawling the entire web system. We are contributing our study to the advancement of current knowledge.

Crawling the Web, in a certain way, resembles watching the sky in a clear night: what we see, reflects the state of the stars at different times, as the light travels different distances. What a Web crawler gets is not a "snapshot" of the Web, because it does not represents the Web at any given instant of time.[15] The last pages being crawled are probably very accurately represented, but the first pages that were downloaded have a high probability of have been changed.

REFERENCE

[1] S. Brin and L. Page. The anatomy of a large-scale hypertextual Web search engine. Computer Networks and ISDN Systems, 30(1–7):107–117, April 1998.

[2] R. D. Burke. Salticus: guided crawling for personal digital libraries. In Proceedings of the .rst ACM/IEEE-CS joint conference on Digital Libraries, pages 88–89, Roanoke, Virginia, June 2001.

[3] M. Burner. Crawling towards eternity -building an archive of the world wide web. Web Techniques, 2(5), May 1997.

[4] S. Chakrabarti. Mining the Web. Morgan Kaufmann Publishers, 2003.

[5] S. Chakrabarti, M. van den Berg, and B. Dom. Focused crawling: a new approach to topic-specific web resource discovery. Computer Networks, 31(11–16):1623–1640, 1999.

[6] J. Cho and R. Adams. Page quality: In search of an unbiased Web ranking. Technical report, UCLA Computer Science, 2004.

[7] J. Cho and H. Garcia-Molina. Synchronizing a database to improve freshness. In Proceedings of ACM International Conference on Management of Data (SIGMOD), pages 117–128, Dallas, Texas, USA, May 2000.

[8] J. Cho and H. Garcia-Molina. Parallel crawlers. In Proceedings of the eleventh international conference on World Wide Web, pages 124–135, Honolulu, Hawaii, USA, May 2002. ACM Press.

[9] N. Craswell, F. Crimmins, D. Hawking, and A. Mo.at. Performance and cost tradeo.s in web search. In Proceedings of the 15th Australasian Database Conference, pages 161–169, Dunedin, New Zealand, January 2004.

[10] A. Czumaj, I. Finch, L. Gasieniec, A. Gibbons, P. Leng, W. Rytter, and M. Zito. E.cient Web searching using temporal factors. Theoretical Computer Science, 262(1–2):569–582, 2001.

[11] A. S. da Silva, E. A. Veloso, P. B. Golgher, B. A. Ribeiro-Neto, A. H. F. Laender, and N. Ziviani. Cobweb -a crawler for the brazilian web. In Proceedings of String Processing and Information Retrieval (SPIRE), pages 184–191, Cancun, M´exico, September 1999. IEEE CS Press.

[12] S. Dill, R. Kumar, K. S. Mccurley, S. Rajagopalan, D. Sivakumar, and A. Tomkins. Self-similarity in the web. ACM Trans. Inter. Tech., 2(3):205–223, 2002.

[13] J. Edwards, K. S. McCurley, and J. A. Tomlin. An adaptive model for optimizing performance of an incremental web crawler. In Proceedings of the Tenth Conference on World Wide Web, pages 106–113, Hong Kong, May 2001. Elsevier Science.

[14] D. Eichmann. The RBSE spider: balancing effective search against web load. In Proceedings of the first World Wide Web Conference, Geneva, Switzerland, May 1994.

[15] N. Eiron, K. S. McCurley, and J. A. Tomlin. Ranking the web frontier. In Proceedings of the 13th international conference on World Wide Web, pages 309–318. ACM Press, 2004.

□□□